This book is dedicated to Aline,
William "Bras de Fer" and Thomas Bjorn "Ironside"

The author of this book Benjamin James Baillie lives and works in Normandy

THE NORMAN CONQUESTS

The complete history of the Norman Conquests

911 – 1402 A.D

Contents

Introduction

Chapter 1
THE SEAWOLVES
"The Viking creation of Normandy and its iron Dukes"

Chapter 2
THE FIRST MAFIA
"The Norman Conquest of Southern Italy and Sicily"

Chapter 3
THE NORMAN CRUSADE
"The First Crusade and the Conquest of the Kingdom of Heaven"

Chapter 4
DOMESDAY 1066
"The Normand Conquest and the destruction of Anglo-Saxon England"

Chapter 5
INTO THE DRAGON'S DEN
"The Normand Conquest of Wales and the Marches"

Chapter 6
THE GREY FOREIGNERS
"The Normand Conquest of Celtic Ireland"

Chapter 7
INTO THE LION'S Den
"The Normand infiltration of Scotland"

Chapter 8
THE FORGOTTEN CONQUEST
"Jean de Bethencourt and the Norman Conquest of the the Canary Islands"

Chapter 9
THE LAST WAR
"Richard the Lionheart and the last war in Normandy"

Introduction

The Normans, Normanni (Latin) Les Normands (French) came from an area in North-Western France named after them. Normandy "land of the North-men" was created by Viking raiders in the early 10th century. Within 150 years of establishing themselves, The Dukes of Normandy had created one to the most feared and organised Principalities in Medieval Europe. As the 12th century approached, the Viking age was coming to an end. The hour of the Normans had arrived; their first expansion took them to the foot of Southern Italy and Sicily. The exploits of the sons of Tancred de Hauteville would become engrained in Norman myth and legend. The penniless Mafia like mercenaries defied the odds and created the Norman Kingdom in the sun. For over two centuries the Norman conquests created a piecemeal Empire that stretched from the wild windswept landscapes of Celtic Ireland and Scotland in the north to the sun drenched shores of Sicily in the Mediterranean and to the very frontiers of Christendom itself in the Outremer (Holy land). Their last conquest, almost forgotten by history would take them to the very edge of the known world. In 1402 A.D Norman adventurer's set sail on an epic journey to conquer the mystical volcanic islands of the Canaries in the Atlantic Ocean.

Chapter 1: **Normandy**

THE SEAWOLVES
"The Viking creation of Normandy and its iron Dukes"
911-1087 A.D

Introduction

For over two centuries the Norman conquests created a piecemeal Empire that stretched from the wild windswept landscapes of Celtic Ireland and Scotland in the north to the sun drenched shores of Sicily in the Mediterranean and to the very frontiers of Christendom itself in the Outremer (Holy land). However the story of the Normans started in the early 10th century in Northern France, where Viking raiders from Scandinavia settled down and created Normandy "land of the North men", which became one of the most feared and organised Principalities in medieval Europe.

The sea wolves: For three centuries Europe was terrorised by a fierce warrior race from Scandinavia that became known to us as the Vikings. The origin of the word Viking itself is far from clear, but it represented the Northern peoples from Norway, Sweden, and Denmark who ventured out in their dragon head ships to raid and trade during the last three centuries of the first millennium. Due to over population and other factors in their traditional homelands, the Viking age of expansion commenced just before the beginning of the ninth century. The Norwegians and the Danes naturally sailed west and south towards the British Isles and Western Europe. The Swedes crossed the Baltic Sea and infiltrated into Poland, the Baltic States and Russia creating the Viking Kingdom of Rus (Novagrad). Using their famous longboats which could hold up to 50 warriors, the Vikings were able to navigate the open seas with ease and sail up the sallowest rivers wherever they went. They travelled far and wide from North Africa and the Mediterranean to the inland rivers of the Dniepner and Volga in central Russia where they became known as Varangians. They even formed the Varangian guard (bodyguards of the Byzantine Emperor in Constantinople). Perhaps their greatest expedition was setting foot on North American soil, some 500 years before Christopher Columbus. The Viking expeditions had three main goals, trading, raiding and later conquest. When the crews returned to Scandinavia with their spoils of booty and slaves they spread the word of the riches that were on offer. By the late 9th century, organised war bands and armies were crossing the seas intent on outright conquest.

The Oseberg Viking ship, Norway

The Kingdom of France

After the fall of the Roman Empire in the 5th century A.D, Gaul was overrun by various Germanic tribes including the Visigoths, Burgundians, Alans and Franks. The Franks occupied Neustria (modern day Northern France) and continued their rise to power under the Merovingian King Clovis. The first recorded legend between the Vikings and Franks can be traced back to the 6th century when Theudebert of Ripuaria killed Hygelac the Dane (the brother of Beowolf) in combat. In the late 8th century, Charlemagne (Charles the Great) the future Holy Roman Empire united most of Western Europe under his rule. His wars against the Germanic Saxons brought Frankish influence and Christianity nearer to the pagan Viking homelands of Scandinavia. Widukind the

Saxon leader, even fled to Denmark and told the Viking peoples of the power and aggression of Charlemagne. The Vikings did not wait for a Frankish invasion and instead brought terror to the very heart of the Carolingian Empire. In the year 799 A.D the Vikings attacked France for the first time near Noirmoutier (Vendée Region of Western France). They pillaged the monastery, striping it of its riches and killed the fleeing monks. Charlemagne ordered the construction of a fleet and defences to be erected on France's Western coastline. These measures kept the Norsemen at bay and France weathered the Viking raids until the death of Louis the Pious in 840 A.D

With the Frankish Empire in disarray, the Vikings took their chance and attacked France. The great inland rivers of the Seine, Loire, Garonne, Saone and the Rhine allowed the Vikings to infiltrate deep into the heart of the Kingdom. In 841 A.D they appeared in the Seine valley and pillaged the rich abbeys of Jumiéges and St Georges de Boucherville. The region's capital Rouen was also sacked and burned to the ground by the sea wolves.

The Seine valley from the Brotonne forest (Normandy, France)

Early Viking raid on a Seine valley settlement

Ragnar's raid on Paris 845 A.D

The raids increased with ferocity during the 840s. In 845 A.D a Viking fleet of 120 longboats sailed the 240 miles from the sea to the French capital Paris. They were commanded by one of the most famous Vikings of them all; Ragnar Lodbrok "hairy breaches". Ragnar's fame was legendary, and his exploits earned him a place as one of the most popular heroes in the Viking Sagas. After ravaging the city of Rouen his pagan war band continued upstream and sacked the modern day town of Chaussy near Paris.

The new Frankish King, Charles II "the bald" raised an army and set out to confront Ragnar's Vikings. He split his army on both sides of the Seine River hoping to encircle the Norsemen, but Ragnar realised what Charles was up to and quickly ambushed the smaller Frankish force, taking numerous prisoners and slaughtering the rest. The 111 unfortunate captured prisoners were taken and then executed on a tiny island in the middle of the Seine, in front of Charles and his remaining men, who watched on helplessly. Seizing the initiative again, Ragnar launched a second bold attack against the remainder of the Frankish forces.

Ragnar "Lodbrok"

Charles fearing for his life fled the field with the remnants of his army and headed for the safety of St Denis. With the Frankish forces destroyed, Rangnar terrorised the region, sacking towns, villages and wasting the land. On Easter Sunday 845 A.D the Vikings broke through the defences of the island city of Paris and plundered the capital. Charles who was still in St Denis behind the Vikings could have blocked off the Seine River and any escape route open to them.

Instead he hesitated, and paid Ragnar off with 7000 pounds of silver. Charles payment became known as the "Dane geld" (Danes pay) or simply, protection money to stop any further aggression. The marauding Scandinavians returned back down the river Seine to Denmark unmolested. As for the Viking warlord Ragnar, legend has it that he met his end when he was shipwrecked on the English coast. After being captured by the Northumbrian King Ælla, he was thrown into a pit of Snakes and bitten to death. His sons Halfdan, Björn Ironside, Sigurd Snake-in-the-Eye and Ivar the Boneless swore to avenge their father's death. In 865 A.D they invaded England with the "Great Heathen Army" and captured York. King Ælla was captured in battle outside the city walls and sentenced to death according to the tradition of the blood eagle (A cruel Viking method of torture and execution).

The great invasions 856-911 A.D

Although Charles had paid off one group of Vikings, within a few years several roaming fleets and armies were attacking his Kingdom. Sometimes these war bands joined forces with each other, as was the case in 856 A.D when the Scandinavians ransacked Paris again. They were not adverse to accepting bribery or even being recruited by the feudal lords of medieval France in their private wars against the King and the other nobility. Just as in England, the Vikings were changing their behaviour and tactics. Raiding was slowly becoming invasion and colonisation. They were spending the winters on the coastal regions and estuaries of France. The island of Oselles (probably modern day Oissel) was fortified by the Vikings and used as a base to strike terror into the Parisian region.

Also somewhere between Saint Wandrille and Jumiéges in the forest of Arélaune (now Brotonne) the raiders had a shipyard where they had access to a huge supply of wood and trees to repair and build their ships.

King Charles II "the bald"

In the campaigning season they actively targeted the rich, but poorly defended centres of commerce. Every year they grew bolder in their ferocious military campaigns against the Carolingian Empire, forcing the Church and nobility to pay the "Dane geld". Charles II position was so threatened that he sought to ally himself with the Anglo-Saxons of Wessex (England) in combating the Viking menace by marrying off his daughter Judith to Æthelwulf (King of Wessex). Charles II had his successes during the 860s. His newly constructed fortifications on the river Seine and Marne succeeded in trapping Weland's Viking raiding party in 862 A.D.

However, just four years later, the Franks were heavily defeated at Melun. When Charles died in 876 A.D the Viking attacks intensified, the united Empire of Charlemagne had disintegrated into fragmented Kingdoms, much easier for the Vikings to infiltrate.

The siege of Paris 885-886 A.D

In 885 A.D a massive Viking fleet, some say as large as 700 ships, sailed up the river Seine under the command of Siegfried. Their target was Paris, and the memories of Ragnar's devastating raid of 845 A.D was still fresh in the minds of the populace. Siegfried demanded the usual "Dane geld" bribe, but this time King Charles "the Fat" refused to pay it. The Frankish nobility including Odo (the Count of Paris) and Joscelin (the Abbot of St Germain des Prés) were tasked with defending the city against the pagan hordes.

In November, Siegfried's Vikings attacked the city walls with scaling ladders and battering rams. The battle was fierce, but the Franks repulsed the Norsemen with everything they had within their arsenal. Hot burning oil was poured down onto the attackers along with flaming arrows and stones hurled from the defensive battlements. Throughout the cold damp winter the Vikings besieged Paris and tried to enter the city by any means possible. In one such attempt they filled the city's moat with the bodies of the executed prisoners and used them as a sort of pontoon bridge to gain closer access to the Parisian fortified towers. In the New Year Count Odo managed to break through the Viking lines and get word to Charles (who was in Italy) of the situation and also requesting urgent assistance. The

Statue of Rollo, Rouen, Normandy

siege dragged on into the summer of 886 A.D with both sides refusing to give in. By the time Charles arrived on the scene, both the defenders and attackers had been decimated by disease. Instead of attacking the remaining Vikings, one of whom may have been a certain Rollo "the Ganger"; Charles offered them the "Dane geld" in return for recruiting them as mercenaries to crush a rebellion within the Empire.

Gongu-Hrolfr / Rollo the Ganger(walker)

The question of the origin of Hrolf/Rollo is still disputed between Norway and Denmark to this day. Norwegian and Icelandic historians firmly believe that the identity of the famous Viking Jarl is Ganger Hrolf (Rollo the Walker). He earned his nickname "the walker" because no one could find a horse big enough to carry the giant Viking warlord, hence he walked everywhere. He is believed to have been a son of Rognvald Eysteinsson (the Norse Earl of More, Norway). After a dispute with the Norwegian King Harald Fairhair, Rollo was forced to leave his homeland and seek fame and fortune abroad.

Like many other Vikings, Rollo found his way to Northern France after raiding and pillaging in the "Great Heathen army" campaign of terror in Anglo-Saxon England. Slowly but surely he gained experience and became one of the main warlords of the late 9th century. Whether or not he was at the siege of Paris cannot be verified, but it is quite possible. What is certain is that by 911 A.D Rollo was in command of the Viking army that attacked Chartres.

The Siege of Chartres 911 A.D

In the spring of 911 A.D Rollo laid siege to the Frankish city of Chartres. The several thousand strong Viking army devastated the surrounding region before encircling the city. Their main camp was located just up steam on the island of "Petits-Pres" on the river Eure. Bishop Guateaume organised the defence of the city and sent out urgent calls for help to the Frankish King

Rollo (Hrolfr) Founder of Normandy 911 A.D

Charles III "the simple" and the local nobility. The strong walls and gallant resistance of the defenders thwarted the Viking assaults to take the city by storm. In July a Frankish army arrived on the scene to break the siege. According to the "annals of Ste Colombe de Sens" the two armies clashed in an epic confrontation just outside the city. After an initial Frankish charge, Viking berserkers forced the Franks back in the vicious hand to hand combat. A local legend says that the Vikings were forced to retreat when Bishop Guateaume and the garrison charged out of the city carrying "Mary's Veil" (a holy relic). Rollo ordered a fighting withdrawal towards a small hill known as Léves on the banks of the river Eure. With the arrival of Frankish reserves under the Count of Poitiers, the Franks began to close in on Rollo's men. As nightfall fell they encamped at the foot of the hill and prepared for a final showdown with the Viking invaders.

Chartres Cathedral, the medieval heart of the city

Rollo was faced with utter annihilation unless he could change the fortunes of his army; the cunning warlord devised a plan to alter the dire situation. He ordered several hand picked warriors to conduct a stealth operation against his foes. The selected Vikings crept down the hill and infiltrated the Frankish camp. At the crucial moment they blew on their horns and tricked the Franks into believing that they were being attacked by the whole Viking army. The camp fell into complete panic, with horses and soldiers fleeing in all directions. Rollo's ruse had worked, while the Franks were in disarray he was able to slip away into the night with the remainder of the army to the safety of his ships. In the morning the Frankish army marched out after the Vikings to give battle, but when they arrived towards the Norse position on the river Eure they were halted by a formidable barricade, hastily constructed out of dead animals, trees and bushes. The Franks may have relieved the siege of Chartres, but they had failed to eliminate Rollo's army. The Vikings were able to return back to the relative safety of Rouen and the Seine valley.

King Charles III decided to try and capitalise on the French victory at Chartres. He did not launch a military campaign against the Vikings, but instead sent emissaries on a diplomatic mission to Rollo's camp.

The Treaty of Saint Clair Sur Epte and the Creation of Normandy

According to Dudo de Saint Quentin (the 10th / 11th century historiographer to the Dukes of Normandy) Rollo and King Charles III met in the small town of Saint Clair sur Epte on the frontier of the Viking colony in 911A.D. King Charles III, accepting that he could not recover Rouen and the coastal regions of Neustria from the invaders, agreed to cede the land from the river Epte to the sea to Rollo if he became a vassal of the Frankish King and convert to Christianity. The terms were that Rollo would be given the title Count of Rouen and legitimately govern the land in the King's name. Charles hoped that by ceding the "Pagi of Caux, Talon, Roumois, Evrecin and Vexin" to Rollo, he would be creating a buffer state to protect France from further Viking attacks. Rollo agreed to the terms, but when he was asked to perform the act of homage and fealty, he refused. Legend has it that to consecrate the Treaty he would have to kiss the King's foot. He replied that;

> **"I will never kneel before another man, nor kiss anyone's foot"**

Rollo ordered one of his men to take his place and kiss the King's foot. The warrior knelt down and took the King's foot in his hands. Instead of kissing it, he hurled the King into the air; Charles III was thrown off his feet and fell over backwards. The scene caused uproar of laughter amongst the Vikings. The land of the North-men "Normandy" had officially been created.

Depiction of the Treaty of Saint Clair Sur Epte

Normandy and the iron Dukes 911-1087 A.D

For Charles the agreement proved to be a success. There were no more Viking raids on his lands and Rollo kept his word and was baptised a Christian in 912 A.D, taking the name Robert. The Roujarl (Count of Rouen), as Rollo was known to his Viking followers, started to transform his new territory. Instead of sacking the churches and abbeys, he began to repair and encourage new ones to be built. The Vikings rapidly integrated into the Frankish majority, adopting their customs and language. Some Viking laws were introduced such as the Counts monopoly on shipwrecks and banishment/exile (utlagr). The Viking "Thing" (assembly or council of free speakers) was never introduced and Rollo seems to have kept most of the power of the fledgling state for himself and a few selected companions.

Some Norse words were adapted into the French language such as vagr = Vague/wave and humarr = homard/lobster. Viking place names in Normandy are in abundance. Most towns and villages ending with tot = symbolise a farm, Yvetot, Ectot, Caltot and so on. The towns of Honfleur and Harfleur are both of Scandinavian origin, Hon = possibly a persons name and Fleur = inlet/cove. Quillebeuf sur Seine = Kilbow in old Norse means village of the bay. Settlements ending with ville usually take the first part from a Viking personal name, Bierville = Bjorn's town/ville. There are over 100 place names ending in bec, meaning a stream or a slope.

Table of some Viking place names in Normandy

Viking	English	Town / village
tot	farm	Yvetot, Ectot, Formetot
bec	Stream/slope	Briquebec, Foulbec
dale/dal	valley	Oudalle, La dalle
hogue	hill	St Vaast de Hogue, Les Hogue
thuit	cleared area	Bracquethuit

The Norman expansion

The Vikings married and assimilated into the local Frankish population and became Normans. In 923 A.D civil war broke out within the Frankish Empire. King Charles III was deposed in a revolt by some of his nobles led by Robert of Neustria. The Franks fought each other, culminating in the battle of Soissons 923 A.D where Robert I was killed by Charles III in single combat. Charles actually lost the battle and was taken prisoner. Meanwhile Rollo exploited the divisions within the Empire and expanded the Norman state. His troops overran most of what is now lower Normandy, capturing the Bessin and Bayeux up to the river Vire. He was also ceded Le Mans in Maine, south of Normandy. Norman aggression did not stop there, in 925 A.D according to Flodoard de Reims;

> "The Normans broke the Treaty and attacked the districts of Amiens and Beauvais"

Arms of Normandy

The campaign did not go all their way, the French Count of Vermandois counter attacked and destroyed the Norman settlement of Eu. In the savage battle for the town the Frankish soldiers managed to breach the town's defences and slaughtered all the male inhabitants. The war raged on and probably sometime in 925 A.D Rollo's son William

"Longsword" took over the reins of power from his father. Towards the end of his life Rollo seems to have gone mad. It is said before he died in 932-33 A.D that he ordered the execution and beheading of 100 Christian prisoners to appease the pagan Gods. Clearly although Rollo had been baptised a Christian he had never forgotten his Viking past.

Tomb of Rollo, Rouen Cathedral, Normandy

William I "Longsword"

William I "Longsword" Count of Rouen continued his father's work to expand and enhance the power of the Norman State. William first had to suppress internal revolts from within Normandy. In 925 A.D the citizens of Bayeux revolted against his rule and then a more serious threat came from Riuf, a Norman/Viking noble who believed that William had become to Frankish. Riulf led a Viking revival and marched his army to the very gates of the Norman capital Rouen. With the city on the verge of being besieged, William sent his pregnant wife Sporta to the safety of the loyalist town of Fecamp on the coast. After continued negotiations, William launched a surprise attack on the rebel camp, scattering the heathens. Riulf's army was destroyed and he was forced to flee for his life.

William consolidated his power by coming to terms with King Raoul who granted him permission to annex the **"land of the Bretons at the edge of the sea"**. This was the Contentin peninsular and the Avranchin. The Contentin was inhabited by Irish-Norwegian Vikings who fought hard against the Count's troops to retain their freedom. The Bretons were forced out of the Avranchin and William resettled the land with a group of Danish warriors under the leadership of Aigrold.

King Raoul died in 936 A.D and Hugh the Great installed Louis (the exiled son of the former King Charles III) on the Frankish throne. Hugh hoped that he could use Louis as a puppet King to further his own ends. Within two years, Louis rebelled against Hugh's guardianship and the Empire was plunged into civil war again.

Norman castle of Fecamp, Normandy

In 939 A.D William "Longsword" intervened and invaded the disputed territory of Ponthieu which lay between Normandy and Flanders. The Count of Flanders retaliated and captured the capital of Ponthieu, Montreuil. The pro-Norman Count of Ponthieu, Herluin fled to Normandy and with William's help raised a Norman army. Herluin crossed the frontier and recaptured Montrreuil, slaughtering the Flemish garrison. The tit for tat war continued and William was excommunicated by the Pope for his continued raids on Flanders/France.

Reconciliation came about in 940 A.D when William traveled to Amiens and committed himself to King Louis IV. Two years later William was tricked into attending a peace conference with the Count of Flanders to settle the disputed region of Ponthieu and Montreuil. During the meeting William was murdered by the Count's men. The event caused a power struggle for the very survival of Normandy itself.

Duke Richard I "the fearless"

King Louis IV never forgot the loyalty of William Longsword and supported his son (Richard I "the fearless) claim to the Duchy. The Viking Aigold, (William's man in Lower Normandy) also allied himself with Richard. The early years of Richard's reign were filled with constant danger. In 943 A.D Tormod led an internal rebellion against the Duke and linked up with a Viking invasion fleet from York under the command of Sigfred Sigtryggsson. Together they headed for Rouen, in the battle that followed Richard and King Louis IV's forces utterly annihilated the rebel and Viking army. Both Tormod and Sigfred were killed in the fighting, reputedly by the King himself.

Richard was the first of the Counts of Rouen to use the title Duke. Relations with the Bretons improved when Conan I Duke/Count of Brittany signed a treaty with Richard. On reaching adulthood with the help of the Norman nobles the Duke managed to distance himself from the politics of the Carolingian Empire and concentrated on strengthening the Duchy of Normandy.

Richard further united ties with the Norman nobility by marrying Gunnora, a reputedly beautiful lady of Danish origin. Legend has it that when the Duke was out hunting he heard of the beauty of forester's wife Seinfreda. The Duke sent out his men to capture her and bring her to him, but Seinfreda hid and the soldiers took her unmarried sister Gunnora instead. Richard was extremely happy and took Gunnora to be his mistress. They had seven children together including Richard II Duke of Normandy, Robert who became the Archbishop of Rouen upon the marriage of his parents and Emma of Normandy who married King Æthelred the Unready of England. After his death she then married the Viking King Cnut the Great of Denmark and England.

Feudalism increased under Duke Richard, and as a result Normandy became more organised and united. The Norman adoption of Carolingian cavalry tactics enabled them to sever the link to the Scandinavian style of fighting on foot. Slowly the Norman war machine was emerging as a force to be reckoned with during the beginning of the 11th century.

Richard II "the good"

When Duke Richard I died in 996 A.D he had ruled Normandy for over half a century. The Duchy passed the hands of his son Duke Richard II "the good". Richard was still in his minority, so the reins of power were held by his uncles and his mother Gunnora. During the first year of his reign, the Norman peasantry revolted. All over the Duchy peasants and free farmers banded together in groups and assemblies. Their objective was to achieve greater liberty and freedom from the increasing demands of the Duke and the aristocracy.

13th Century manuscript showing Duke Richard and his children

Duke Richard II and his half uncle Rudolf D'Ivry got word of the growing discontent and brutally crushed the rebellion with vicious zeal. The rebels were captured and had their hands and feet cut off to serve as warning to other would-be troublemakers.

During the reign of Richard II the Norman age of expansion started. Norman adventurers and mercenaries such as the sons of Tancred De Hauteville flocked to Southern Italy to seek fame and fortune (see Chapter 2). A certain Roger De Tosny (later known as Roger de l'Espagne) fought against the Moors in Spain. On one such occasion in Iberia, he and a troop of 40 men were ambushed by 500 Moors. Roger fought like a wild boar and killed over 100 of the enemy. When he returned to Normandy a hero, he built the Abbey of Saint Pierre at Conches en Ouche (L'Eure).

Richard II supported King Svein Forkbeard of Denmark Viking invasion of Anglo-Saxon England, from whom he received a proportion of the spoils. He may even have sent Norman mercenaries to fight in the battle of Clontarf (Ireland). In 1014 A.D the Duke gave refuge to his nephews (the Anglo-Saxon heirs) Alfred and Edward (later King Edward the Confessor of England). In 1026 A.D Duke Richard died and was buried in the Abbey of Fecamp alongside his father.

Duke Richard II with the abbots of Mont St Michel

Tomb of the Dukes of Normandy, Richard I, Richard II, Fécamp

Richard III and Robert "the Magnificent"

Richard III was already an experienced military commander before he was proclaimed Duke. His military skills were put to the test when his brother Robert, who was unhappy with only receiving the County of Hiémois, rebelled against his rule. Richard harried the rebels and laid siege to the great castle of Falaise in lower Normandy. With the odds stacked against him Robert capitulated and made peace with his brother. Richard III returned to the Norman capital Rouen but suddenly became ill and died. Robert who had the most to gain from his brother's death was suspected of poisoning him. Whatever the truth maybe Robert was proclaimed Robert I Duke of Normandy. The New Duke faced various revolts and uprisings from the ever increasing powerful Norman aristocracy, including his Uncle Robert the Archbishop of Rouen, Hugh the Bishop of Bayeux and the Count of Belleme. But Robert quickly quelled the disturbances and restored order to the Duchy.

Alain III of Brittany took advantage of the internal strife in Normandy and invaded the Avranchin. In a lighting campaign against the Bretons, Robert forced Alain III to submit, acknowledge him as his overlord and concede Brittany as a vassal state of the Dukes of Normandy. The Duke also helped and gave military assistance to his overlord, the King of France, who bestowed upon him the important region of the Vexin between the river Epte and Oise. At the zenith of his power Robert decided to go on pilgrimage to the Holy land. Before departing he made the Norman nobility accept his illegitimate son, William "the bastard" as his rightful heir. On the return journey from Jerusalem in 1035 A.D Robert died in Nicaea (Turkey). Later a mission was sent by his son William, to bring his body back to Normandy. When the envoys learned that William had died they decided to intern Robert's body in Norman Auplia (Southern Italy).

Falaise castle, Calvados lower Normandy

The Iron Duke

William II "the bastard, before the Conqueror"

Legend has it that Robert "the Magnificent" laid eyes on a beautiful young lady from the castle of Falaise. Her name was Herleva/Arlette (the daughter of a tanner or embalmer). Apparently she was dying leather garments, and when Robert saw her his lust was uncontrollable. She was brought to the castle where they became lovers.

The legend of Herleva (Robert Wace "Roman de Rou")

"I dreamt that a tree was coming out of my body and rising up into the sky above; the whole for Normandy was covered by the shadow cast from its branches"

Herleva did indeed have something growing in her body and in 1027/1028 A.D she gave birth to a baby boy. The boy was named William and in time his shadow just like in his mother's dream did come true and cover all of Normandy and later England as well.

The fountain of Arlette, below Falaise castle, according to legend this is the exact spot where Robert encountered Arlette.

Duke William II became the Conqueror, the most famous of all the Normans. His Conquest of Anglo-Saxon England earned him a place in history and 1066 A.D still is the most famous date in the island's history. Before William became the Conqueror he was known to his contemporaries as William "the bastard". As the illegitimate son of Robert "the magnificent", William was catapulted into the limelight when his father died in 1035 A.D.

Robert the Archbishop of Rouen (William's great uncle) upheld the wishes of Duke Robert and proclaimed young William, who was only seven years old, Duke William II of Normandy. William was sent to Paris to perform the act of fealty and homage where he received the consent as the rightful Duke from his overlord King Henry I of France. In March 1037 A.D his great uncle Robert died and the Duchy descended into chaos.

William of Jumieges wrote:

"Conspiracies and plots were hatched and the Duchy was ablaze with fire"

The Norman castle of Bricquebe, Contentin, Normandy

From the very start of his reign, William's life was in mortal danger. Some of the Norman nobles and even some of William's relatives refused to accept his rule and sought to have him murdered. On one such occasion, Osbern de Crespon (William's guardian and the Seneschal of Normandy) had his throat cut in front of the boy's eyes. In 1042 A.D William was coming of age, he was knighted at the siege of Falaise, where he forced Turstein, the Viscount of Hiémois, to submit and surrender.

In 1046 A.D the conspiracy against the young Duke deepened when Guy de Bourgogne (a grandson of Duke Richard II) and various Norman nobles assembled in Bayeux and swore to destroy him. William was resting in the castle of Valognes (Contentin, Western Normandy) when he was awoken by Goles, the court jester, who told him he had overheard a plot to kill him. William crept out of the castle and fled on horseback. He continued riding hell-for-leather cross the entire region to reach the safety of Falaise. Under the cover of darkness he passed through the treacherous marshes of the Contentin and crossed the river Vire near the modern day town of Isigny-sur-mer. In the morning William sought refuge with Hubert de Ryes, who gave the young Duke a fresh horse and provisions. Hubert advised William to avoid Bayeux and travel to Falaise via the old Roman road through the Orne valley. The Norman countryside was swarming with rebel soldiers eager to capture or kill the Duke, but William avoided capture and reached his hometown of Falaise.

Duke William II from an early manuscript

The Battle of Val es Dunes 1047

In 1047 A.D William was determined to crush the Western rebels once and for all. With the help of the faithful Norman barons and King Henry of France, the Duke pushed into lower Normandy and prepared to give battle to Guy De Bourgogne, Grimont de Plessis and the rebels. Just outside the great medieval city of Caen the two armies confronted each other.

Robert Wace, Roman de Rou:

"You should have seen the divisions and their leaders stretched out across the vast plains: there was not one Lord nor man of influence present who did not have either a war banner or flag near him. You could have seen the battlefield tremble, horses were charging into the attack, spears were raised, lances brandished. There was an almighty noise when the two armies clashed, the very ground beneath them was disturbed and shook"

Although outnumbered by the rebels, William and King Henry decided to attack. As the loyalist forces advanced a third army came into view. Raoul Tesson de Thury Harcourt had not joined either the rebels or the Duke's forces. Both sides sent urgent envoys to try and convince Raoul and his retinue to commit to their side.

Although Raoul had been one of the rebels who had sworn to destroy William at the secret meeting in Bayeux, in the end he decided that he could not make war against his rightful overlord, Duke William and the King of France. He met the Duke and struck William in the face with his glove. Raoul said: **"my oath is complete, I had sworn to smite you and by this act I have. Henceforth I will do you no further harm, for I am your liege man"**. Raoul returned to his men and waited on the side lines between the two armies.

The battle commenced with the fully armoured mounted knights riding at full gallop against one another. The chivalry of Normandy now clashed together in the fierce mounted hand to hand combat. The King's division crashed into the rebels from the Contentin. Lances were broken into the bodies of the horses and their riders, and then swords were drawn and plunged into the mail coats of the Norman and French knights.

Monument to the Battle of Val es Dunes

A rebel Norman knight charged straight through the Royal household and struck King Henry on his hauberk (helmet). The King was beaten off his horse and fell to the ground, unharmed but a little shaken. He immediately remounted and continued to fight in the fray. The better organisation of William and the loyalist forces were holding their own against the overwhelming rebel numbers. William fought like a lion, hacking the limbs off his enemies and killing all in his path.

Then two incidents turned the battle in favour of the Duke. One of the rebel's leaders, Haimo/Hamon de Creully, nicknamed "Le Dentu" was killed in the fighting; his death caused panic amongst his men, who were starting to look for an exit route from the bloody field. Then Raoul Tesson decided the time was right and attacked the rebels in their rear. Raoul and his men charged in, shouting the war cry "TUR AIE" forging a path deep into the enemy ranks. The remaining rebels broke formation and fled for their lives. Many died whilst trying to ford the Orne River, weighed down by their heavy armour; they drowned in the bloody water. William relentlessly pursued the rebels, killing and capturing many men. The victory was complete for the Duke, who had fought the first major battle of his career.

The rebel leadership had been smashed, but Guy de Bourgogne escaped and took refuge in the formidable castle of Brionne in the valley of the Risle (Central Normandy).

William's cavalry charge at the Battle of Val es Dunes 1047

Many of the surviving, rebels were pardoned, but Grimont de Plessis who had been captured after the battle trying to flee to his castle in the Bessin, was sent to Rouen and later died in imprisonment. A gruesome tale circulated that William, who hated Grimont had him torn apart, piece by piece using a wooden knife. He was skinned, and his skin was made into a saddle cover. William set about restoring order to the Duchy. Firstly he besieged Guy's castle of Brionne. The siege lasted for three years until Guy requested terms of surrender. In the end he was pardoned and left Normandy to return to Burgundy.

The Duke also enlisted the help of the church, who agreed to impose the "Truce of God". This agreement stated that private wars were forbidden between Wednesday evening and Monday morning. They were entirely prohibited during the holy periods of Advent, Easter, Lent and Pentecost. Only the Duke and the King of France were exempted from the treaty, but anyone else who violated the truce would be excommunicated. In 1049 A.D William negotiated with Baldwin of Flanders for the hand of his daughter Matilda, in marriage. When Pope Leo IX heard about this proposal he forbid the marriage on the grounds that William and Matilda were too closely related (both were distant cousins and descendants of Rollo, the Viking founder of Normandy). Pope Leo IX was the same Pope who was defeated and captured after the Battle of Civitate by the Norman

Conquerors of Southern Italy. The real reason may have been political, for both the French King and the Holy Roman Emperor, Henry III were concerned about the creation of a Norman-Flemish power block in Northern France. William took no notice of the interdiction and went ahead with the marriage. Matilda was escorted to the great frontier town of Eu, where William was waiting for her. In the church of Notre Dame et Saint Laurent d'Eu the happy couple was married.

To the south of Normandy, Geoffrey Martel, the Count of Anjou, had been busy extending his domains. He had encroached on the disputed region of Maine, which in the past had acknowledged the Dukes of Normandy as their overlords. When Count Hugh IV of Maine died, Geoffrey seized his chance and took over the entire region, including the strategic castles of Domfront and Alencon on the Norman border. King Henry of France was growing concerned about the increasing power of both Normandy and Anjou decided to play one side off against the other. He requested William attack the Count lands, hoping both sides would be weakened by the conflict.

William launched a major military assault on the castle of Domfront, but was unable to take it by force. On hearing the news from Domfront, the citizens of Alencon, confident of withstanding the Norman attack, hung animal skins from the battlements, in reference to William's ancestry as the illegitimate son of Duke Robert and a tanner's daughter. When Alencon fell to the Normans, William ordered the leading citizens of the town to be brought before him. For mocking him, he had their hands and feet cut off in front of the rest of the town. When the garrison of Domfront got wind of the story they immediately surrendered under a promise of mercy. William's victory enabled him to annex the Plassais region into the Duchy of Normandy.

William of Poitiers commented that William said in the words of Julius Caesar:

"I came, I saw, I conquered"

Further insurrections, Arques 1053

No sooner than having returned from his victorious campaign in Southern Normandy, William was faced with yet another insurrection. Since leaving the Norman host during the siege of Domfront, William de Talou (the Duke's uncle) had been busy stirring up trouble for his nephew. From the formidable castle of Arques in Eastern Normandy, he openly defied the Duke. William immediately invaded the county and nearly took the castle by surprise. Arques was too strong to be directly assaulted, so William besieged the castle and blockaded the surrounding area using the loyalist lords of Longueville to supervise the siege. King Henry of France decided to support the rebels covertly, and sent Enguerrand II (son of the Count of Ponthieu) to relieve the siege. William expected such a plan and had stationed a mobile force of mounted knights in the vicinity. As Enguerrand II approached St Aubin, his force was attacked by a small detachment of Norman knights who conducted a feinted flight. Thinking the knights were retreating, Enguerrand II charged after them, not knowing that he was being drawn into an ambush. From the wooded undergrowth around him appeared the main body of William's mobile force. It was carnage as the French soldiers tried in vain to flee the bloody scene. The relief force was completely annihilated including Enguerrand II, who was killed in the melee. The Normans allegedly used the same successful tactic 13 years later at the Battle of Hastings.

With no hope of relief from the outside world, the garrison surrendered in the winter of 1053 A.D. William's rebellious uncles were banished from Normandy never to return again. The King of France, who was left embarrassed by the whole debacle, decided that he would have to lead the army directly against Duke William in the next campaigning season. He formed an alliance with his old enemy, Geoffrey Count of Anjou and planned an invasion set for the spring of 1054 A.D.

The remains of the formidable castle of Arques, Eastern Normandy

The Battle of Mortemer 1054

King Henry I of France and Geoffrey Count of Anjou invaded the Duchy (Evreux region) in early 1054 A.D. While Duke William faced the threat on the south side of the river Seine, the defence of upper Normandy was entrusted to Robert, Count of Eu, William de Warenne, (later 1st Earl of Surrey) Hugh de Gournay, Roger de Mortemer, Hugh de Montfort and Gauthier Giffard. The French incursion was commanded by Count Odo (The King's brother) and Count Rainald of Montdidier.

The invasion force entered the Eastern borders of upper Normandy sacking and pillaging the district in the custom of the time. They captured and encamped within the small town of Mortemer en Bray on their way towards Rouen, to link up with King Henry who had been ravaging the Evreux region. Count Odo was over confident and neglected to secure the area, unaware of the presence of the Norman defence force.

Just before dawn, while the French were still sleeping, the Normans with the local knowledge of Roger de Mortemer, encircled the town, cutting off any escape routes. They then set fire to the thatched houses and buildings. Within minutes the dark sky was ablaze with fire and smoke bellowing out the town's dwellings. The French were in total disarray, and the panic stricken soldiers tried to gather their booty and flee the town. Unfortunately for them, the Norman knights and militia attacked them at this crucial moment, charging out of the darkness into the burning rubble of the town. The battle for Mortemer became a slaughter; in the burning streets the Normans wreaked a bloody revenge on the invaders. By the end of the day the carnage and rout of the French army was complete.

Mortimer arms, St Laurence church, Ludlow

Although Count Odo (King Henry's brother) had managed to escape, many valuable French prisoners were captured including Rainald Count of Montdidier. The battle of Mortemer had inflicted a crushing defeat on the French. Duke William is said to have thanked God for the victory and sent Ralph de Toeni / Tosny to give the good news to the French King and the Count of Anjou.

The Norman chronicler Orderic Vital reported that Ralph crept up to the French camp and shouted

"FRENCHMEN! FRENCHMEN! ARISE, ARISE! PREPARE FOR FLIGHT, YE SLEEP TOO LONG! AWAY, AND BURY YOUR FRIENDS WHO HAVE BEEN SLAIN AT MORTEMER!"

On hearing the woeful news from Mortemer, King Henry called off the invasion and fled a hastily retreat back across the Norman border. One of the heroes of the battle was Roger de Mortemer. In the rout that followed he captured Rainald de Montdidier, who was actually his father in law and also his feudal lord for lands within the French Kingdom. Roger released the Count, but without the consent of the Duke. William was outraged at the release of an important prisoner and ransom.

Orderic Vital commented that Duke William said:

"I banished Roger from Normandy for this offence, but became reconciled with him soon afterwards."

Carving of Norman knights, Eardisley church

Mortemer was pardoned, and his successors became one of the most powerful Marcher Lord families of the English-Welsh border after the Norman Conquest (see chapter 5).

The final showdown, The Battle of Varaville 1057

The Battle of Mortemer practically put an end to the internal divisions within the Duchy. William had only to contend with the outside threat from the King and the Count of Anjou. In 1055 A.D William decided to take the offensive against his enemies. He invaded the County of Mayenne situated on Normandy's Southern border. The Duke constructed a new castle at Ambrieres which he intended to be used as a forward base for the conquest of the County. The local lord, Geoffrey de Mayenne, appealed to his overlord Geoffrey Count of Anjou for assistance. The Count headed north and a standoff between the Normans and Angevins ensued. Geoffrey tried in vain to besiege the castle of Ambrieres, but was thwarted by the presence of the Duke's army. He retreated back to Anjou and conspired with King Henry, who was determined to destroy his vassal William, once and for all.

Royal arms of France

In the summer of 1057 A.D the Royal host of King Henry and the Angevins crossed the border and invaded Normandy. They ravaged the countryside, destroying the corps and burning all the settlements in their wake. Even the city of Caen was sacked. William was gathering his forces in Falaise waiting for the right moment to attack. When his spies brought word to him that the invaders were planning to cross the marshes of the Pays d'Auge, the Duke seized his chance and marched out with the army. As the invaders crossed the Dives estuary, laden down with their spoils from the campaign near Varaville, disaster struck. Duke William waited until half the French had crossed the bridge then gave the signal to attack. The Normans ferociously pounced upon the French rearguard. Caught completely by surprise, the French soldiers tried to force their way over the wooden causeway. Under pressure from the sheer weight and numbers, the bridge collapsed into the rising waters of the estuary. King Henry watched the disaster unfold; he could do nothing but look on in despair, as his army was annihilated. The entire rearguard was killed, captured or drowned. Even the Norman peasants armed with clubs and crude farm weapons joined the battle.

Monument to the Battle of Varaville 1057

William de Poitiers described the battle;

> **"Caught by complete surprise on this side of the estuary, under the watchful eyes of the King, almost all fell under the strokes of the sword, apart from those who were terrified, and preferred to throw themselves into the waters".**

For King Henry it was nothing less than a total disaster. He left Normandy with his tail firmly tucked between his legs, never to return to the Duchy ever again.

Robert Wace commented;

> **"The King went back to France, filled with anger and despair. He no longer bared arms and never again set foot in Normandy."**

William's position in Normandy was now stronger than it had ever been. Within two years after the battle of Varaville both King Henry and the Count of Anjou were dead. They were succeeded by infant heirs and William was almost given a free hand to strengthen and enhance the power of the Duchy of Normandy.

The Conquest of Maine 1062

The historic region of Maine lies between Normandy and Anjou with Le Mans as its capital. In 1051 A.D Geoffrey Count of Anjou had banished Count Hebert II who took refuge in Normandy. Herbert II allied himself with William and promised that if he died without issue, his title as Count of Maine would pass to the Duke. William also arranged the marriage between his son Robert and Herbert's younger sister. In the spring of March 1062 A.D Herbert II died childless in Normandy. William at once gathered his troops and invaded Maine to uphold his claim. The Duke was opposed by his old enemy Geoffrey de Mayenne. The fighting was difficult, but slowly the Normans gained the upper hand. In 1063 A.D William broke through the defences of Le Mans and entered the capital where he had his son Robert crowned Count. The last sparks of resistance were snuffed out with the capitulation of the great

The remodelled medieval castle of Sillé-le-Guillaume, Mayenne

border fortress of Sille le Guilliame and the capture of Geoffrey de Mayenne. A legend states that Geoffrey was held up in the castle of Mayenne with food and provisions. William preferring not to risk a long drawn out siege bribed two children, who entered the castle and set fire to it, forcing Geoffrey to abandon the fortress and surrender.

In 1064 A.D William invaded Brittany and forced Conan II to recognise him as his overlord. In one of the strange coincidences of history, Harold Godwinson actually fought alongside the Duke during this campaign. William had beaten all of his enemies and secured the Duchy against any potential threats. Now he embarked on the greatest gamble of his life, the Conquest of a Kingdom far greater and more prosperous than his own, England (see chapter 4)

Normandy after the Conquest of England

In the spring of 1067 A.D William returned to Normandy. No longer was he regarded as William "the bastard" but as William the Conqueror. Against all the odds the Duke had triumphed and was now the King of England. William began a tour of the Duchy visiting the abbeys of Fecamp, St Pierre sur Dives and Jumieges where he held court. Trouble was brewing in England and by the end of the year William set out to restore order in his new Kingdom.

In 1070 Count Baldwin VI of Flanders (William's brother in-law) died. William supported the claim of his nephew Arnulf to the County, and sent his most trusted loyal friend William Fitz Osbern to look after his interests. Another one of the boy's uncles, Robert, disputed his nephew's claim and with the help of the King of France destroyed the Norman-Flemish forces at the battle of Cassel in 1071 A.D. In the encounter both William Fitz Osbern and Arnulf were killed. Encouraged by the absence of William and the defeat of the Norman forces in Flanders Maine

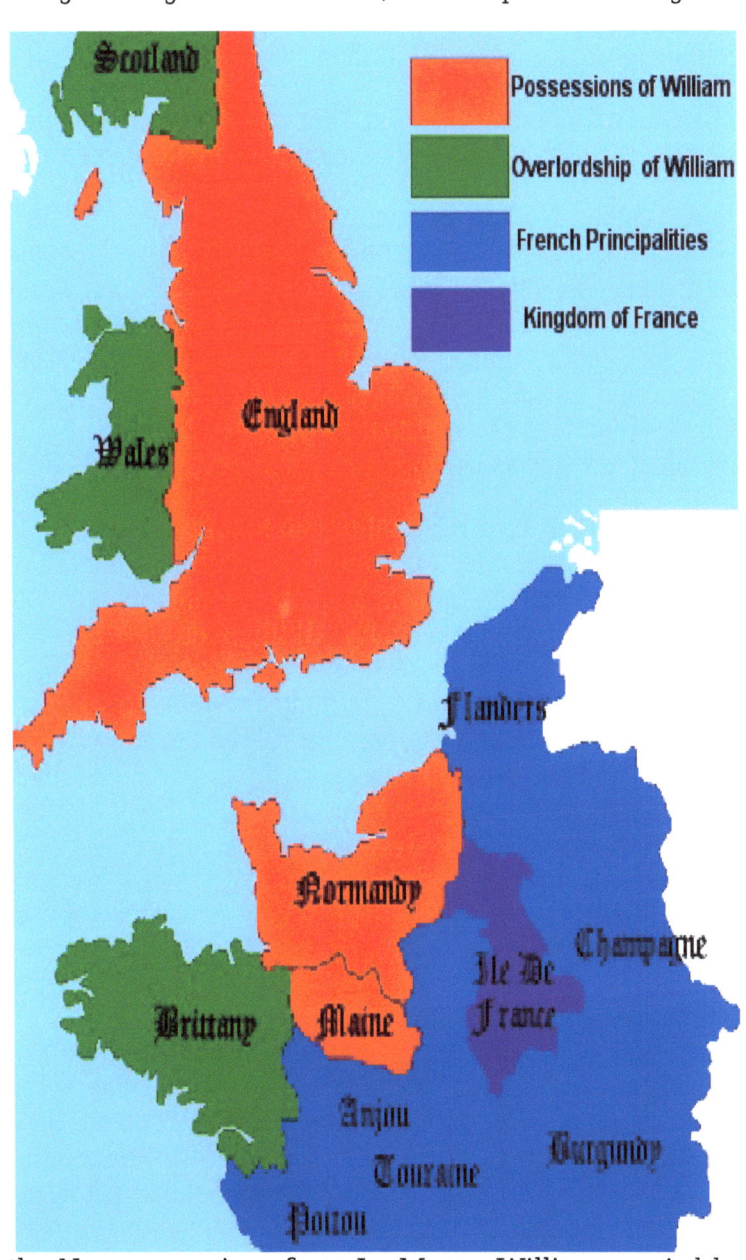

erupted into open revolt and expelled the Norman garrison from Le Mans. William worried by events on the continent returned to Normandy with an army of Norman and English soldiers. He swiftly surprised the rebels in Maine and recaptured Le Mans. In a shrewd political move he defused the threat from Anjou by recognising the Count of Anjou as overlord of Maine, thus leaving Robert his son to control the County free from any interference. The last years of William's life were spent mostly in Normandy trying to assert his authority over the advances of his nobles and the King of France. William suffered his first defeat at the hands of the French King at Dol, on the Norman-Breton border. He was forced to lift the siege and retreat back to Normandy. Undeterred William fought on and inflicted a defeat against the Angevins in 1077 A.D. His Son Robert, nicknamed Curthose (probably given to him because he wore short trousers known as Courte heuse) rebelled against his father and joined the King of France.

William is said to have told Robert:

"It was with Norman valour that enabled me the conquer England, and Normandy is mine by hereditary descent and I will never relinquish it up while I live".

Robert raided Normandy from the castle of Gerberoi on the Norman - Picardie border until his father arrived on the scene and besieged the castle. Legend states that both father and son fought each other beneath the walls of the castle. Robert wounded his father killing his horse from underneath him. William was only saved when an English knight called Tokig of Wallingford, gave the King his horse. William's family troubles continued: his half brother Odo, the Bishop of Bayeux and Earl of Kent was arrested in 1082 A.D for raising an army against the wishes of the King. When Odo pleaded that as a Bishop he could not be arrested, William replied that he was not being arrested as Bishop of Bayeux, but as the Earl of Kent.

In 1087 A.D the aged King set out on his final military campaign. The French garrison of Mantes had crossed the border and raided the Norman Vexin, William was determined to punish the offenders and reclaim the whole of the Vexin which had actually been ceded to his father back in the early part of the 11th century. William crossed the river Epte and harried the land, destroying the crops and vines as he made his way towards Mantes. When the Duke arrived in Mantes the French garrison fled in terror, burning down the town to try and halt the Norman advance. As the Duke ventured through the burning rubble his horse became spooked and threw him against his saddle. William seems to have suffered some internal bleeding and was carried back to the Norman capital Rouen in a litter. Unable to sleep because of the noise of the city, William was taken to the priory of St Gevais just outside the city walls. On the 9th of September 1087 A.D William Duke of Normandy, who had ruled the Duchy for 52 years and had been King of England since 1066 died. William's legacy continued through his sons Robert, William, Henry and his granddaughter Matilda "the Empress".

Within 150 years of establishing themselves, The Dukes of Normandy had created one to the most feared and organised Principalities in Medieval Europe. As the 12th century approached, the Viking age was coming to an end. The hour of the Normans had arrived; they would spearhead the invasions and Conquests of Anglo-Saxon England, the Celtic Kingdoms of Wales, Ireland, and Scotland and become Christianities, iron fist in the re-conquest of the Holy-land. However their first expansion took them to the foot of Southern Italy and Sicily. The exploits of the sons of Tancred de Hauteville would become engrained in Norman Myth and legend. The penniless Mafia like mercenaries defied the odds and created the Norman Kingdom in the sun.

Chapter 2: Southern Italy and Sicily

THE FIRST MAFIA
"The Norman Conquest of Southern Italy and Sicily"

The arrival of the Normans in Southern Italy has been shrouded in mystery for centuries. Some say the first Normans were pilgrims returning from the Holy land, others say they were mercenaries banished from their homeland of Normandy searching for employment and news lands to settle. Whatever the truth may be their impact on the Italian mainland and the island of Sicily was as dramatic as the conquest of Anglo Saxon England and the Celtic Kingdoms of the British Isles. The exploits of the sons of Tancred de Hauteville would become engrained in Norman Myth and legend. The De Hauteville Mafia defied the odds and created the Norman Kingdom in the sun.

THE FIRST ARRIVALS 999 A.D -

Unlike the Norman conquest of England in 1066 A.D where we have a specific date of conquest (14th of October 1066 A.D) and a detailed account of Duke William's campaign, the Norman conquest of Southern Italy took decades of cunning, bravery and ferocious determination before being united under the leadership of the De Hauteville brothers. Amatus of Montecassino (a Benedictine monk from the abbey of Montecassino) who was writing over 80 years after the events, records that a group of Norman Pilgrims were returning from pilgrimage in the Holy land before the year 1000 A.D.

Salerno and Monte Gargano
999 A.D

En route home back to Normandy they stopped off at Salerno in southern Italy. During their rest a Muslim army from Sicily (the island then was still under the control of the Muslim Emirs of North Africa) attacked the town, seeking retribution for the town's none payment of tribute money. Knowing the fate of the town, if it were to fall into Saracen hands, the Normans galvanised themselves into action. They asked Guaimar (the local lord) to provide them with arms and armour, which he did happily. They then immediately attacked the besiegers and killed many Saracens, the rest fled in terror from the men of the North wind. Guaimar so impressed, asked the Normans to stay and to encourage more of their compatriots to come to the land of flowing milk and honey (Southern Italy). Another chronicler William de Apulia writing a few years later describes how again the first Normans were also pilgrims. In his account they were visiting the shrine of Saint Michel at Monte Gargano. Saint Michel was indeed one of the Normans favorite warrior saints whom they also worshipped in Normandy, Le Mont de Saint Michel (Manche, lower Normandy)

St Michel, Monte Gargano, Italy

At the shrine they encountered Melus de Bari (an Italian/Lombard nobleman) who had recently lost his lands and been forced into exile by the Byzantines who controlled most of the Southern Italian Adriatic coast. The leader of the Norman pilgrims was Rainulf /Rudolf who had also been exiled from Normandy. Melus and his brother Dattus hatched a plan together with the help of the Normans to return to power. In the spring of 1017 A.D the Italian/Norman forces raided deep into Byzantine Apulia. They defeated the Byzantine forces in several skirmishes, but their attempt to capture the fortified town of Trani failed. By the winter the Byzantines sent over their general Basil Boiannes to regain control of the situation. In 1018 A.D the successes of Melus and his Norman mercenaries had been checked. In an encounter at Cannae (the same place where Hannibal had defeated the Roman army in 216 B.C) the Italian/Norman forces were defeated. Gilbert one of the Norman leaders was killed in the battle and Melus fled north to raise support from the German Emperor who claimed to be overlord of all Italy in his capacity as Holy Roman Emperor. After the defeat at Cannae the few surviving Norman mercenaries enlisted in the armies of the highest bidder. Indeed the Byzantine General Basil Boiannes even employed some Normans to garrison Troia.

Divide and Conquer

In the years of civil strife between the Byzantines, Italians and Lombards, the only winners were the Norman mercenaries who played one side against another. William de Apulia states that;

Norman Carving in the Duomo, Aversa, Italy

"The Normans never desired any of the Lombard factions to win decisively, in case this should be to their disadvantage. But now supporting the one, and then aiding the other, they prevented anyone from being completely destroyed. Gallic cunning deceived the Italians, for they allowed no one to be at the mercy of a triumphant enemy"

From an early stage the Norman "Kingmakers" were setting themselves up for a complete takeover.

Aversa 1030 A.D

In 1030 A.D the Norman warlord Ranuif was installed by Duke Segius IV as Lord of the town and newly built castle of Aversa some 15 miles outside Naples. He had also given the Normans the right to control the surrounding land and take tribute from the local towns and villages. Ranuif had now secured the first Norman fief on the mainland. By 1038 A.D the Holy Roman Emperor Conrad II came down to Italy to re-assert his authority over the Italian nobles. Ranuif gained even more autonomy by being officially recognised as the new "Count of Aversa".

The Byzantine campaign in Sicily 1038 A.D

Also in the same year the Byzantine Empire planned to re-conquer the Island of Sicily. Guaimar was asked to supply troops for the invasion to which he sent 300-500 troublesome Normans. In September the Norman mercenaries and the elite Byzantine Varangian Guard spearheaded the invasion force and crossed the straits of Messina into Sicily.

The Varangian Guard was led by an outstanding Viking warrior, Harald "Hardrada" who in time became King of Norway and who launched the last Viking invasion of England in 1066 A.D. At the Battle of Stamford Bridge his mighty army was utterly annihilated and Hardrada himself lost his life in the battle. King Harold Godwinsson and the Anglo Saxon victory did not last long as he had to rush from York to the south coast of England to face the Norman invasion by William the Conqueror. After the initial success in capturing the city of Messina the fighting was hard going. In 1040 A.D the Byzantines managed to capture Syracuse in which a Norman knight William De Hauteville distinguished himself during the fighting and earned the nickname "Iron arm". The Muslim garrison sallied out from the city and attacked the Byzantines. Its commander cut down many Byzantine men until William "Iron Arm" charged into the fray, killing him single handed. The campaign ended because of the heavy handed treatment of the Lombard contingent and distribution of spoils by the Byzantine commander. Back on the mainland Byzantine authority started to crumble and the Italians and Normans exploited the situation by invading Apulia. In 1041 A.D the Italian-Norman army inflicted a heavy defeat on the Byzantine forces at Montepeloso. Then in late 1041 A.D/early 1042, the Normans gained control of the important town of Melfi. They chose William "Iron arm" as their leader. The De Hauteville Clan had arrived.

Castle of Melfi (Apulia) Italy

The De Hauteville Mafia

The De Hauteville family came from a small village called Hauteville Le Guiscard in the Manche region of lower Normandy. William and his brother Drongo were the first of the family to seek fame and fortune abroad. They were two of six children from their father Tancred de Hauteville's first marriage. Tancred married again and produced a further seven children of whom five would also come to Italy. With the installation of William "Iron arm" at Melfi the Normans extended their gains in Apulia by annexing Ascoli, Venosa, Lavello, Trani, Acerenza and several other towns and villages. The Byzantine Empire was suffering from incursions in Asia Minor and on the Danube front, and was unable to send major reinforcements to Italy; consequently its Italian colonies had to fend for themselves. The new Norman lordships were created not from permission of the Holy Roman Emperor or from the Pope in Rome, but through sheer brute force. A Byzantine monk from Lucania commented that it was the **"invasion of the heathen".**

Norman Castle of Lamezia Terme (Apulia, Italy)

The Normans became the first real mafia in the region. They extracted tribute money from the towns, confiscated food reserves, burned holy places to the ground and brutality punished anyone who stood in their way. With a steady arrival of reinforcements from Normandy their grip on the southern Italian peninsular was taking shape. Anti-Norman feeling erupted in 1045 A.D when the Norman Count Rudolf from Aversa and his entourage were ambushed in the Town of Montecassino. The Norman knights were pulled from their horses and murdered by the angry mob. Only Count Rudolf was spared, he was kept in prison by Abbot Richer of Montecassino until his ransom was paid and he promised never again to attack the abbey lands.

In the year 1046 A.D Robert De Hauteville, half brother of William "Iron arm" who had recently died, and Drongo (who became the new count) arrived in Italy. Robert was a true Norman; hence he had come to Southern Italy hungry for land and fortune. Robert came to the court of his half brother, but Drongo could not accommodate him with any lands and sent him out to Calabria. After a few months in the wilds, Robert again returned and as Amatus put it:

"Robert returned and told his brother of his poverty. For he was very thin in the face and underweight, but Drongo turned away and sent Robert away again".

Robert first went to garrison the Norman outpost at Scribla, he then moved on to the hilltop of San Marco Argentano. From his rocky outcrop he raided the surrounding countryside. On one occasion after arranging a meeting with a noble representative from a local town, Robert seized the man from his horse and carried him off for ransom. He received the nickname "Guiscard" (the cunning).

Robert "Guiscard" De Hauteville
1015 - 1085

William of Auplia describes how Robert came up with an old Viking plan the gain access to a fortified city which he was unable to take by force. He pretended that one of his warriors had been killed and asked for the coffin to be buried in the city's church. Once inside the coffin bust open to reveal the warrior very still much alive, with the help of the false mourners they opened the gates and let Robert's forces inside, enabling him to capture the city.

Robert Guiscard's Castle at San Marco Argentano

The New Holy Roman Emperor (Henry III) upset the power balance in Southern Italy with his dispute with the Principality of Benevento. The Emperor instructed the German Pope to excommunicate the Beneventians and gave the green light to the Normans to attack them at will. The Normans needed little encouragement and attacked the Principality with vigor. All over Southern Italy they caused havoc.

In 1050 A.D Pope Leo IX came south on a visit to the region and was shocked to what he saw.

"He journeyed to the borders of Apulia, to repair the Christian religion which had all but disappeared. He tried to bring about peace between the Italians and Normans. The princes had recruited the Normans to help them drive out their enemies, but now the Normans have become savage tyrants, they have destroyed the land and its people".

When he reached Benevento in 1051 A.D the townspeople forced Prince Pandulf III to flee the city, asking the Pope to rid them of the Norman menace and take direct control of the Principality. The Pope ordered Count Drongo to cease attacks against Benevento. Drongo agreed, but in truth how much control he had over the various Norman factions is debatable. The Wolves had been let loose and they were hungry for more booty and territory. In the summer of 1051 A.D Count Drongo was assassinated, some say in a Byzantine/Lombard plot, although the Normans had enemies all around them. Drogo's younger brother Humphrey stepped into his brother's shoes as Count, but was unable to control the escalating Italian-Norman violence. The Byzantines sent ambassadors to the Pope and German Emperor to conclude an alliance against the Norman invaders. By 1053 A.D an anti Norman alliance had been concluded. Leo received several hundred elite Swabian troops from Germany and by May this force was boosted with troops from

Benevento, Abruzzi, Capua and other disaffected regions from Southern and Central Italy. Only the Duchy of Salerno stayed neutral and refused to join the coalition. The Papal army's plan was to march in force into Apulia and link up with the forces of the Byzantines; together they could then crush the Norman menace once and for all.

The Battle of Civitate 1053A.D

For the first time since they had arrived, the Normans were faced with complete annihilation. In this uneasy situation all the different factions had no choice but to unit. Count Humphrey commanded the Norman forces along with Richard De Aversa and Robert Guiscard. Their force was made up of mostly 3000 heavily armoured Norman knights and their objective was to stop the Papal and Byzantine armies from joining together at all costs. The outcome of the fore coming battle would decide the fate of Southern Italy and the medieval world. Near the ancient settlement of Civitate by the Fortore River the Normans intercepted Pope Leo's army. At first the Normans sent envoys to try to settle a negotiated peace. The Pope was after all their spiritual leader and God's representative on earth. Their peace proposals were rejected and they were told with influence from the Germans in the Papal Army that they must leave Italy or face death.

With no hope of a peaceful settlement, the Normans were left with only one option, to give battle at once. As the two armies squared up to one another the Pope watched the battle unfold from the safety of the town of Civitate. The Normans although heavily outnumbered, charged directly at the Papal forces. Richard De Aversa on the Norman right smashed into the Italians. So fierce was his charge that the Italians broke rank and fled. In the centre the fighting was difficult, the Swabians with their gigantic two handed swords held the line with ferocious fighting spirit, cutting men and horse in two. Robert Guiscard brought his Norman knights into the centre to try to finish off the Germans. Three times he had a horse cut down from under him, and three times he mounted another and returned into the fray. Only when Richard De Aversa returned from routing the Italians was the battle decided. Surrounded on all sides, the Swabians fought desperately to the last man, no quarter was asked and no quarter was given. The Normans against all odds and against an army probably twice their size had triumphed. The citizens of Civitate were at first defiant, only when the advancing Norman army approached the town and threatened it with complete destruction did they decide to promptly hand over the Pope to the Normans in fear of retribution. Almost embarrassed by the capture of the Holy Father, the Normans treated Pope Leo IX with respect, asking for his pardon and forgiveness. The hapless Pope was carted off to Benevento and kept a prisoner for the next nine months.

After the battle of Civitate the Norman position was even stronger than before. They would never again face any substantial threat to their power on the mainland. In 1054 A.D Pope Leo died followed by the Byzantine Emperor in 1055 A.D and then the Holy Roman Emperor (Henry III) in 1056 A.D. During the 1050s the Normans continued to annex and create new lordships in Calabria, Apulia and Capua. Count Humphrey died in 1057A.D and was succeeded by his half brother Robert Guiscard. Under Robert's leadership and that of his newly arrived brother Roger, the De Hauteville mafia became a force to be reckoned with. The legitimization of the Norman regime and reconciliation with the Papacy came about in 1059 A.D. Pope Nicholas II needed the support of the powerful Norman Lords to secure his Papal throne against a rival candidate Benedict X. He granted Robert Guiscard the new title of Duke of Apulia and Calabria.

"By the Grace of God and St Peter Duke of Apulia and Calabria and, in the future Lord of Sicily"

He also confirmed Richard De Aversa as Lord of Capua. Most important of all he gave Robert the Papal Banner with the right to conquer the island of Sicily and bring it back into the Christian fold, taking it back from Saracen hands.

Robert Guiscard, invested by Pope Nicholas II as Duke of Apulia, Calabria and Sicily

Holy war: The Crusade in Sicily

The Mountainous island of Sicily lies only a few miles off mainland Italy separated by the strait of Messina. In the 11th century it was at the very edge of the Christian world. The majority of Sicily remained under Muslim control with a few Byzantine enclaves in the east of the island. The reconquest would be led be the Pope's new right hand "The Normans" and its outcome would determine Papal international policy that would have repercussions to this day. For the Normans Sicily represented a new challenge and land to conquer. Sicily's strategic position was fundamental in controlling any trade in the Mediterranean. Always eager for new territory and power they began preparations for the invasion and conquest of the island. In 1061 A.D Guiscard's Normans conducted some reconnaissance operations to assess the feasibility of the invasion. In May Roger landed the advanced guard on the shores outside Messina at night to avoid being detected by the Saracens. In the morning the Normans ambushed and destroyed a relief force sent from the Sicilian capital Palermo. On hearing the news the garrison of Messina fled in terror and abandoned the city. With Messina and its important harbor safely in Norman hands the main army under Robert Guiscard crossed over into Sicily. With over 2000 troops 1000 of whom were mounted knights Robert and Roger set about conquering the Island.

At Enna (Castrogiovanni) the Normans encountered a Saracen army composed of several thousand African and Sicilian troops. Robert aligned his army into battle formation. Roger led the vanguard followed by Robert in the centre. Just as at Civitate the Norman cavalry charge cut deep into the Saracen army. Robert encouraged his men hacking through the Saracen ranks, soon the battle turned into a rout as the Muslims turned and fled the battlefield. The victorious Norman army marched on to Enna, but was unable to take the fortified city. Instead Robert sent Roger with a large mounted force south to reconnoiter the southern shores of the island. He raided the Agrigento region, but was unable to attack the fortified hilltop towns and cities without siege equipment.

Robert also used the Norman policy so successful in the conquest of the Southern Italy "divide and conquer". Quick to exploit the differences between the various Muslim factions, Robert exacted protection money and promised assistance in the disputes between the different Emirs. With the onset of winter Robert and Roger returned to Messina and then back to the mainland to prepare for the next campaigning season. Sicily would not be an easy conquest, after the initial shock of the Norman invasion the Muslims rallied and fought tooth and nail to hold on to the island. In 1062 A.D Roger captured the town of Petralia only 40 miles from the Sicilian capital Palermo. Although the war in Sicily was a "Holy war", when possible both Robert and Roger tried to negotiate the peaceful transfer of loyalties from town to town. Indeed there were few too many Normans to conquer and garrison the whole island. During the winter of 1062 A.D at Troina the townspeople who had once welcomed the Normans as liberators, revolted against them and besieged Roger's wife (Judith d'Evreux) who had come over from Normandy. Roger arrived just in time before the garrison was overwhelmed, but then found himself besieged by the town's Muslim and Byzantine population. The siege lasted all winter and only ended when the besiegers got drunk and neglected their defensive lines. Roger seized the opportunity and with a few remaining knights charged out from the citadel and killed the drunken besiegers. With Troina back in Norman hands, the town's burgers were publicly executed to set an example for disobeying Norman rule.

The battle of Cerami

Fresh Saracen reinforcements were sent from Africa to try to bolster up Muslim moral on the island. Not far from Roger's forward base of Troina (Cerami) a several thousand strong Saracen Army squared up against Roger and his squadron of 150 knights. After three days of stalemate Roger gave the signal to attack and charged directly at the enemy camp. His nephew Serlo led the charge and distinguished himself in the fighting. Roger urged caution before being persuaded by Roussel De Baillieul, a Norman knight from the Seine maritime region of Upper Normandy, to pursue the Saracens and complete the divine victory. It was said that the Normans saw Saint George himself on the battlefield and this image encouraged them to rally and cut down over twenty thousand Saracens. Roger killed the Saracen Commander Arcaduis in single combat just as his half brother William "Iron arm" had done at Syracuse twenty years earlier. After the battle four captured Saracen camels were sent to Pope (Alexander III) in Rome as a present. Never again would the Saracens risk open battle against the Normans.

The hilltop Citadel of Troina (Sicily) Scene of the famous Siege of 1062

Palermo 1064 A.D and Misilmeri 1068 A.D

In 1064 A.D Robert returned to Sicily with a further 500 armoured knights. Together the two brothers marched on to besiege the Sicilian capital Palermo. The army pitched camp on a nearby mountain later called Monte Tarantino. Indeed the mountain was covered with tarantula spiders which caused much discomfort to the Normans and forced them to change camp. The siege continued for three months, but Robert's forces were not numerous enough to take the city by force and in the end he had to abandon the siege. In a retribution chevauche the Normans attacked and burnt the town of Bugamo, its inhabitants were sent back to Italy and sold off as slaves. The war dragged on and on, with Roger launching long distant raids all over the island affecting Saracen moral. The greed of the Hauteville mafia to control more land and territory was limitless; no matter how long it took Roger, he would keep on fighting.

In 1068 A.D the Normans were raiding in the vicinity of Palermo. At Misilmeri the Saracens tried in vain to ambush Roger's forces. It was a disaster; Roger got wind of the plan and slaughtered them all. Knowing that the citizens of Palermo were waiting for news about the encounter Roger devised a despicable plan. Carrier pigeons were used in the middle ages to transfer long distance messages. Using the captured Muslim carrier pigeons, Roger's men dipped and wrote messages not with ink, but with the blood of the dead Muslim soldiers. They then released the birds free to return home to Palermo. When the birds arrived in the city and the messages were read out, it caused panic and a general collapse of moral.

Palermo 1071 A.D

Even after the defeat at Misilmeri in 1068 A.D, the Muslims refused to surrender the capital Palermo. Only when Robert arrived in 1071 A.D did the two brothers have enough resources to put pressure on the capital. Robert sent Roger to the south east of the island by sea to capture Catania, the objective was to ruse to trick the Saracens into thinking the campaign would be conducted on the south of Sicily and a possible invasion of Malta, instead of the capital. The ruse worked and the Muslim emirs of North Africa and Sicily diverted forces from the capital accordingly. In a lighting strike Roger captured Catania, he garrisoned the city and re-joined Robert who had already surrounded Palermo with the main Norman army. The siege lasted five months, and only ended when a plan was devised so that Roger would faint an assault on the landward side of the city walls, so that Robert could secretly lead three hundred knights through the city gardens on the seaward side of Palermo. While the Muslim garrison fought off Rogers's men, Robert and his knights scaled the city walls and entered the city by stealth. Within minutes they opened the gates and the main army rushed into city outmaneuvering the defenders. The same plan would be used by the Normans during the siege of Jerusalem many years later. With no hope for reinforcements from outside, the city elders agreed to surrender the city avoiding anymore bloodshed. Robert was indeed generous, and allowed the Muslims to continue the practice of their religion, possibly understanding that with a shortage of manpower the Normans could not hope control the whole of Sicily unless they adopted a tolerate attitude towards the island's inhabitants. Robert returned to the mainland and never came back to Sicily. He left Roger to continue the conquest.

The great city of Palermo, from Capo Gallo (Sicily)

The death of Serlo

It might be easy to think that after the surrender of Palermo, the conquest of Sicily had been completed, but Muslim resistance would continue for many years yet. Indeed in 1072 A.D personal tragedy would befall the De Hauteville mafia. The Count and Duke's nephew, Serlo who had acted so courageously at the battle of Cerami was lured out from the Norman fort near Enna, Castrogiovanni (still in Muslim hands). Serlo and seven Norman knights were ambushed by several hundreds Saracens. Unable or refusing to flee, Serlo had his horse killed from under him. He and his remaining knights climbed up to a rock (which became known as Serlo's Rock) and fought on valiantly against the hordes of enemy soldiers swarming around them. Like a wounded lion with his back against the rock face, Serlo hacked off the limbs of his assailants, until he was finally struck down. The Saracens stripped Serlo's body naked, disemboweled him and ate his heart so it is said; they could share in his bravery. The dead Norman knight's heads were sent back to North Africa as a present to the Emir. Serlo's severed head was placed on a pike and paraded around the Muslim towns and cities of Sicily.

Serlo De Hauteville's last Stand on (Serlo's Rock)

When Roger heard the news he was greatly saddened and grief stricken. Only Robert could snap him out of his lament.

Robert said:

"Women are allowed to be full with sorrow; we should however put on our armour and avenge his death".

The last years of Conquest

In 1075 A.D while Roger was on the mainland, the Normans were ambushed again. This time Roger's son in law Hugh de Gerce and his illegitimate son Jordan were ordered to protect Catania and remain on the defensive until the Count's return, but the young Knights were eager for fame and recognition. When the Saracen warlord Ibn-el-Werd set a trap for them outside the city, they disobeyed Count Roger's orders and charged straight in. Disaster struck just as it had at Enna in 1072 A.D for Serlo. The Normans were massacred and only Jordan and a few Knights managed to escape the carnage back to the fort. Only when Roger returned in 1076A.D were the Normans able to go on the offensive again. Roger's wrath had no bounds; he destroyed everything in his wake. The region around Noto and Syracuse was completely destroyed; the crops and harvest were burned to cause widespread famine and suffering.

Taormina (Sicily) Looking towards Mount Etna

Roger's message was a simple and tried method: resistance is futile and those who resist will be annihilated. In 1078 A.D Roger began the Siege of Taormina; he constructed a network of 22 forts. Whilst traveling between the fortifications with only a small entourage, he was ambushed by Slav mercenaries/bandits. As the Slavs moved in for the kill, one of Roger's Knights (Eviscardus a Knight from Brittany) put himself between the Slavs and Count Roger, saving his life, but also being killed in the process. The attack was repulsed, but danger in Sicily was never far away. The Saracens had learned the art of guerrilla warfare. In open pitched battles the Normans were near enough invincible, but in the mountain passes and ravines that covered the island, they were extremely vulnerable. It took another 13 years to subdue the last remaining Muslim enclaves in Sicily. In early 1091 A.D the Muslim stronghold of Noto finally surrendered to the Normans without a fight, ending some 30 years Saracen resistance.

Roger extended Norman power south by annexing the island of Malta, although he allowed its Muslim governors to continue rule the island. It had taken the Normans 30 years to conquer the mountainous island. The De Hauteville brothers' conquest of Sicily in the name of Christianity had started off a chain of events that would lead to the very capture of Jerusalem itself. Four centuries of Muslim expansionism had now been halted by the Normans; the conquest of Sicily enabled the Christian powers of the west to go on the offensive and reclaim the Holy land.

Robert Guiscard against the Byzantine Empire 1061-1085 A.D

Since the re-conquest of the Western provinces of the Roman Empire by the Eastern Roman Emperor Justinian I in the Sixth century A.D, the Byzantine Empire had been the major power player in Southern Italy. The arrival of the Normans threatened the "Status Quo" in the region. Indeed after the defeat of the Papal army at the battle of Civitate and their reconciliation with the Pope in 1059 A.D the Normans re-directed their aggression against the last remaining strongholds of the Byzantine Empire on mainland Italy.

Mosaic of the Byzantine Emperor Justinian I, Church of San Vitale, Ravenna

The siege of Bari

During the 1060's the Normans chipped away at Byzantine territory until by 1068 A.D Robert Guiscard was strong enough to attack the great Byzantine Catapanate of Bari. Bari was the center of Byzantine power in Southern Italy, controlling the Adriatic Sea and the gateway to modern day Albania and the former Yugoslavian states. Although the Normans surrounded the city by land and sea, the citizens of Bari were highly confident of beating off the Norman menace. They gathered together their valuables and treasures, displayed them on the battlements and taunted the Normans with rude gestures. Robert intern shouted back:

"The treasures you have shown me, are mine, keep them safe for now, for you will miss them in the future when I take them and give them away"

The Medieval fortifications of Bari (Italy)

The Baroits conceived a plan worthy of Robert himself. They sent Amerinus (an assassin) to kill the Duke. During one evening Amerinus crept into the Norman camp armed with a poisoned javelin. As Robert was dining in his tent Amerinus took aim and launched the javelin. It tore straight through Robert's cape missing his body and hit the ground. The assassination attempt failed, but the incident exposed the dangers Robert faced against a determined enemy. As the siege tightened around the city, its citizens prepared to surrender. Just before the news was announced, Byzantine reinforcements arrived. Count Roger of Sicily also arrived on the scene and in a naval battle just outside Bari he captured the Byzantine commander named Joscelin.

Even with the blockade and the daily pressure the Normans were applying, Bari held out for another three years. In April 1071 A.D with no hope of relief from Constantinople, Bari finally surrendered. Robert entered the city and instead of sacking it (as medieval law allowed) he let many of the city's laws and customs continue intact. The last great bastion of Byzantine rule had been extinguished in the West.

The year of Crisis for the Eastern Empire

1071 A.D was a catastrophic year for the Byzantine Empire. Not only did they lose control of their Italian colonies, but in a campaign against the Seljuk Turks they were also heavily defeated at the battle of Manzikert, thus losing control of most of modern day Turkey. During the battle of Manzikert a curious character appeared, none other that Roussel De Bailleul (the Norman Knight who had fought for Count Roger at the Battle of Cerami, Sicily).

Roussel de Bailleul commanded some of the western mercenaries in the Byzantine army. As the battle unfolded the Emperor ordered Roussel and his mercenaries to attack. Roussel possibly with his past experiences of warfare refused, perhaps knowing the fate of himself and his men if he did. The battle should have been a Byzantine victory securing Aisa minor against further Seljuk incursions, but it ended in a total defeat for the Emperor Romanus. The defeat at Manzikert shook the Byzantine Empire to its very foundations; the Emperor Romanus IV was captured and his army destroyed. Roussel de Bailleul gained his freedom and continued in the service of the Byzantines until 1073 A.D when he turned renegade. He had by then decided to create a new Norman Principality for himself in Galatia (Turkey). From his powerbase in Amasya he ruled over Galatia defeating various plots and armies sent to overthrown him from power. For the next four years he played the age old Norman tactic of playing one side off against another until he was finally captured by the Seljuk Turks in 1077 A.D. The Seljuk's handed him over to the Byzantines, who promptly brought him back to Constantinople where he was executed.

With the Byzantine Empire fighting on all fronts, they drew up a plan to pacify Robert Guiscard and the Normans on their western front. Romanus IV proposed that one of his sons marry Robert's daughter to seal a peace agreement, but after his defeat at Manzikert this proposal was shelved. His successor the Emperor Michael VII, offered the hand of his son Constantine to Robert's daughter Olympias and also the Byzantine imperial title of "Nobilissimus" to Robert along with substantial sums of gold. Robert agreed and in 1076 A.D Olympias arrived in Constantinople. However by 1078 A.D the wheel of fortune had turned again. The Emperor Michael VII was deposed in a coup d'etat and replaced by the new Emperor Nikephoros III who decided against the marriage. He also stopped the payments of gold and pensions to Robert and his supporters.

Invasion of the Empire

The Byzantine Emperor Alexius I

Robert's excuse if ever there was one, had now been justified. With his daughter now a prisoner in Constantinople, his funds drying up and with military coups rife within the Byzantine regime, the time was right to launch the biggest gamble of his career. Under the pretext of restoring the deposed Emperor Michael VII back onto the imperial throne, Robert launched the invasion of the Byzantine Empire itself.

In 1080 A.D Geoffrey De Malaterra describes how a man claiming to be the former Emperor Michael VII came to Apulia asking Robert to restore him to power. The man was an imposter, as the real Michael had been forced to become a monk in Constantinople, but this may have been Robert's plan all along in order to enlist Papal support for his campaign. By 1081 A.D the invasion of the Byzantine Empire had begun. After an early reconnaissance mission around the island of Corfu, (the island became the springboard to attack the Balkan mainland) Robert embarked with 1300 Knights and a vast army of over 20,000 men. The Normans landed on Corfu and stormed the fortress of Casopoli. Within days the whole island capitulated. Robert then embarked on the mainland proper. The Normans ravaged the Albanian countryside laying siege to Durazzo (the region's main city). Events in Constantinople took another turn as Nikephoros III was deposed by another general Alexius Commenus.

The Battle of Durazzo 1081A.D

As Robert continued to lay siege to Durazzo, the new Emperor Alexius gathered together all the last remaining resources of the Empire to combat the Norman invasion. Ambassadors were sent to Venice and the Holy Roman Empire to form an anti-Norman alliance. By 1081 A.D all the preparations had been concluded, the Venetian's fore filled their promises by attacking the Norman fleet in the Adriatic, this tactic was designed to cut off the Norman supply lines from Southern Italy. Alexius assembled his forces in Constantinople, with the elite Varangian Guard at its head. Then the huge imperial army set out to relieve the beleaguered city of Durazzo. On October the 18th 1081 A.D Alexius reached Durazzo; Robert ordered the Norman ships in the bay to be burned. His message was a simple one: his men must fight or die, for there would be no escape.

After the early morning mass the two armies squared up to one another. The Byzantines advanced in three divisions with Alexius commanding the center. Robert's army was also drawn up into three divisions: Robert in the center, Bohemond, his son, on the Norman left and the Count of Giovinazzo on the right. The Emperor then gave the signal to the commander of the elite Varangian Guard to advance towards the invaders. These warriors had a personal score to settle with the Normans as they were largely made up of Anglo-Saxon Huscarls who had left England after the Norman Conquest by William the Conqueror, some may have even been veterans of the battle of Hastings (1066 AD). Robert sent in a detachment of Norman cavalry, but they were beaten back by the Anglo-Saxons with their huge double handed battle axes. Both armies clashed together in a titanic confrontation. Some of the Normans fled the battlefield towards the beach, followed by the Byzantines thinking victory was close. This left the Varangian guard exposed in the open. Robert seizing the chance at once launched a devastating attack on them. Spearmen cross bowmen and Norman shock cavalry crashed into their exposed flanks. The survivors made their way to the church of St Nicholas where they made a final desperate last stand. Refusing to surrender, they fought on with tremendous courage, fighting to the last man. Unable to budge the last of the Anglo-Saxons from the church, the Normans set fire to the roof, burning them alive. The second battle of Hastings ended in the same result, a Norman victory! Meanwhile on the beach, the Normans were railed by Robert's wife Sikelgaita, who urged them to return to the battle. The Normans then regrouped and closed in on the Byzantine center. They were within inches of killing Alexius who was struck on the head and was lucky to survive the debacle. Dazed and bloody faced, the Emperor was protected and ushered away to safety by his personal bodyguard.

With the Varangian Guard annihilated the rest of the Byzantine army lost heart and fled the field in terror. Victory was complete; Robert halted his men from continuing the pursuit of the Byzantines and instead contented himself by ransacking the Emperor's camp.

The Balkan Campaign

With winter setting in, Robert fortified himself and his army on the River Daemoni, within striking distance of Durazzo. Robert entered into secret discussions with Dominic (one of the Castilians of Durazzo) he offered the hand of his niece if Dominic handed over the city to him. Dominic could not resist the offer and agreed. On a cold February night he lowered rope ladders from the city's battlements. Through guile and treachery the Normans captured Durazzo. Geoffrey de Malaterra wrote:

"No enemy is more dangerous than the enemy from within".

With a secure city now in his hands, Robert extended the conquest of the Balkans by capturing Kastoria and advancing into modern day Greece, but envoys from Pope Gregory arrived with urgent news from Italy.

The German Emperor Henry IV had invaded Italy in conjunction with his agreement with the Byzantine Emperor Alexius. The panic stricken Pope was besieged in Rome and pleaded for Robert's return. More worrying was that the Norman nobility had also risen up in revolt and were causing untold damage to Robert's authority on the mainland. Robert left Bohemond, his son, in charge to prosecute the war against the Byzantines while he returned to Italy to restore order.

The ramparts of the city of Durres / formerly Durazzo (Albania)

Bohemond advanced into Greece and captured the towns of Ioanninia and Ochrid. On two separate occasions Alexius was defeated in battle by Bohemond, but a decisive victory proved elusive. The Normans rampaged their way through central and southern Greece. Only at the city of Larissa were they stopped. After the recent defeats Alexius changed his tactics and decided to bolster up the defences of the major cities instead of facing the Normans on the battlefield. His strategy proved successful, after a six month siege, Bohemond's army had been depleted and he was forced to abandon the siege of Larissa. Alexius now advanced with his newly recruited army and gave battle. This time the Norman cavalry was ticked into charging the Byzantines. When the distance was great enough between them and their infantry, the Byzantines struck. The Count of Brienne managed to escape the field with his few remaining horses, but Bohemond's camp fell into Byzantine hands. Larissa was the first major defeat of the Normans. With his supply lines stretched to the limit and with no hope of reinforcements from Italy, Bohemond abandoned the campaign. Had Robert been there, the two energetic commanders may have been able to topple the Byzantine Empire itself. Alas for the Normans their window of opportunity had passed and they would never again be in such an advantageous position.

Mainland Italy 1083-84 A.D

As soon as Robert landed, news reached him that the rebel Geoffrey de Conversano was laying siege to the city of Oria. Robert mustered his tiny force and rode off to Oria. On hearing that the Duke was on his way, Geoffrey lifted the siege and retreated immediately. Robert summoned his brother Roger to come to his assistance and bring his Sicilian army with him to help put down the revolt of Jordan (Prince of Aversa). Jordan's fief was laid to waste and both Robert and Roger besieged him in his castle at Capua. By early 1084 A.D Jordan had been forced to submit to his uncles. With the last of the rebels punished the De Hauteville brothers turned their attention to helping their overlord Pope Gregory in Rome. Since March 1084 A.D Pope Gregory had been cooped up in the Castle Saint Angelo and besieged by the German army under Henry IV (The Holy Roman Emperor, still not crowned by the real Pope). By May Robert had gathered together an immensely strong relief force. Troops from his estates in Italy, Norman mercenaries and even Muslim soldiers under the banner of Roger of Sicily were seconded. The Normans now marched on Rome.

Prince Jordan's Castle at Capua, Italy

On hearing the news and size of the Norman army which was descending on the capital Henry IV was forced to flee north in order to avoid battle. Robert Guiscard's reputation as a fearsome warrior proceeded him wherever he went and the Emperor dared not risk everything in battle as the Byzantine Emperor had so at Durrazo in 1081A.D. With the departure of the German Emperor, Rome and its citizens were panic stricken. Robert and over 1300 mounted knights arrived in the eternal city and entered unmolested through the San Lorenzo gate. The main army battered down the city gates and stormed in, shouting out their war cry GUISCARD….GUISCARD. In a show of force they marched to the Castel Sant'Angelo where they released the Pope. After three days in the city the Romans who had been quiet, rose up in rebellion and tried to ambush the Normans. Devastation followed as the Norman troops went on the rampage and ransacked the city. Robert set fire to the centre of Rome and cornered the surviving rebels on a bridge over the river Tiber, where they were massacred to the last. The position of the Pope could not by upheld without Norman protection and Gregory reluctantly left the city with the Normans on their return to Apulia.

The mighty fortress of Castel Sant'Angelo (Rome, Italy)

The last days of Robert Guiscard

With order restored back in Southern Italy and the German Emperor put back firmly in his place, Robert returned to the unfinished business of the conquest of the Byzantine Empire. Two years had passed since he had last been on the Balkan mainland. Although Bohemond had been in command, the campaign had wavered and needed Robert's personal influence to carry it through. In September Robert set sail from Otranto with 150 ships. Operations began as soon as Robert landed, but the onset of winter and more worrying an outbreak of "the burning flu" depleted his army. William de Apulia noted that over 500 knights were lost to the disease and even Bohemond was taken ill and had to return to Italy. Robert arrived on the Greek island of Cephalonia in July 1085 A.D to be greeted by his wife and son Roger "Borsa", but he had already contracted the deadly disease. On the 17th of July 1085 A.D the greatest adventurer of his age died. Robert was probably over seventy years old when he died, a remarkable age for the time. William the

Conqueror, King of England and Duke of Normandy encouraged his knights by saying: **"It would be a disgrace to show less bravery than one whom he surpassed in rank"**.

Perhaps the epitaph on Robert's tomb says it all.

"Hic terror mundi Guiscardus"

"Here lies Guiscard, terror of the World".

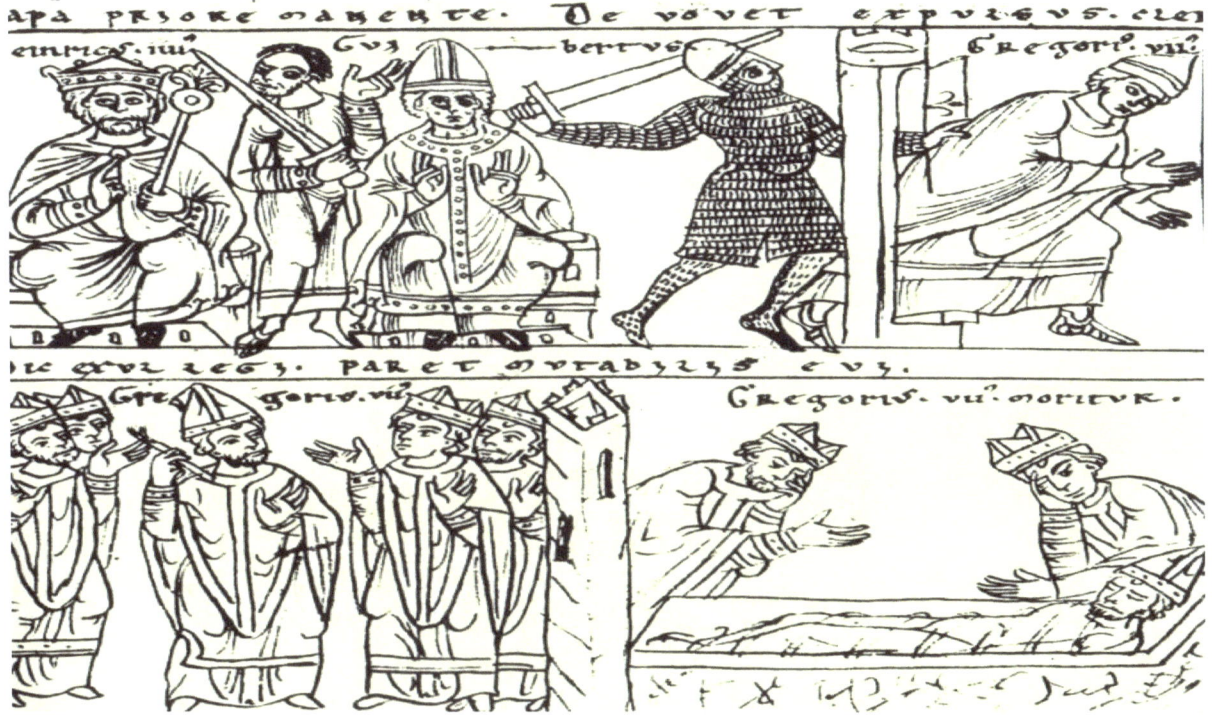

Miniature of the events in Rome 1083-1084, note Robert Guiscard in armour ushering the Pope out of the Eternal city

The Normans after Robert Guiscard

1085-1154 A.D

After the death of Robert Guiscard the campaign against the Byzantine Empire ended. The challenge would be left to his son Bohemond to continue in the years ahead. Robert's body was taken back to Italy to be laid to rest in the abbey of Venosa. Bohemond had been excluded from Robert's will as he may have been intended to receive the Byzantine crown after the conquest. Instead his son from his second marriage Roger "Borsa" inherited the Apulian Dukedom. Although Roger "Borsa" became Duke, his authority was never secure. By 1087 A.D Bohemond rebelled along with Jordan de Capua and Southern Italy was thrown into chaos. Only with the support and intervention of his uncle Roger (Count of Sicily) was order restored. Bohemond was given various towns and cities including Bari and Taranto to compensate him. In 1094 A.D both

Bohemond and Count Roger of Sicily were besieging the rebel lord of Castrovillari, William de Grandmesnil. After a prolonged siege William gave up, but was forced to flee to Constantinople when Duke Roger "Borsa" confistcated his lands. Bohemond was encouraged by his half brother and uncle to participate in the First Crusade to get him out of the way. Count Roger knew his nephew Bohemond only too well and understood he wanted greatness, and that Italy would not be sufficient for him. Bohemond indeed headed off for the East and became one of the leaders of the First Crusade (see chapter 3)

"Regnum Siciliae" and Roger II De Hauteville "King Roger"

Because Sicily is an island and had been conquered solely by the De Hauteville brothers, there were no great political families on the island before the conquest. For this reason Count Roger's power was supreme. The conquest had been a holy war, but now to run the island correctly and profitably Roger practiced toleration towards Sicily's population. A greater part of the population was Greek in the east and mostly Muslim in the south and west. This attitude of toleration bore its fruits and the island became one of the most important medieval states in Europe. As great as his brother Robert Guiscard, Count Roger had laid the foundations of the great island state when he died in 1101 A.D. He was succeeded by his son Simon who died an early death in 1106 A.D. Simon's younger brother Roger II became Count in the same year. During the first years of Roger's reign, Sicily was governed by his mother Adelaide. A curious tale recounts that King Sigurd of Norway stopped off in Sicily on his way to the holy land and was so impressed with the island that he called little Roger not a Count, but King Roger. By 1112 A.D Roger was coming of age and was ready to rule in his own right. Again like his father before him Roger ruled the island well, treating all the different peoples with respect and tolerance. King Baldwin of Jerusalem proposed a marriage between himself and Roger's mother Adelaide and if no heir was produced then the crown of Jerusalem would go to Roger. In 1116 A.D King Baldwin was extremely ill; Roger was on the verge of becoming King; only the Patriarch of Jerusalem opposed the transition of power, forcing a dying Baldwin to repudiate his wife Adelaide. Roger never forgot the way his mother had been treated and never again supported the Crusader states.

De Hauteville family arms (Montreale, Sicily

King Roger of Sicily (Santa Maria dell'Ammiraglio (*Martorana*) Palermo, Sicily)

Opportunity on the Mainland

In 1122 A.D Roger's cousin, Duke William of Apulia, asked for Roger's military help to restore order in the Duchy. In exchange William renounced all his fiefs and properties in Sicily and Calabria to Roger. With his cousin's support William crushed the rebellion and lived out the rest of his life in peace. William died childless in 1127 A.D. Roger at once claimed all the possessions of his cousin and invaded the mainland to push home his claim to the Duchy. In 1128 A.D Pope Honorius II invested Roger as Duke of Sicily, Calabria and Apulia. When Honorius died in 1130 A.D there were two claimants to the Papacy. Inocent II gained the support of the German Emperor Lothaire III, Louis VI of France and King Henry "Beauclerc" of England, while the Antipope Anacletus II received the support of Roger in exchange of giving him the title of "King Roger of the Kingdom of Sicily". On Christmas day 1130 A.D Roger was crowned King in the cathedral of Palermo. It was a proud moment for the De Hauteville family, as in just over 100 hundred years they had risen from the landless sons of a minor noble in Normandy to the rulers of medieval Europe's newest nation state.

The Battle of Nocera

Unlike his father and uncle Robert Guiscard, Roger II had no real experience of war. In 1132 A.D Roger led his army into battle against the rebel Norman lords of Capua and Alife. At Nocera Roger engaged the rebels, but medieval battles were very unpredictable affairs. Roger gained the upper hand at first, but when Count Ranuif charged in with 500 mounted knights the battle turned into a rout. Roger II tried to galvanise his men, but to no avail. The King was forced to flee back to the protection of the city of Salerno. The German Holy Roman Emperor Lothaire III invaded Italy and by 1136 A.D Roger II was forced to leave the mainland and retire to his island fortress of Sicily. As the case with many an invasion, Roger II bided his time until Lothaire tired of the campaign and returned home to Germany. In 1137 A.D Roger II again came to the mainland to restore order. He was however again defeated by his nemesis Count Ranuif De Alife at the battle of Rignano. In the encounter not far from the abbey of Mount Gargano, the King's son another Roger, led the cavalry charge against the rebels and forced them to retreat towards Siponto. King Roger's charge followed, but was beaten back. As a result, the royal army lost heart and retreated. Although defeated,

King Roger from the (Liber ad honorem Augusti)

Roger II changed his strategy and avoided pitched battles. Instead he concentrated on sieges and reducing the enemy strongholds. When the Anti-pope Anacletus II died Roger II became reconciled with Pope Innocent II. Count Ranuif retreated to Troia where he was besieged by Roger's forces. He died from fever in 1139A.D before the castle fell. Roger II, in a callous act, had the Count's body exhumed and thrown into the castle ditch.

Multicultural Sicily

The last years of Roger's reign were filled with joy and prosperity. Roger II started the building of some of the finest Norman churches in the world. Craftsmen and women from the Arabic, Byzantine and Latin communities all left their mark. Their magnificent work can still be seen today in the churches of Santa Maria dell'Ammiraglio (*Martorana*) Palermo, the abbey of Montreale, Palermo's Cathederal and many more. Roger II also commissioned the Tabula Rogeriana "the book of Roger": this amazing book was created by Muhammad al-Idrisi (an Arabic subject of the King) and took over 15 years to complete. Inside the book were maps of the known world and details on the geography, population and resources of each region. Roger II was secure enough by the late 1140s to launch an attack on Muslim North Africa, briefly capturing Tunis, Susa and Tripoli. He also attacked the old enemy Byzantium. More a raid of piracy rather than military campaign, Roger's Norman raiders sacked Athens and even attacked the Byzantine capital of Constantinople. On the 26th of February 1154 A.D King Roger II died leaving the Norman Kingdom in the sun to his son William.

King Roger II mantle with the two lions of Normandy in Arabic style.

The Norman Kingdom 1154-1194 A.D

William ruled from 1154 to 1166 A.D in which time the Normans lost their recent conquests in North Africa and in the Balkans. His son William II became King in 1166 A.D and achieved the high watermark of the Norman Empire in the south by marrying Joan, the daughter of Henry Plantagenet (King of England) and Eleanor d'Aquitaine. She was also sister to Richard the Lionheart and the future King John of England. William also achieved peace with the German Emperor by marrying off his aunt Constance (King Roger's II daughter) to the Emperor's son Henry IV. The King finally revived an alliance with the Crusader states by attacking Saladin's resurgent Saracens in Egypt. When he died heirless in 1189 A.D the crown passed to Tancred de Lecce, but he was unable the hold off the advances of the German Emperor Henry IV who believed that the crown should have gone to himself. In 1194 A.D Henry IV invaded the Kingdom and on Christmas day he was crowned King of Sicily. Tancred's son William III is said to have been blinded, castrated and disappears from the records. The time of the Norman Kings had come to an end, but the Kingdom of Sicily would last for over 700 years until the time of Garaboldi. The blood of the De Hauteville mafia would live on through the exploits of Bohemond and the Norman Princes who would conquer the Kingdom of Heaven.

King Roger's II tomb (Palermo Cathedral, Sicily)

Chapter 3: The Holy Land

THE NORMAN CRUSADE
"The First Crusade and the Conquest of the Kingdom of Heaven

Christianity's counterattack had started long before the First Crusade in 1095. Three centuries had passed since Charles Martel had halted the Muslim invasion of Europe at the battle of Poitiers in 736 AD. By the 11th century the Christians were on the offensive. The legendary El Cid had started the fight back against the Moors in the Iberian Peninsula and just before the turn of the century the Normans under the De Hauteville brothers had conquered the Muslim stronghold of Sicily. In 1071 Seljuk Turks captured the Holy city of Jerusalem from the more tolerant Fatimid Muslims and by 1076 they had all but closed off the city and Holy land to pilgrims. In 1095 the call to arms by Pope Urban II would lead to the First Crusade and embitter Christian and Muslim relations for centuries to come and still have consequences to this very day.

The call to arms

In 1095 ambassadors from the Byzantine Emperor Alexius arrived at the Papal court asking for help against the Seljuk Turks who had conquered most of Byzantine Anatolia (Turkey). The Emperor hoped that with western military support he would be able to regain Byzantine territory lost to the Turks.

Clermont Ferrand 1095

"He, who welcomes to me, let him deny himself, take up his cross and follow me".

In November 1095 the Council of Clermont gathered in the medieval city of Clermont Ferrand (France). Pope Urban II gave a rousing speech to the people. He called upon all of Christendom to take up arms and liberate the Holy land from the Muslims. The crowd and clergy responded with the Crusader chant: "DIEU LI VOLT" (God wills it!) The Pope offered anyone who went on Crusade absolution from sin and it was firmly believed at the time that participating in the Crusade was an act of the highest good. The Pope's agenda was not just a spiritual belief in the ideals of Crusade, but also a chance to pull into line the Heretic church of the Eastern Roman Empire (The Byzantine Empire) and to cement Papal supremacy over the Kings, Emperor and Princes of Europe.

The Council of Clermont, November 1095

After the Pope's speech the idea of Crusade spread around Europe like wildfire. Old and young, noble and poor were galvanized into action. In an age where the power of religion was far more important to people than in the present day the Crusade offered the opportunity to guarantee a place in Heaven

The 3000 mile journey and the gathering of the Titans

The first Crusaders to make the 3000 thousand mile journey were badly organized. Peter the Hermit led a fanatical peasant army across Europe causing widespread damage in Hungary before they reached Constantinople in the summer in 1096. While Peter stayed in Constantinople many of his followers continued into the hostile lands of the Seljuk Turks. It was a disaster, with no central command, the small Crusader groups were massacred by their Seljuk foes.

In August 1096 the main Crusader armies set off for the Byzantine capital of Constantinople. Some of the most famous and richest warriors of the age made up the major contingents. From the Anglo-Norman world came Robert Duke of Normandy (son of William the Conqueror). Bohemond De Hauteville (son of Robert Guiscard) Tancred his nephew, Rainulf son of William "Iron arm" and other members of the De Hauteville family led the Italian-Normans. From France came Raymond Count of Toulouse who had already fought against the Muslim Moors in Spain, Godfrey of Bouillon, Robert Count of Flanders, Stephen Count of Blois, Baldwin, Godfrey and Eustace III of Boulogne and Adhemar Bishop of Le Puy.

Constantinople 1096-1097

By the spring of 1097 all the major contingents had arrived in Constantinople. For the Byzantine Emperor Alexius this was not what he had envisaged, instead of the western mercenaries that he had hoped for, he now had thousands of zealous Crusaders in and around his capital.

He was extremely suspicious of the motives of some of the Crusader commanders, especially Bohemond De Hauteville whom he had previously fought before during the wars against Robert Guiscard and the Normans. The Emperor's daughter Anna Comnena commented:

"Bohemond is psychically strong, brave and has an unruly wild temper. He is the exact stamp of his father Robert Guiscard, and is a living model of his father's character. During their war against us in the Balkans they were nicknamed the Caterpillar and the Locust. For whatever escaped Robert, his son Bohemond grabbed and destroyed"

Robert Duke of Normandy (Gloucester Cathedral)

Alexius demanded that the Crusader commanders swear an oath of allegiance unto him and that any former Byzantine land conquered during the campaign should be returned to the Empire. Some of the Normans refused to swear allegiance. Tancred and Richard of the Participate escaped from the city and rejoined the Crusader army on the other side of the Bosporus.

The attack on Nicaea 1097

Nicaea was the first major Muslim city that stood in the way of the Crusader march to the Holy land. The capital of the Sultanate of Rum would have to be captured to avoid the supply lines being cut or being attacked from behind. On the 6th of May 1097 the Crusader forces of Robert de Normandy, and Stephen de Blois surrounded the city and began the siege. When the other contingents arrived, the besieging force swelled to over forty five thousand professional troops. A further 3000 Byzantine troops were sent by Alexuis under the command Tatikois and Tzitas.
A Turkish relief force tried to break through, but were held at bay by the troops of Raymond de Toulouse and then annihilated when the Count of Flanders men smashed into their flank. After a month of siege the city surrendered not to the besiegers, but to the Byzantines. At the same time as the negotiations were taking place the Crusaders were scaling the city walls.

The gates opened only to reveal the Byzantine Imperial banner flying from the citadel. It was a huge disappointment, the Crusaders wanted to sack the city and receive the spoils of war. They were even more galled when the Turkish garrison received safe conduct from the Byzantines.

The Battle of Dorlaeum

The army marched off into the hostile interior of Asia Minor led by the Byzantines, then followed by the Normans of Bohemond and Robert of Normandy. In late June the Norman scouts returned to the column and announced that the Turks were preparing for battle. Bohemond ordered the Crusaders to form up into a defensive position near a swamp until the second contingent of Crusaders arrived. The Turkish cavalry unleashed a deadly barrage of arrows and spears at the Crusaders. This was the first time the westerners had been subjected to such harrying tactics. They were completely shocked by this new form of warfare and fled towards their defensive camp. Robert Duke of Normandy rallied the men by lifting up his helmet, and Shouting **"NORMANDIE, NORMANDIE",**

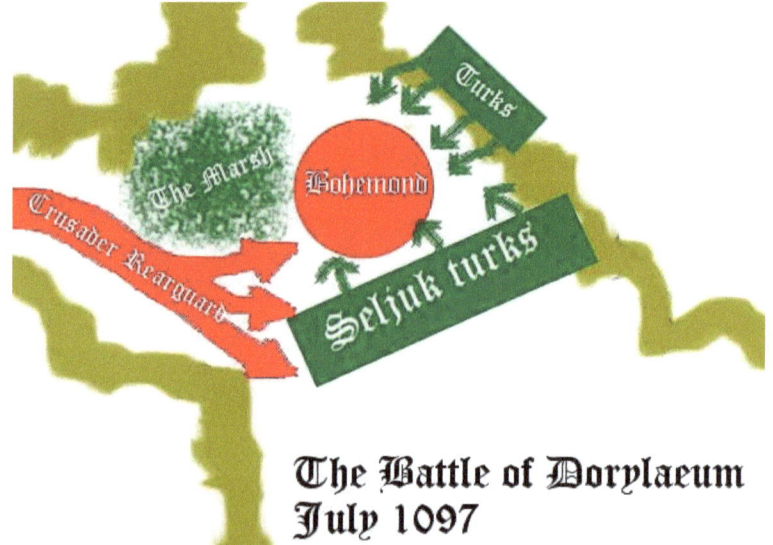

Just as his father had done before him at the Battle of Hastings in 1066. Confined to a defensive position they held off the Turkish attacks for over 7 hours. The sky turned black from the volleys of Turkish arrows, but the Crusaders held firm protected by their heavy armour. Indeed the Turkish gave them the name "The Iron people" afterwards. Reinforcements from Adhemar Bishop of Le Puy and Godfrey of Bouillon arrived in the nick of time and bolstered up the Crusaders ranks.

The Battle of Dorylaeum July 1097

Both sides fought hard until the third contingent of Crusader heavy cavalry arrived on the Turkish left and steamrolled over their archers. Bohemond said **"if it pleases God today, you will all become rich"** the Christians rallied and afterwards ransacked the Sultans camp. Victory was complete and although it had been a shaky start, the Crusaders were convinced that God was on their side and they were invincible. After the defeat at Dorylaeum Sultan Kilij Arslan I withdrew from the region and left the Crusaders to march on virtually unmolested. The local Christian and Greek communities of the cities and towns opened their gates and welcomed the Crusaders as liberators.

Robert Duke of Normandy (The Battle of Dorylaeum 1097)

The Crusade splits

The Crusaders had forefilled their part of the bargain with the Byzantine Emperor Alexius by recovering most of Anatolia for him. So far as the Crusaders were concerned it had been a one sided deal. They had done all the hard work for little reward. Indeed some members of the Crusade were now thinking about carving out a Kingdom for themselves. On the Roman road outside Heraclea a Turkish host hoped to ambush the Crusaders. It was routed by Bohemond and the Normans in the advanced guard. They marched into the Tarus Mountains and at the Cilican gates Tancred De Hauteville and Baldwin De Boulogne split from the main force and headed south into Cilicia and northern Syria.

It is probably certain that both men intended to secure fiefs for themselves. Baldwin's wife had died on the long march after the battle of Dorylaeum and with her any reason he had for returning to France. Tancred may have all along used the excuse of the Crusade to further his designs on a new Norman State in the east. They both laid siege to Tarsus then Tancred spurred on and captured Adana and Mamistra. The two hot headed commanders nearly came to blows at Mamistra. Tancred headed south towards Antioch. Baldwin received a curious offer from Thoros of Edessa who offered him the chance to become the Lord of the County of Edessa when he died in exchange for the military muscle of Baldwin's Crusaders. In March 1098 Thoros was assassinated and Baldwin was proclaimed Lord of Edessa. He established the first Latin Crusader state in the Holy land.

Baldwin, the first Crusader lord of Edessa 1098

The siege of Antioch

In October 1097 the main Crusader army reached Antioch. Antioch is situated on one of the great trade routes between east and west and was one of the most important cities in the Middle East since its foundation by Alexander the Great.

When the vast Crusader army came into view Yaghi Siyan (the Turkish Governor) sent out ambassadors to every corner of the Muslim world requesting urgent help and assistance. Raymond De Toulouse wanted to the attack the city immediately, but Bohemond urged caution and suggested a siege. Indeed the mighty Byzantine built walls around Antioch were virtually impregnable.

Stephen De Blois;
"We found before us the city of Antioch. It is very large and fortified, with the greatest strength and almost impossible to be taken by force alone".

The Crusaders encircled the city and began the siege. Antioch would be their greatest test of faith to date. If they were to fail here there would be no going back. Each Crusader contingent blocked off access to the main five gatehouses of the city.
The coastal port of Latakia was captured by an Anglo-Saxon fleet in the service of the Byzantines. These warriors were probably refugees from England after the Norman Conquest and were led by Edgar the Atheling (the Anglo Saxon heir to the throne of England). Without the supplies brought in from the captured ports the Crusader siege around Antioch would have failed. As the Siege dragged on throughout the winter conditions became terrible.

Stephen De Blois;
"Throughout the whole winter we suffered from excessive cold and enormous torrents of rain. What some say about the impossibility of bearing the heat of the sun in Syria is untrue, for the winter here is very similar to our winter in the West."

With supplies dangerously low and the extreme cold effecting Crusader moral Bohemond and Robert of Flanders set out with 20,000 men raiding the neighboring districts for food. At the same time Duqaq of Damascus was leading a Muslim relief army towards Antioch.

The Battle of Harenc December 1097

Duqaq's scouts returned to him and reported that the Crusader army was close and unaware of their presence. At once Duqaq ordered a forced march and attacked Robert of Flanders division. The Saracens came into view and quickly overwhelmed and surrounded Roberts force. Desperate hand to hand fighting ensued. Robert's men were on the verge of complete annihilation when Bohemond who was also in the vicinity saw the swirling clouds of dust in the distance and realized what was happening. He spurred his horse and ordered a direct cavalry charge. The Saracens were now enveloped by Bohemond's Norman Crusaders. It was pure carnage; the Crusaders from inside the envelopment fought their way out as Bohemond's troops rode down the Saracens trying to escape. The remnants of the Damascene army retreated and had to abandon their attempt to relieve Antioch.

Although the Crusaders had again won a great victory, the area was too dangerous to continue foraging. They returned triumphant to Antioch ,but also empty handed.

Antioch, December 1097

When Yaghi Siyan saw that Bohemond and Robert of Flanders troops had withdrawn from Antioch he decided to try and defeat the remaining Crusaders who surrounded the city.
In a daring nighttime raid the city's garrison attacked the main Crusader camp. Although initially surprised by the assault, the Crusaders rallied and Raymond de Toulouse's men forced the Turks to retreat back into Antioch. The siege continued into the New Year. Both sides were suffering from hunger and the weather. On a cold February night Peter the Hermit one of the Crusades most ardent religious followers attempted to leave the siege. Fearing a general collapse of nerve and moral if he escaped, Bohemond ordered Tancred to capture him and bring him back to camp. Tancred forced Peter to return under pain of death, thus avoiding the crisis.

The second battle outside Antioch

The Crusaders got wind of another Saracen plan to relieve Antioch. This time Ridwan, Lord of Aleppo was marching towards the city with a huge army. Bohemond was chosen to lead the remaining 700 armoured knights into battle. Indeed Bohemond may have used his childhood knowledge of guerilla warfare in Sicily from his father Robert Guiscard and uncle Count Roger to defeat the Saracens. As although outnumbered he would use the terrain to defeat them. Near the Iron Bridge Bohemond sent a detachment of knights to attack the Turks. The knights charged in and then conducted a feinted retreat. The Turks who thought they were retreating chased after them, not realizing that they were been being drawn into a trap; it was too late, with the river Orontes on their left and the lake on their right. The area was unsuitable for them to use their vast numbers. At the last moment Bohemond led the Crusader heavy cavalry directly into the ranks of the surprised Turks. They simply rode down everything in their path. Bohemond hacked down man and horse; the Christian knights were in frenzy, covered from head to toe in the blood of their enemies. Victory was complete and the legend of the Crusader heavy cavalry now spread throughout the Muslim world.

Spring 1098

In the spring of 1098 spies brought disturbing information to the Crusader commanders, Kerbogha of Mosul was raising an almighty army of over 75.000 men to destroy the Christian besiegers. The Crusades leaders discussed the situation. Bohemond suggested that Antioch should be given to whoever could take it and once captured it should not be handed over to the Byzantines. Since the Byzantine representative Taticius had left the siege the leaders saw no reason why Antioch should be handed back. After all they had suffered throughout the siege with little help from the Emperor Alexius. By May 1098 Kerbogha's army fell upon the fledgling Crusader state of Edessa. The Saracen army laid siege to Baldwin's hilltop fortress but was unable to budge him from his defensive position. After a month of futile besieging Kerbogha gave up and headed off to confront the Crusaders at Antioch. Meanwhile Bohemond had entered into secret negotiations with Firouz, one of Antioch's castellans, to hand over the city to him. After over eight months of terrible conditions and destroying two armies sent against them, the Crusaders moment had come.

On the 2nd of June Stephen de Blois left Antioch fearing he would be killed by the approaching Saracen army. The rest of the Crusaders pretended to leave the siege and marched off to confront Kerbogha, in reality they secretly returned during the evening. Bohemond's Normans assembled beneath the tower of the Two Sisters, then Firouz gave the signal from the battlements. Fulk de Chartres climbed a ladder along with a party of 60 Knights and entered Antioch. They crept along the city walls, dispatched the guards and with the help of some Christian inhabitants opened the mighty St George gate. The main army who were waiting outside stormed into the city. Shouting their war cry **"GOD WILL'S IT!"** the Crusaders went on the rampage, ransacking and massacring the Muslim population, soon the streets were filled with the bodies of the slain. The frustration built up over eight months had been unleashed upon the people of the city. The slaughter of Antioch brought out all the horrors of the medieval sack. Bohemond commented; **"We wept for their wives, children and servants"**.

Antioch's Governor Yaghi Siyan chose the cowards tried to flee the city but was set upon by some Armenian peasants who pulled him from his horse and decapitated him. His head was sent back to Antioch and given to Bohemond as a present. The remnants of the garrison held out in the citadel, but surrendered within a short time afterwards. Bohemond claimed the city for himself, but there was little time to celebrate as Kerbogha's army was only a few miles away. Antioch was made as defensible as possible during the circumstances. More Crusaders deserted the city fearing the worst. William de Grand-Mesnil slipped out and joined up with Stephen de Blois who was heading towards the Byzantine Emperor's camp at Alexandretta. Indeed when they arrived they told the Emperor that he should return to Constantinople as all was lost at Antioch. Guy, Bohemond's half-brother tried to persuade Alexuis to go on to the assistance of the Crusaders, but to no avail as the Emperor decided not to risk everything in what he believed to be a lost cause. When the news reached Antioch that there would be no assistance from the Byzantines, the rank and file and many of the nobles cursed them for not having the courage to help their fellow Christians, the Crusaders were on their own.

The Discovery of the Holy Lance

Kerbogha's army surrounded Antioch and cut off any supplies from entering in and out of the city. The Crusader's moral dropped and many feared this was the end of their epic journey in the quest to retake the Holy Land from the infidel.

The mood inside changed on the 14th of June when Peter of Bartholomew a priest /pilgrim in Count Raymond's retinue, came forward and preached to the crowd that he had been visited in his dreams by St Andrew. The Saint had told him he would find the Holy Lance that had pierced Jesus inside the church of Saint Peter. Peter immediately started digging up the floor within the church. Knee deep in dirt and rock Peter started to sing and shout. The Crusader onlookers were amazed when he held high above him the relic of the Holy Lance. The discovery of the Holy Lance was seen as a good omen and with their faith renewed the Crusaders decided to take the fight to Kerbogha instead of huddling behind the walls of Antioch.

The Final battle for Antioch

On the 28th of June 1098 the Crusader army opened the Bridge gate and marched out to confront the Saracens. Adhemar Bishop of Puy commanded the Crusader left flank which was protected by the river Orontes. Bohemond led the centre with Robert Duke of Normandy. Hugh de Vermandois commanded the right wing with the last remaining cavalry. Kerbogha could not believe that the Crusaders dared attack his mighty army and sent in the Saracen cavalry and archers who conducted a feinted flight. This maneuver backfired when the rest of the Saracen army saw them retreating, and thought they were in full flight. Paninc set in and Kerbogha set fire to the grassland to try and halt the Crusader advance. The Crusaders saw cloud formations that resembled Saint George in the sky and pressed home their attack on the retreating Saracen army.

Bishop Adhemar held up the Holy Lance and stated;

"Behold soldiers, St George, St Maurice, St Theodore have come to your help"

It was a slaughter with the Crusader heavy infantry cutting down everything in its way. By the time they reached the Iron Bridge the battlefield was littered with thousands of dead Muslim warriors. Kerbogha abandoned the field and returned to Mosul a broken man. For the Crusaders it was the ultimate God given victory and it seemed nothing could stop them now. For the remaining half of 1098 the Crusaders instead of marching on Jerusalem fought amongst themselves. Bohemond claimed Antioch and refused to give it up. He had led the Crusade from the front and won many battles against the enemies of Christendom, but now he decided for him the Crusade was over. The Byzantine Emperor sent a letter to Antioch

"You know the oaths and promises which you all took in Constantinople. Now you break them by retaining Antioch and other cities. The right thing to do is to leave these cities so not to provoke more wars and trouble".

Bohemond replied;

"It is not I, but you, who are the cause of all this. For you promised you would follow us with a vast army, but you never made good your promise. When we reached Antioch we fought for months under great difficulty both against the enemy and against famine, which was more severe than had ever been experienced before, with the result that most of us ate of the

very foods which are forbidden by law. We endured for a long time and while we were in this danger even Taticius, your Majesty's most loyal servant, whom you had appointed to help us, went away and left us to our danger. Yet we captured Antioch unexpectedly and utterly routed the troops which had been sent to destroy us. In what way would it be just for us to deprive ourselves willingly of what we gained by our own sweat and toil? "

The final battle for Antioch June 28th 1098, left of the picture Bishop Adhemar holds before him the Holy lance

Jerusalem 1098-1099

The Fatimid Government in Egypt decided to launch their own offensive not against the Crusaders, but against the Seljuk Turks who had their hands full against the Crusaders and Byzantines in Asia Minor and Syria. They retook Jerusalem from the Seljuk's without much bloodshed. Indeed the Islamic world was torn apart by division. The Fatimid regime still believed that the Crusaders were just mercenaries working for the Byzantines. If they had understood that the Westerners were intent on destroying Islam and conquering the entire Holy Land they may well have joined forces with their fellow Muslim brothers. In December 1098 the Crusader army attacked Maaret en Numan and sacked the city. It was one of the worst atrocities that the Crusaders had committed thus far. Man, woman, child and dog were slain in an unparalleled act of brutality. Muslim  chroniclers wrote that the Crusader soldiers were so starved and hungry that they resorted to cannibalism, eating the flesh of the slain. Some of the Crusader commanders had been stalling the march on Jerusalem in order to create their own Principalities like Bohemond had done with Antioch. Many of the ordinary soldiers were fed up and decided to march on towards the Holy City. The army swelled with the arrival of some Anglo Saxon soldiers and sailors who burned their ships and joined the Crusader march on Jerusalem.

The ordeal of Peter of Bartholomew

Ever since discovering the Holy Lance at Antioch, Peter of Bartholomew had been targeted as a fraud and charlatan by various members of the Crusader army. Peter refused to admit that the whole episode had been a scam to lift Crusader moral. In April 1099 Peter decided to undertake a trail by fire to prove his innocence. The disbelievers constructed a huge fire with logs and bush wood. Peter holding the Holy lance above him walked into the fire and then came out at the other end alive. The watching crowd was in total awe, it was a miracle he had survived but, sadly he would never see the Holy city as he had been terribly burned in the fire. For nearly two weeks he clung on to life but on the 20th of April 1099 the hero of Antioch died. The Crusaders crossed the Dog River and entered Fatimid territory for the first time. The local Fatimid rulers tried to halt the advance of the Crusader army, but nothing could stop them from reaching their goal of advancing to the Holy city. Most of the towns and villages were abandoned by their Muslim inhabitants fearing the wrath of the western holy warriors. The garrison at Jaffa burned the fort to the ground to avoid it being used by the Crusaders. Panic ensued and the whole region was in complete terror as to what would happen next. The advanced guard led by Tancred de Hauteville captured Bethlehem and raised the De Hauteville Banner from the tower of the Church of the nativity (the birthplace of Jesus) in early June. Three years had pasted since many of the Crusaders had taken their vows to re-conquer the Holy land. On the 7th of June 1099 the fanatical Crusader army arrived at their rendezvous with destiny. After a 3000 mile journey they had reached the gates of Jerusalem.

Church of the Nativity, Bethlehem

The Siege of Jerusalem 1099

Jerusalem is considered the holiest city for the Christian and Jewish faiths and the second holiest place in the Muslim world. The city had been fought over many times before the Crusaders arrived in 1099, but the siege would be remembered by the Islamic world with consequences to this very day. Jerusalem's governor Iftikhar al-Dawla, poisoned the wells outside the city to deny the Crusader army any fresh local water. He also expelled the remaining Christian population from the city in case of any assistance they might give towards the Crusaders. Jerusalem would have no "Third column" traitors from within who would give up the city just like what had happened at Antioch. The Crusader army began to surround the city. Although depleted, the army was still a formidable fighting force. It consisted of about 15,000 soldiers, 2000 of which were mounted knights and thousands of followers

The First assault and the bare footed procession

Godfrey de Bouillon, the Count of Flanders and Robert Duke of Normandy besieged the City form the north side. Raymond of Toulouse camped next to the great tower of David. The Crusaders constructed a few scaling ladders with the little material they had and made their first assault on the city at the Damascus gate. The trumpets sounded and the attack on the walls began. Although they attacked with fanatical zeal it was a complete failure, after six hours of hard fighting the attack was called off. Jerusalem would be a hard nut to crack and many believed that they would be in for a long siege similar to that of Antioch.

The formidable mighty walls of Jerusalem

The Crusaders were forced to forage far and wide in search of water and supplies. They were often ambushed by the Saracens in the dangerous passes and hills that surrounded the city. In mid June their luck changed when a Genoese fleet managed to slip through Fatimid lines and arrive in Jaffa. With the Fatimid war galleys closing the net on them their Captain decided to scuttle his ships and use the wood to construct siege machines for the attack on Jerusalem. Tancred also managed to discover a large supply of timber located in a cave just outside the city. With these extra provisions of wood the Crusaders set about constructing two mighty siege towers and extra scaling ladders ready for the final assault. Peter Desiderius had a vision that Bishop Adhemar de Le Puy (who had died after the last battle of Antioch) had visited him in his dreams and said;

"Tell all the Princes and People that they must march bare foot around Jerusalem invoking God'. If you do this then on the ninth day the city will be captured".

On the 8th of July 1099 the entire army and its followers marched around Jerusalem. The city's garrison mocked the Crusaders, insulting them and hurling abuse towards them. It would be a gesture that the defiant garrison would live to regret. The procession arrived at the Mount of Olives where the Clergy gave sermons encouraging the moral of the Crusaders. The high ranking leaders discussed their strategy for the final assault. Tancred may have told the story of how his Grandfather Robert Guiscard devised the plan to capture the Sicilian capital Palermo. The Normans attacked one side of Palermo's walls, drawing the city's garrison to combat them. Robert led the real attack on the other side of the city, enabling him to enter the capital via deception. The plan was decided upon; the Crusaders would simultaneously launch diversion attacks from several directions, allowing Robert of Normandy, Robert of Flanders and Tancred to launch the strongest attack.

The final assault

On the 13th of July 1099 judgment day had arrived, there was to be no going back now. All the Crusader contingents readied themselves for the final assault on the city. The night before the attack the great siege towers were moved in some cases over a mile to throw the garrison off guard. When the morning came the Saracens were astonished. The attack commenced with the Crusader stone throwing machines hurling great pieces of rock at the city walls and gates. Flaming arrows dipped in pitch, peppered the walls and houses inside the city. Hell was unleashed upon Jerusalem, the fighting continued all day and one Crusader commented that:

"It was hard to believe how great the efforts were made on both sides during that day"

On the second day the vicious fighting continued with both sides struggling to keep up the momentum. Legend has it that a lone knight began to wave his shield around on the Mount of Olives encouraging the Crusaders to continue the attack. On the 15th of July the breakthrough came. Crusader archers managed to ignite cotton bales the defenders were using on the city walls. The flames engulfed the ramparts and forced the defenders to fall back. At once the Crusaders dropped the drawbridge on one of their towers and descended upon the battlements. Lethold and Engelbert, two Flemish Knights were the first to enter, closely followed by Tancred and the Duke of Lorraine.

The Massacre of Jerusalem

As the Crusaders pilled into the city their rage became uncontrollable. They went berserk slaughtering everything within the city. The amount of blood they shed that day was incredible. An eyewitness wrote:

"Some of our men cut off the heads of our enemies; others shot them with arrows, so that they fell from the towers into the flames. Piles of heads, hands and feet were to be seen in the streets of the city". The massacre at Antioch had been vicious, but Jerusalem was pure uncontrolled religious fever.

"It was necessary to pick one's way over the bodies of men and horses. But these were small matters compared to what happened at the temple of Solomon, if I tell you the truth, it will exceed your powers of belief. So let it be suffice to say this much, at least, that in the temple and porch of Solomon, men rode in blood up to their knees and bridle reins".

On the roof of the temple the Crusaders climbed up and beheaded the survivors, men women and children. The Jewish population of the city was treated no better. The main synagogue was burned to the ground with the people inside it. Following the massacre of the city the bodies of the dead were removed to stop the spread of disease and some kind of order was restored. Raymond of Toulouse was offered the title of King of Jerusalem, but he refused it. It was offered to Godfrey De Bouillon who refused the title, but accepted to become Advocatus Sancti Sepulchri (Advocate of the Holy Sepulchre). On the 22nd of July 1099 the Crusader Kingdom of Jerusalem was created.

The few Muslim survivors that managed to escape the carnage of Jerusalem spread the terror to what they had seen. Shockwaves went around the Islamic world. The Fatimid government in Egypt raised an army to crush the Crusader upstarts. The Saracen relief force assembled in Ascalon in early August. In Jerusalem the new Patriarch (Arnulf of Chocques) discovered a relic of the True Cross, possibly another ploy just like the Holy Lance at Antioch, in order the raise Crusader moral. Raymond d'Aguilers circulated a story that the Saracens intended to capture all the Crusaders under 20 and mate with them, so they could create a race of superior warriors to fight for Islam. The story only encouraged the Christians to fight on to the bitter end. A last ditch diplomatic effort was sent to try and reach a compromise, but the Crusaders rejected the offer and launched a pre-emptive attack against the Fatimids.

The Battle of Ascalon

The Crusader army left Jerusalem on the 10th of August 1099. At the head of the Army was Raymond d'Aguilers carrying the Holy Lance from Antioch. He was followed by the Patriarch with the relic of the Holy cross. Tancred led a surprise attack on Ramalah and captured many men and provisions. On the 11th the Crusaders caught the Fatimid army off guard and in disarray beneath the walls of Ascalon. Although outnumbered by perhaps 5/1 they decided to attack and formed up into battle array. The vanguard was led Tancred, Robert of Normandy and Robert of Flanders. On the left wing was Godfrey de Bouillon and on the right was Raymond of Toulouse. The battle began with a Fatimid charge. They were stopped in their tracks by the Crusader archers who let their deadly volleys of arrows rain down into their ranks. The Crusaders now counter attacked. The battle was hard fought in the centre, Ethiopian troops fought with great courage until Godfrey de Bouillon arrived and charged deep into their ranks. The battle turned into a rout, Raymond of Toulouse pursued the fleeing Saracens towards the coast. The Fatimid camp was overrun by Tancred and Robert's Normans in the centre. Godfrey's men chased the remaining Fatimids to the very gates of Ascalon itself. For the Fatimids it was a disaster losing up to 10-15,000 men, but for the Crusaders saw it was seen as another divine victory. During the night they camped in the former Fatimid camp expecting to give battle the next day. Instead the Fatimid army broke up and headed home. The Muslim commander Al-fdal's personal banner had been captured and was returned to Jerusalem as a trophy of war. After the battle most of the Crusader leaders forefilled their vows in Jerusalem and started returning home.

The creation of the Kingdom of Heaven

The First Crusade had now officially come to an end. Indeed for the Medieval Christian world it would go down in legend as a miraculous affair. No other Crusade after it would be as so successful. 400 hundred years of Islamic expansion had come to an end and the time of the Kingdom of Heaven had arrived. Rising up out of the ashes of the First Crusade were the fledgling Crusader states of Antioch in the North, The County of Eddessa in the east, Tripoli on the coast and the Kingdom of Jerusalem to the south. Most of the Crusader states were almost always on a state of alert after the end of the First Crusade in 1099. They had enemies virtually all around them. Bohemond's personal struggle against the Byzantine Empire to hold on to Antioch raged on for years. The Norman warrior tried to extent the Principality, but in 1100 while coming to the assistance of an Armenian ally, his small force of 300 knights was ambushed by Danishmend Turks at the battle of Melitene. Bohemond himself was captured along with his fellow family member Richard of the Principate and held ransom by the Turks until 1103. Fearing a complete takeover either from the Byzantines or the newly rejuvenated Turks the leading magnates of Antioch offered Tancred Bohemond's nephew the regency. Tancred proved an able regent and secured the Principality's independence. Bohemond managed to raise the ransom for his release by 1103, not without difficulty from the Byzantines who were trying to lay their hands on the Norman Prince. In 1104 Bohemond decided to return to Western Europe to recruit reinforcements and settle the disputed claim of Antioch with the Pope. Tancred was again left as regent during his absence. Bohemond arrived home in Italy and began a tour of Europe, recruiting an army not to attack the Saracens in the East, but to wage war on his old enemy Alexius, the Byzantine Emperor. The Norman warlord even managed to secure the hand of the King of France's daughter. All the preparations had been made by 1107 to launch a campaign against the Byzantines.

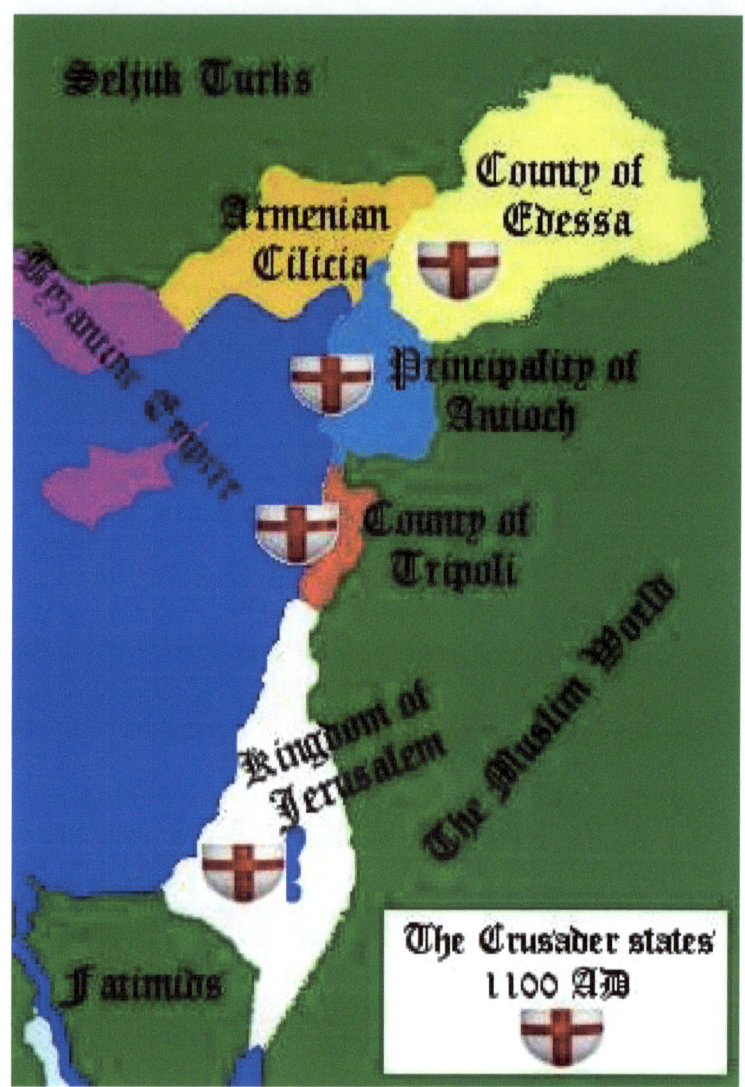

Bohemond, continuing his Father's work 1107

The campaign against the Byzantine Empire had become a personal grudge between the Norman De Hautevilles and Alexius ever since Robert Guiscard (Bohemond's father) had attacked the Eastern Empire in the early 1080s. After receiving mass in the church of St Nicolas (Bari) Bohemond set sail for the Albanian mainland. The Norman army that invaded the Balkans was extremely large; over 30,000 men from Italy, France, Normandy and even England crossed the Adriatic that winter. The army captured Canina and then Bohemond laid siege to Durazzo for the second time in his career. Fear struck the Byzantine court except for Alexius who said;

"Let us eat now, we shall see about Bohemond afterwards".

Failing to take the city by force, the Normans began the long siege, but just like his campaign thirty years earlier the realities of warfare set in. Hemmed in by the Byzantines who held the mountain passes and cut off from supplies from Italy the offensive faltered. In the Spring Alexius arrived on the scene and negotiations started. In the end Bohemond became a vassal of Alexius and was granted: Antioch, the port of St Simeon and other towns within the Principality of Antioch. Bohemond returned to Italy and by 1111 he was raising another army with the intention of returning to the East or maybe of attacking the Byzantines again? He died in Norman Apulia (Italy) on the 7th of March. He never achieved his dream of overthrowing the Byzantine Emperor Alexius, but his contribution towards the success of the First Crusade remains impressive.

Bohemond's Mausoleum Canosa, Puglia, Italy

Without his daring, guile, leadership and determination the First Crusade is likely to have failed. Bohemond may have sworn to become a vassal of Alexius, but Tancred held the reins of power in Antioch and refused any part in the deal. With the support of the other Crusader states the Byzantines had no chance of taking back the mighty city from Tancred. Within a year Tancred died and Bohemond's son (Bohemond II) became regent under the guidance of Roger de Salerno. Roger was another Norman who defended the Principalities rights, defeating the Seljuk Turks in several battles and skirmishes. He was cut down in 1119 at the battle of the Ager Sanguinis (the Field of Blood). Bohemond II continued the De Hauteville family trade of warfare throughout the 1120s. In 1130 he was lured into an ambush and was killed in the fighting. A horrible tale says that he was decapitated and his head along with his blond hair was embalmed, placed in a silver box and sent to the Caliph as a gruesome gift. Antioch became a vassal state of the Kingdom of Jerusalem until its capture by the Baibar Muslims in 1268.

Toros Roslin wrote:

"Antioch was captured by the wicked Caliph of Egypt, many were killed and became his prisoners, all the holy temples, houses of God, which are in it were destroyed by fire." The empty title of "Prince of Antioch" passed, with the extinction of the Counts of Tripoli, to the Kings of Cyprus, and was sometimes granted as a dignity to junior members of the royal house".

Bohemond De Hauteville
"Prince of Antioch"

The Kingdom of Jerusalem 1099-1187

When Godfrey de Bouillon died in 1100 the crown of Jerusalem passed to Baldwin Count of Edessa. After a short campaign against the Fatimids Baldwin was proclaimed King of Jerusalem on Christmas day 1100. Baldwin was an energetic King who strove to expand the power and territory of the Kingdom. He captured the costal towns of Caesarea and Arsuf from the Saracens in 1101. In September he again defeated a Fatimid army at Ramalah. It was a glorious victory against the odds, his army of only 250 armoured knights and 1000 infantry defeated Saad el-Dawleh's 10,000 strong Saracen force. The battle was a close run-thing with both sides fighting hard and was only decided when Baldwin personally led a direct counter attack then routed the Fatimid centre.

The Coronation of Baldwin I "King of Jerusalem" 1100 A.D

In 1102 reinforcements arrived from Europe including Stephen De Blois, the nobleman who had deserted the First Crusade back at the siege of Antioch. At the second battle of Ramlah Baldwin overreached himself. The Crusaders were overconfident and decided to give battle not knowing the strength of the enemy. Unable to escape they had no choice but to launch a direct cavalry charge at the Fatimids. Baldwin managed to escape with a few knights to a fortified tower, but the remainder of the army was wiped out including Stephen de Blois. Baldwin was ferried out of Ramalah by an English pirate Godric of Finchale who took him to Jaffa. There he raised another army with the help of newly arrived German and French Crusaders and defeated the Fatimids at the battle in Jaffa. During the next few years he continued the struggle against the Saracens and by 1109 the Crusaders captured Tripoli and established the last great Crusader state in the Outremer (Middle East).

The crisis came in 1113 when Baldwin faced a combined assault from the Saracens of Damascus and Mosul. At the battle of Al-Sannabra the Crusaders were enticed into attacking the Saracens who used a feinted flight to entrap them. The Crusaders retreated to a nearby hilltop and fortified themselves on it. Norman reinforcements arrived from Antioch and Tripoli and stabilized the situation. The Muslim attack on the Kingdom subsided when infighting broke within their camp and their leader Mawdud was assassinated. A great period of castle building commenced during the reign of Baldwin I. In 1115 he built the castle of Montreal (Mont Royal) in the south of the Kingdom.

Montreal castle (Jordan) built by King Baldwin 1115

The Military Orders

In the wake of the First Crusade the Kingdom's Holy Military Orders were created. Hughes de Payens and Godfrey de Saint Omer founded the Knights Templar in 1118. They set up the monastic order on the ruins of the Temple of Solomon in Jerusalem. The other great Military order was the Knights Hospitallers. They originally looked after the sick and pilgrims visiting Jerusalem, but after the First Crusade they became the defenders of the Holy land.

These Orders grew in power and became the standing army of the Kingdom of Jerusalem in times of trouble.

Bernard de Clairvaux of them wrote;

Arms of the Knights Templar

Arms of the Knights Hospitaller

"A Templar Knight is truly a fearless warrior, and secure on every side, for his soul is protected by the armour of faith, just as his body is protected by the armour of steel. He is thus doubly armed, and need not fear either demons or men."

Baldwin II

King Baldwin I died a broken man in 1118, he was forced to repudiate his wife Adelaide (The mother of the Norman King Roger II of Sicily). The crown passed to his cousin Baldwin de Bourcq. Most of his reign was spent defending the precarious Crusader states from invasion. The King was captured while defending the frontier of Edessa in 1123. Eustace Grenier was elected Constable of Jerusalem during the King's captivity. He defeated the Fatimid invasion of the Kingdom in 1123 at the battle of Yibneh. The legendry Crusader cavalry charge broke the spirit and will of the Sudanese infantry.

Fulcher of Chartres said;

"The battle did not last long because when our foes saw our armed men advance in excellent order against them their horsemen immediately took flight as if completely bewitched, they went into a panic instead of using good sense. Their foot-soldiers were massacred."

King Baldwin II

In 1124 King Baldwin II escaped from his imprisonment and returned to Jerusalem. The Crusaders also captured the important coastal city of Tyre establishing a colony and trading links with the new sea power of Venice.

Baldwin took the offensive against the Seljuk Turks laying siege to Aleppo in 1125 and although the siege was broken off after three months, Baldwin defeated the Turks at the Battle of Azaz. The King tried to capture Damascus in the following year, but again the Crusader forces were not strong enough to finish the campaign. The King died in August 1131 after a reign of over 13 years of non stop-fighting and warfare.

A period of instability struck the Kingdom after the death of Baldwin II. By 1132 the Crusaders were fighting themselves. Fulk Count of Anjou reigned as co-consort. He was the Grandfather of Henry Plantagenet, Future King of England and Duke of Normandy. By the 1144 the Kingdom was on the verge of total collapse. Fulk had died and the Kingdom was in the hands of a boy (Baldwin III). Worse still the Crusader State of Edessa fell to the Saracens which send a shockwave back towards Western Europe and led to the Second Crusade.

The Second Crusade 1145-1149

The call to arms did not fall upon deaf ears in the west, Louis VII King of France and Conrad III the German Emperor pledged their support. The two monarchs arrived in the Holy Land in 1147. Instead of attacking Aleppo, which if captured would have allowed them to re-take the County of Edessa, they decided to attack Damascus. The ill conceived strategy proved disastrous. The Crusaders laid siege to Damascus in the summer of 1148, but under constant attack from the Saracens and no real plan of action the Crusade started to fall apart. The Crusaders fought a desperate battle in the orchards outside Damascus. Conrad the German Emperor led a cavalry charge, but was forced to continue to fight on foot. The Crusaders could not manoeuvre their heavy cavalry in the orchards and decided to move camp. With three Kings but no one in supreme command the Crusade was destined to failure. After four days the different Crusader contingents retreated back towards Jerusalem. The Second Crusade was a missed opportunity to bolster up the defence of the Kingdom and achieve a memorable victory. Blamed on sin, it only made the First Crusade seem even more miraculous. Conrad III returned home to Germany while Louis stayed in Jerusalem for another year until his marriage with Eleanor D'Aquitaine broke down.

The Battle of Ascalon 1153

The Saracen Fortress of Ascalon had been a thorn in the side of the Crusaders for over 50 years. In May 1153 King Baldwin besieged the city. The siege dragged on for four months. In August after heavy bombardment and mining part of the wall tumbled down.

The Three Kings Baldwin, Louis and Conrad III
The Second Crusade 1148

At once Bernard De Tremelay (Grand Master of the Templars) stormed through the breach into the city. However he and his knights were surrounded and killed. Their heads were cut off and displayed on the city gates. The Saracens were ecstatic, but their joy was short lived when the Crusaders finally stormed the city on the 19th of August in force. Although Baldwin ruled well, the dynastic struggles between the Crusaders nobles undermined the strength of the Kingdom. Rumors circulated that the King had been poisoned from conspirators within the court upon his death.

The rise of a united Muslim World

The debacle of the Second Crusade gave rise to the Zengid Dynasty. The Zegrid Muslim Turks began to unite the Muslim world under the leadership of Nur ad-Din. He united the former County of Edessa with Mosul, then Aleppo and Damascus in 1154. His power was checked by King Baldwin whom he had a mutual respect for.

When Baldwin III died William de Tyre reported that Nur ad Din Said;

"We should sympathize with their grief and in their pity, spare them, because they have lost a King such as the rest of the world does not possess today."

The new King of Jerusalem Amalric I started his reign well. He formed an alliance with the Byzantines and at the Battle of Al-Buqaia defeated Nur ad Din. Overconfident he invaded Egypt in 1164. This left the Kingdom open to attack from Nur ad Din who had recovered from his previous defeat. In 1164 he crushed the combined Crusader and Byzantine army at the battle of

Harim. The defeat was a severe blow for the Crusaders. Some of the leading barons in the Kingdom had been captured, Raymond III of Tripoli, Joscelin III of Edessa, Bohemond III of Antioch and Hugh de Lusignan. Amalric rushed back from Egypt to stop a complete collapse of the Crusader states. The next few years were filled with constant warfare. In 1169 a nephew of one of Nur al Din's commanders became Sultan of Egypt. The man's name would become world renowned in time, for he was Saladin "The champion of the Islamic world"

Saladin and the Leper King

Amalric I died in 1174 and his 13 year old son Baldwin IV became King (commonly known as Baldwin the leper). Saladin's power continued to grow during the 1170s and Baldwin IV had to use all the virtues of Kingship to stop the destruction of the Kingdom.

Success came in the winter in 1177 when Saladin invaded the Kingdom. King Baldwin along with Raynald of Châtillon, Odo De Saint Amand (Grand master of the Knights Templar) Joscelin III of Edessa and the Ibelin brothers headed for Ascalon to garrison the city. Saladin bypassed the fortress and sent a small force to besiege it while he continued his march on Jerusalem.

The Young King Baldwin IV showing the signs of Leprosy

The Battle of Montgisard 1177

The Saracen force that had been sent to hold up the King in Ascalon was by no means strong enough for the task. The Crusaders broke out from the siege and began to gather their forces. Saladin who was unaware of the movements behind him carelessly divided his forces, terrorising the local countryside. Near Montgisard Baldwin's army caught Saladin completely off guard. The King who was quite ill had the relic of the True Cross paraded in front of his knights to encourage them. With no more time to lose the Crusaders unleashed their heavy armoured knights against the unprepared Saracens. The Knight himself led the charge hacking down the Saracen soldiers in his way. He was within inches of killing Saladin who was only saved by nightfall and the bravery of his Mamluk guards. The Saracen army was wiped out and the Kingdom was saved for the time being. A truce was agreed between the King and Saladin in 1180. It was broken by Raynald of Châtillon who attacked trader caravans passing through his fief on countless occasions. Baldwin's leprosy affected his health and led to his early death in 1185. He had been co-ruling the Kingdom with his nephew Baldwin V since 1183, but the real power in the Kingdom now lay with the leading Barons. When he died, his mother Sibylla and her husband Guy de Lusignan took up the reigns of power.

The Gigantic Crusader castle of "Le Krak des Chevaliers" Syria

The Battle of Hattin and the fall of Jerusalem

With Jerusalem weak and fractioned, Saladin decided the time was right for the destruction of the Kingdom. In May 1187 he crossed the river Jordan with an army of over 40,000 men. His first target was Raymond of Tripoli's castle of Tiberias. Guy was now forced into mobilising the army of Jerusalem to combat the invasion. The fore coming titanic battle would decide the fate of the Holy Land. Guy had two choices, either let the castle fall and defend his current position, or push on to relieve the siege. Foolhardy voices from within the Crusader camp urged Guy to march on and give battle. On the 3rd of July a reluctant King Guy marched off towards Tiberias. They reached the small village of Turan, the last watering spring before Tiberias at midday. With still over eight miles to go the Crusaders marched out in the afternoon, into the barren rocky landscape. As soon as they left Turan, Saladin sent his men to capture the village and effectively cut off the Crusaders from any retreat. With the trap now set Saladin attacked the beleaguered Crusader army as it made its slow progress in the sweltering heat of the summer sun. By evening they were forced to make camp on a plateau that became known as the Horns of Hattin. When the Crusaders awoke on the morning of the 4th of July they found themselves completely surrounded. Their situation deteriorated further when Saladin set fire to the grassland vegetation all around them causing terrible suffering from the heat and the smoke. Raymond of Tripoli despaired;

"God, our war is over! We are all dead men-and the Kingdom has come to an end."

Faced with no alternative, but to fight their way out of the trap the Crusaders formed up into battle array. Raymond of Tripoli led the Vanguard, King Guy in the center and Joscelin III of Edessa to the rear. In a desperate attempt to breakout Raymond charged the Saracen lines twice. He managed to breakthrough on the second time, but did not have enough men to counterattack, and with the weight of Saracen number beginning to tell he fled the field. The King was less fortunate, when his knights became separated from the infantry the slaughter began. Vicious hand to hand fighting continued all day until the last remaining Crusaders surrendered.

The Battle of Hattin 1187 (Matthew Paris)

The highly ranking captives were brought to Saladin's royal tent. Saladin offered King Guy water to drink, after a few sips Guy offered the cup to Raynald of Châtillon. Before Raynald could drink it Saladin knocked the cup out of his hands and accused Raynald of being an oath breaker.

Raynald of Châtillon ;
"Kings have always acted thus. I did nothing more."
Saladin had heard enough and with one fatal swoop of his sword he cut Raynald in two. King Guy was shook by the act and fell to his knees expecting the same treatment.
Saladin; **"Have no fear. It is not the custom of Kings to kill Kings."**

The battle was a total victory for the Saracens. The Crusader field army had been smashed which left the Kingdom virtually defenceless. By late summer he had taken Jaffa, Acre, Nablus, Sidon, Beirut and Ascalon. In September 1187 his army began the siege of the greatest prize of all, Jerusalem. After a futile defence of the city by Queen Sibylla and Balian De Ibelin the city surrendered on the 2nd of October. Saladin was magnanimous in victory. He allowed pilgrims to visit the Holy City and even allowed the Church of the Holy Sepulchre to remain Christian. The Kingdom of Heaven would live on until its final defeat at Acre in 1291, but the shockwaves of the Saracen capture of Jerusalem would lead to the coming of the Normans again. The Third Crusade was spearheaded by another titanic Anglo-Norman Warrior: Richard the Lionheart, Duke of Normandy, Aquitaine and King of England.

Chapter 4: **England**

DOMESDAY 1066
"The Norman invasion and the destruction of Anglo-Saxon England"

In the night time sky over the Kingdom of England Halley's comet burned brightly. For many it was seen as a bad omen and sign of impending doom. Fear gripped the nation and could be seen in the eyes of the newly crowned King Harold II. Indeed the year of 1066 would decide the fate of Anglo-Saxon England and the destiny of Western Europe. Two Kings and Europe's most powerful warlord would confront each other in a titanic battle for the control of the island of Britannia.

Following the departure of the last Roman Legions in 410AD the island of Britannia was invaded by the Jutes, Angles and Saxons. These Germanic warrior tribes pushed the Romano-British population into Wales and the Western fringes of Britain. By the ninth century Wessex, Mercia and Northumbria made up the Heptarch of the newly created Kingdom of England. In 793 AD a new invader came to the shores of England. They were the "Sea Wolves" who spread terror across all of Europe and they were called the Vikings. Firstly they only came for plunder but by the 860s they were intent on full scale conquest and invasion of the island. Over the next 15 years they destroyed the Anglo Saxon Kingdoms of Northumbria, East Anglia and Mercia. Only Wessex stood in their way of complete domination over England.

Alfred the Great and the Danelaw

On the verge of complete annihilation Anglo-Saxon England found in itself a leader and King who would combat the Viking menace and save the Kingdom. In 871 Alfred and his brother King Ethelred fought five almighty battles against the "Great Heathen army". At the battle of Ashdown Alfred led the Anglo-Saxons like a "wild boar". Five Viking warlords were slaughtered and the myth of Viking invincibility was vanquished forever. After four years of respite the Vikings attacked again, this time under the command of Guthrum, a cunning wrlord. In 878 Guthrum launched a daring winter campaign against the Anglo- Saxons.

Alfred's royal residence at Chippenham was destroyed, Alfred and his family were forced to flee to avoid capture. He roamed the countryside like a fugitive escaping to the Isle of Athelney. Welcome news arrived from Devon where the Vikings had been defeated losing their sacred raven banner in the process. Galvanised into action Alfred raised an army and at the battle of Edington inflicted a crushing defeat on Guthrum's pagans.

A chronicler wrote; **"Fighting ferociously, we formed a dense shield-wall against the whole army of the Pagans, and with great bravery...at last, Alfred gained the victory. He defeated the Pagans with great slaughter, and pursued them as far as the fortress of Chippenham".**

After the defeat, Guthrum left Wessex and settled in East Anglia. In 884 both leaders concluded a treaty known as the Danelaw "lands controlled by the Danes / Vikings". England was effectively cut diagonally in half following the old Roman road of Watling Street with the Vikings controlling the north of the country and the Anglo-Saxon controlling the south.

Alfred ruled well and started to strengthen the Kingdom by building fortified towns commonly known as "Burghs". When he died 899 his son Edward the Elder was ready to take the offensive against the Scandinavian invaders. Instead of all out war, Edward slowly advanced each year into the Danelaw and captured or bought land and towns from the Vikings.

Alfred the Great statue, Winchester

He then fortified them into Burghs. His strategy made very good sense for when the Vikings attacked they used up all their energy on attacking the well defended settlements losing many men in the process. By 924 Edward had reclaimed most of England up to the river Humber. He also showed his greatness as a ruler by encouraging both Anglo-Saxon and Dane to live together. This policy allowed the two communities to work together and united the fragmented regions into the Kingdom of England.

Athelstan "King of Britain"

When Edward died in 924 his son Athelstan was proclaimed King by the Saxon free council, the Witan. Athelstan did not disappoint, when Viking raiders from Ireland invaded Northumbria Athelstan marched north and captured York, the capital of the northern England. In July 927 the three Kings of Celtic Britain (Constantine of Scotland, Owain of Wales and Hywel of Strathclyde) paid homage and submitted to Athelstan. It was a crowning moment for the King who received the accolade:

Viking ship Dragon head carving

"I Athelstan, King of the English, elevated by the right hand of God, which is Christ, to the throne of the whole Kingdom of Britain"

In 937 Athelstan faced a formidable coalition against his rule. At the battle of Brunanburh Athelstan's Anglo-Saxons were pitted against the armies of King Constantine of Scotland, the Viking King Olaf of Dublin and Owen I of Strathclyde. At the end of an October day the battlefield was littered with thousands of brave warriors from both sides. Athelstan emerged victorious and undisputed King of Britain.

Normandy and the Confessor King

By the turn of the century the Vikings returned again to England. Years of bloody conflict continued decade after decade. On the other side of the channel in Northern France, the Vikings had also conquered large areas of territory. In 911 they forced King Charles III of France to recognise their conquests and officially create the Duchy of Normandy. Unlike the Vikings in England who kept their Scandinavian origins, "The Norseman" became the Normans and quickly adopted Carolingian feudalism. They inter-married the local aristocracy and after a generation spoke Norman-French as their language. Their ability to assimilate was their key to successfully creating the Norman state. In 1013 two young boys Edward and Alfred accompanied their mother Queen Emma into exile to Normandy. Emma was the wife of King Ethelred and the sister of the current Duke of Normandy Richard II "the fearless".

King Edward the Confessor

After the Viking takeover, England was not a safe place for the heirs to the Anglo-Saxon throne. Alfred was ticked back into returning to England in 1036. He was betrayed by Earl Godwin of Wessex and brutally put to death. Edward remained in Normandy until 1041/1042 when the Viking King Harthacnut asked him to return and become his co-ruler. When Harthacnut died, the Anglo-Saxon Witan elected Edward as his successor. In 1043 Edward was crowned in Winchester Cathedral. England had changed since the glory days of Athelstan, the great Saxon Kingdoms had been reduced to Earldoms in the years of Viking dominance. With no powerbase like his predecessors Edward was forced to rely on the support of the powerful barons, Earl Godwin of Wessex, Siward Earl of Northumbria and Leofric Earl of Mercia. Edward never forgave Earl Godwin for the death of his brother and the uneasy peace erupted into open warfare in 1051. In a short campaign by the King, Earl Godwin and his family were forced into exile.

Edward then jeopardised his position in England by giving out offices and titles not to Englishmen, but to prominent Normans and Frenchmen. Duke William of Normandy was invited over on a state visit by Edward to show his gratitude towards the Normans who had sheltered him during his years in exile. Edward who was childless may even have offered the English crown to William during his visit. The King was caught off guard when the Godwins returned and forced him to submit to them and dismiss the Norman officials in the Kingdom. Legend has it that during a banquet the King accused Godwin of murdering his brother Alfred. The Earl invited God to choke him if it were true; low and behold the Earl died before finishing his meal. After his father's death, Harold Godwinson became the real power behind the throne. Edward sent him to the Welsh border to restore order and check the aggressions of Gruffydd Ap Llywelyn. Harold earned a reputation as a great general in several campaigns against the Welsh.

Brothers in arms, Normandy and Brittany 1064

In 1064 Harold was shipwrecked on the Northern coast of France. The truth may never be known about the incident; some say he was blown off course during a fishing expedition, others report that he was sent to France on an official mission to secure the release of hostages. He and his men were captured by the local lord Count Guy I of Ponthieu. When Duke William heard the news he marched north and ordered the Count to hand over the important prisoner. Harold was treated well by the Normans and entertained in the Ducal capital of Rouen. He also accompanied Duke William on campaign into Brittany.

On the Norman–Breton border at Le Mont de Saint Michel Harold rescued two of William's knights from sinking into quicksand. He also distinguished himself on the field of battle; Harold fought well showing great courage and tenacity. The Norman war machine raided deep into Celtic Brittany capturing the towns of Dol de Bretagne, Rennes and finally Dinan. The Breton Duke Conan submitted and handed over the keys of the town to William where he knighted Harold for his services. Harold also gained valuable experience of how the Normans fought on horseback, which was very different to the Scandinavian style of fighting mainly on foot back in England. He even set up a cavalry unit copying the Norman knights on his return to England.

← **Overleaf: Harold and the Norman Attack on Dinan**

The chronicler Orderic Vitalis wrote of Harold:

"He was very tall and handsome, with remarkable physical strength, his courage and eloquence, his ready jests and acts of valour. But what were these gifts to him without honour, which is the root of all good?"

The infamous Oath of fealty

According to the Norman sources and the Bayeux Tapestry, on their return to Normandy, Harold swore an oath of fealty on sacred relics to uphold William's claim to the throne of England. The story may have been true; Harold would have said anything in order to escape back to England.

Harold swearing his oath of allegiance to William, Bayeux Tapestry

In January 1066 old King Edward died. He had given no clear instructions as to who should inherit the crown. England was not a hereditary based system and anyone who had Royal blood running through their veins could put forward a claim. The Anglo-Saxon elected council, "The Witan", would then decide who to proclaim King.

In 1066 there was no shortage of claimants; the strongest claim came from Edgar 'the Atheling" who was the grandson of Edmund "Ironside" and who could trace his linage back to Alfred the Great. The problem was that Edgar was only a boy, lacking in experience and authority. Harold Godwinson was the most powerful nobleman in the Kingdom and had proved himself as an able commander against the Welsh during the reign of King Edward.

Dark forces also had an eye on the throne of England, the famous Viking warlord King Harald III "Hardrada" who had captained the elite Byzantine Varganian Guard fighting alongside the Norman conquerors of Sicily before becoming King of Norway, claimed that the English crown had been promised to his nepthew King Magnus "The Good" by King Harthacnut.

The fourth candidate was Duke William of Normandy. William claimed that King Edward had promised him the crown and Harold had confirmed this under his oath of fealty in 1064/65.

The coronation the Harold Godwinson 1066

On the 6th of January Harold Godwinson was proclaimed King of England. 1066 would be the year of destiny for King Harold II and Anglo-Saxon England.

The King was confronted by threats of invasion from both Harald "Hardrada" in the north and William Duke of Normandy in the south. Firstly Harold secured an important marriage union to Edith the sister of Morcar, the Earl of Northumbria and Edwin, Earl of Mercia. This marriage united the Kingdom from any internal division.

1066, Hardrada's Viking invasion of the North

Harold's brother, Tostig had been the Earl of Northumbria since 1055. His rule was harsh and he oppressed its people. One chronicler stated; **"he repressed the Northumbrians with the heavy yoke of his rule".** By 1065 the northern Thegns (minor nobility) rose up in rebellion and ousted Tostig and his officials. At the royal council of Oxford Tostig was stripped of his title. In a furious row he accused Harold of instigating the rebellion. At the end of the council he was banished from the Kingdom. Tostig headed for Flanders where he plotted his revenge. In the spring of 1066 he raided the south coast of England before being forced to flee when King Harold headed south the confront him. He reappeared off the coast of Northern England ravaging the coastline before being decisively defeated by Mocar and Edwin. During the summer months he made contact with Harald Hardrada urging him to invade England. The Viking King raised a colossal army of 10,000 warriors and a fleet of over 500 ships. The scene was set for the biggest Viking invasion of England in living memory.

Harold like a spider on a web waited on the south coast for the fore coming invasion from Normandy. Weeks turned into months, but nothing came. Then during the first week of September Harold allowed the English Fryd to break up and return home to gather the Harvest.

"The provisions of the people were gone, and nobody could stay in the south any longer"

With the campaigning season coming to an end it seemed that England was safe from invasion for another year, but then on a misty September morning Hundreds of Viking dragon-head ships sailed into the mouth of the river Humber. Invasion had come not from William Duke of Normandy, but from the dreaded King Harald III "Hardrada".

The greatest Viking invasion of England in living memory was underway; at Ricall they disembarked and headed for the capital of the north, York (Jorvik in Old Norse). On the 20th of September at Fulford just outside York Harald's men were confronted by an Anglo-Saxon army under the command of Earl Edwin of Mercia and Earl Mocar of Northumbria. Harald formed up his army into battle order, the left flank resting on the river and the centre and right wing along a parallel ditch. The King ordered his famous land-ravager flag to be brought forward and placed deep into English soil. The Earl's men advanced and spotted that the Norse army was weakest on their right flank.

They ordered the whole Saxon army to concentrate their attack on the ditch section. The fierce Saxon charge smashed straight into the Norse formation. Axe, spear and sword were all used to deadly effect in the unrelenting combat. Encouraged on by their initial success, the Saxons broke through the Norse ranks. At this crucial moment, Harald the hero of a thousand battles entered the fray. He ordered a general charge with the land-ravager flag carried before him. His best troops and Viking berserkers pushed Edwin and Morcar's men back into the ditch, where many were slain. Some Norse troops may have also outflanked the Saxon position by crossing the marsh via the old Roman road. The battle turned into a rout and by the time the Saxons were in full retreat, the ditch was so full with bodies that the Norse could cross it without getting their feet wet.

Heimskringla Saga:

"Brave Harald drove along.
Flying but fighting the whole way.
At last, demoralised, they could not fight.
And the whole body took flight and fled".

Both Edwin and Morcar escaped the carnage of Fulford, but the Norse victory caused a general panic back in York and much of Northern England. Harald had won a great victory which strengthened his claim to gain the English crown. He advanced to the very gates of York and received the surrender of the Northern capital. The city was spared the dreaded sack, but was ordered to send hostages to a designated rendezvous point several miles outside the city at a place called Stamford Bridge.

The last Viking victory in England, Fulford, York 1066 AD

The last battle, Stamford Bridge

After the submission of York, Harald returned to his ships at Riccall. On the 25th of September 1066 A.D the King marched out back towards Stamford Bridge, leaving a large proportion of his army at Riccall under the command of Olaf his son and Eystein Orre.
Overconfident and believing that the English had been utterly defeated Harald allowed many of his men to leave their heavy armour and mail coats with the fleet. When they arrived at Stamford Bridge they could see clouds of dust swirling up into the sky. Harald asked Tostig who it could be and the Earl replied that it was probably English friends and allies coming to submit and join the Norse army. Tostig was completely wrong, and it became clear when they saw the "Fighting man banner" of Wessex that it was the full military might of Anglo-Saxon England under the command of King Harold Godwinsson. After the news of the invasion, King Harold had marched north and covered the some 200 miles from London to York in lightning speed.

As the English army approached Harald had little choice but to stand his ground and hope to delay the battle until his main force could arrive from Riccall. He sent some messengers on horseback at full speed to gather the remainder of the Norse army to join him at Stamford Bridge. Harald was caught completely unaware, yet only one battle stood in his way of re-uniting the great North Sea Empire of King Cnut. He organised his outnumbered and lightly armoured troops into a circular shield wall formation with the sacred Land-Ravager flag in the centre.

Then twenty riders came forward from the English position. One of them asked if Tostig was in the army. When Tostig replied that he was, the rider said that he had a message from King Harold. The message was that if he deserted the Norse he would be re-instated as Earl of Northumbria and also given a third of the Kingdom to rule. Tostig replied what would be given to King Harald "Hardrada" for his trouble, to which the rider answered.

"Seven foot of English soil, for he is taller than most men"

As the English rode back to their lines Hardrada asked Tostig if he knew the man who had spoken so gallantly. Tostig said he did and that was King Harold Godwinsson himself. Harald observed to his close comrades;

"What a little man is Harold Godwinsson, yet he sat up well in his stirrups"

With the formalities at an end the Anglo-Saxons attacked and overwhelmed the Norse contingent stationed on the western side of the river. Their advance was checked by a lone Viking berserker who heroically defended the footbridge over the river Derwent. He single handedly cut down ever English soldier who challenged him. The duel was ended when a Saxon warrior crept beneath the bridge and speared the berserker from below.

Battle of Stamford Bridge commemoration plaque

As the giant Viking warrior fell to the ground the English shouted out a deafening battle cry and advanced towards the Norse position. There have been many theories as to why Harald did not defend the bridge and use it is a choke point until the arrival of the Norse reserves. As the most experienced and battle hardened warrior of his day he would have certainly have recognised this tactical advantage.

The answer to this debate may be in the actual origin of the placename of Stamford. The Germanic origin of the word "ford" meaning a shallow river crossing. The river Derwent may have been exceptionally low due to the warm and dry weather conditions of 1066 A.D, allowing the Anglo-Saxon army to cross the river in force without needing to rely on the footbridge.

According to the Heimskringla saga the English attacked on horseback. Although the Anglo-Saxons used horses like the Vikings for transport they are not known to have fought as cavalry, but if the sagas are correct this may have been a detachment of King Harold Godwinsson's royal huscarls. Harold had fought with Duke William of Normandy on campaign in Brittany and had been very much impressed by the Norman mounted cavalry.

When he returned to England he created a unit based on the Norman mounted knight. The English threw everything at the Norse shield wall, but each assault was repulsed and thrown back. The green Yorkshire grass turned red with blood and the field was littered with the dead and wounded from both sides. Soon the lack of armour and overwhelming English numbers began to tell. At the crucial moment just like at Fulford Harald bust out from behind the shield wall and charged straight into the English ranks hoping the break the deadlock and turn the battle to his favour. The King flew into a violent berserker rage and hacked down everyone in his way. Nonone could withstand the fury of his charge as he forced his way through the Saxons ranks infront of him. Harald's Norse charge nearly broke the spirit of the English who were being pushed back and on the verge of fleeing the field.

Then disaster struck, Harald "Hardrada" was hit by a stray arrow in the windpipe. The great warrior King was stopped dead in his tracks, dropping to the ground like a felled mighty oak tree. It was perhaps befitting that he died sword in hand "the Viking way" fighting until his last breath, the way he would have wished. Harold Godwinsson offered quarter to his brother Tostig and the remaining Norse soldiers, but they refused to surrender and fought on to the last man defending Harald's body and the sacred land-ravager flag.

Shortly afterwards Eystein Orri arrived on the battlefield with the Norse reinforcements from Riccall. Although exhausted from the forced march they entered the bloody conflict in a furious rage. Taking charge of the raven banner they inflicted many casualties upon the English. After a short while they ditched their armour and shields in order to carry on fighting, but this made them easy targets for the English archers who decimated their numbers. As darkness fell on the battlefield the last great Viking army to assault England had been annihilated.

Some of Harald's men managed to escape the carnage and return to Riccall with the land-ravager banner. The victorious English King Harold made a peace treaty with King Harald's son Olaf, allowing him and the remaining Norse to return home back to Scandinavia. Only 24 ships out of over 300 were needed to take the Norwegian survivors home. So great was the slaughter of Stamford Bridge that piles of bones still littered the battlefield well into the 12th century.

The Normans invade

Harold had won a great victory, but he had lost many good men at the battle of Stamford Bridge. Three days after the battle disaster struck Anglo-Saxon England, the Normans had landed on the south coast.

The Normans disembark on the English coast

During the spring and summer of 1066 William had been preparing for the invasion of England. He had even secured Papal blessing for the invasion from the Pope in Rome. Although it was extremely late in the campaigning season, William's spies brought back news that Harold was in the north and the south of the island was virtually undefended. Just at the right moment the winds changed in the Channel making it possible to launch the invasion.

On the 28th of September 1066 the Norman fleet carrying 7000 thousand soldiers from Normandy, Brittany, Maine, France and even Southern Italy disembarked on the shingle beaches of the Pevensey Bay. As William came ashore he fell over into the sand. Many around him thought it was a bad omen until William stood up holding two handfuls of English sand and acclaimed

"See, my lords, by the splendour of God, I have taken possession of England with both my hands. It is now mine, and what is mine is yours."

The Normans set up their headquarters inside the ruins of the old Roman fort at Pevensey. William's strategy was to devastate the local towns and villages, not only to supply his army but also to lure Harold south and bring him to battle. William could have marched on London before Harold returned south, but the Hastings peninsula offered a good opportunity for him to choose the field of battle best suited towards the Norman cavalry. With access restricted to only one road in and out, William could not be surprised as to which direction Harold would come. The only problem would be that if Harold could contain the Normans in the peninsula, they would effectively be trapped with no hope of being re-supplied from Normandy and worst of all no escape.

Harold took the Norman bait and headed south to confront the invaders. After a forced march from York he arrived in London where his brother Gyrth suggested that they destroy the land around Hastings, denying the enemy the much needed provisions before risking battle. The King refused the idea of causing any more suffering on his people and decided to attack and drive the invaders into the sea. After only six days of mustering troops in London, Harold impatiently headed out to his rendezvous with destiny

The Normans ravaging the local towns and villages

The Battle of Hastings 14th October 1066

On the evening of the 13th of October Harold and the English army of 8000 men arrived at Caldbec Hill blocking off the road to London and any access out of the peninsula. The situation looked bad for the Normans when the Anglo-Saxon Fleet arrived in the bay, cutting off any hope of escape back to Normandy. For William there was no option but to fight of die. He ordered the camp to be put on full alert and prepare for battle in the morning. Many men on both sides would have had a sleepless night knowing the fate of a nation would be decided by the outcome of the fore coming battle. As the sun rose on a cold October morning, William heard mass and adorned the sacred relics around his neck before ordering the army to strike camp and move out towards the Anglo-Saxon lines.

He acclaimed; **"You shall see the name of a Duke changed into King today"**

The Normans marched down into the valley looking up at the English on the hill in front of them. It was a menacing sight as the Dragon banner of Wessex and King Harold's personal banner of the Fighting man fluttered in the wind above, the English hit their shields and let out the war cries "Out, Out, Out and "Godemite" (God Almighty). William launched a pre-emptive strike and sent in his archers and crossbowmen to soften up in English line. The uphill trajectory and the Saxon shield wall made it extremely difficult for them to inflict heavy casualties upon the English. Next came the turn of the Norman infantry who slogged their way up the steep slope. When they were within a few meters of the English lines, they were met with an almighty barrage of spears, javelins, arrows, rocks and even Viking throwing axes. The whole Norman front line reeled back with men dropping like flies to the ground. When the surviving infantry reached the English lines, vicious hand to hand fighting ensued, it was a brutal struggle to the death.

Seeing his men wavering, William sent in some of the Norman elite cavalry to support the infantry. It was during this stage of the battle that Harold's brothers Gyth and Leowine were probably killed. The Saxon housecarls fought with tremendous fighting spirit chopping man and horse in two with their huge battle axes. The Knights charged in hoping to find holes in the English defence. Instead they were met with axe, spear and sword. The Saxon shield wall stood firm and unbroken. It was said that the English ranks were so dense that no even the dead could fall to the ground. The bodies of the slain were strewn all along the slope of the ridge.

On the Norman left flank the Bretons were suffering enormous casualties; they began to panic and started to flee back down the slope. The Norman centre now pulled back fearing they might be outflanked and surrounded. A rumour spread through ranks of the Normans that the Duke had been killed. Eustace De Boulogne used the Papal banner as a rallying point, pointing at the Duke. William was forced to raise his helmet showing his men that he was very much still alive. **"Look at me; here I am; I live, and by God's help will conquer."** He shouted out great words of encouragement and also reminded them that there was no escape.

William shows himself, rallying the Normans

Harold had given strict orders to hold the defensive position on the hill. He had first hand experience of how dangerous the Norman cavalry could be during his time with them in Brittany. The temptation was just too much for some of the English who had lost their leaders Gyth and Leowine. In an uncontrolled frenzy they started charging down the hill after the Bretons. Had Harold ordered his entire army to commit to a frontal assault, the sheer weight of numbers and the momentum might have won the day for him.

Instead he allowed William the precious time to rally his men and take the initiative. The pursuing Saxons were now at the bottom of the slope far from the safety of the Shield wall. William spotted the opportunity and counter attacked with a detachment of armoured knights. The English were massacred with only a handful managing to escape back up the hill.

The final attack

There was a lull in the fighting with both sides recuperating and accessing the damages. William reorganised his troops ready for the final assault. At the height of the afternoon William sent in everything he had left at his disposal. The Normans had to win the battle by nightfall or all would be lost. Harold's losses were being replenished by more troops arriving from all over England. The chronicler William de Poitiers describes how the Normans used feinted flights to lure the English out of their shield wall. They would attack the English then retreat, the English would then chase after them, allowing the knights to cut them down in the open. Holes were starting to open up along the ridge, but every time the Norman knights broke the shield wall, more Saxons filled the gaps from the rear. One Norman Knight came within distance of striking at the Dragon banner of Wessex. He was surrounded, pulled from his horse and hacked to pieces. William was also in the fray and had three horses killed from under him.

The Normans combined their archers, infantry and cavalry, in a desperate attempt to force the Saxons from their

Duke William of Normandy
1066

hilltop position. The English fought on with desperate bravery holding their ground until disaster stuck. King Harold was hit in the face by a stray arrow. As the King stumbled a group of Norman knights charged through the English ranks and finished Harold off.

The death of King Harold II at Hastings 1066

It was the decisive moment of the battle. Harold's personal bodyguard refused to yield and fought on to the last man protecting the body of the King and the Sacred Dragon banner of Wessex. In the melee the "fighting man flag" was pulled down. Afterwards it was sent to the Pope in Rome as a present for his support. The death of the King was a hammer blow for the English who were now left leaderless. Most of the survivors fled the hilltop for the safety of the forest behind them. Some Norman knights pursued the Saxons into the woods. Although beaten the English railed in the forest at a place later called "Malfosse" bad ditch. The overconfident knights were ambushed and butchered. The few remaining Normans led by Eustace of Boulogne started to retreat until Duke William arrived on the scene. As the Duke reprimanded the Count, a missile hit Eustace in the shoulder knocking him unconscious. William attacked the ambushers, armed only with a broken lance before returning to the battlefield.

The "Malfosse" incident

The battle had been a close run thing indeed. Had Harold not been killed, the English would have probably been able to keep control of the ridge until nightfall. Harold died valiantly, but had neglected his solemn duty of protecting the English people.

Even losing the battle would not have been a total disaster for him, for he could have retreated and raised another army just as Alfred had done before him. Instead he fought bravely to the death, but left a nation leaderless at the mercy of a foreign invader who would destroy Anglo-Saxon England and change the face of Britain forever.

The Norman Conquest

William rested his weary men for five days after the Battle of Hastings. He expected the last remaining nobles of Anglo-Saxon England to come forth and submit to him, but no one came.
The Duke now set out in a show of force. Instead of heading north for the capital he headed east towards the vital port of Dover. Old Romney, Lympne and Folkestone were sacked and razed to the ground. William's policy of terror became a trademark of his character. Dover submitted without a fight. The capture of the port enabled William to receive supplies and reinforcements from France. He built a Norman castle within the old Roman fortress overlooking the town. The Normans now marched on the Kentish capital of Canterbury. Again the town's citizens came before him and submitted. William stayed in the city for a few weeks due to a baut of dysentery.

The mighty Norman castle of Dover, the gateway to England

After recovering from his illness William set out on the long march to terrorise the English into submission. In a surprise attack on the capital, a contingent of his army tried to take London Bridge before being forced to retreat, burning down Southwark in the process.

The Duke's army circled the capital like a lion hunting its prey. Guildford, Farnham and Basing were all destroyed before William turned north towards Wallingford. When the Normans captured Winchester (the ancient capital of Wessex) Saxon resistance started to crumble. London was in a state of panic, some of the clergy and nobility tried to elect Edgar the Atheling as King, but the hapless boy had no authority and no plan of action against the Norman invaders. In mid December, just outside Hertford, a delegation from London arrived at William's camp. Aldred the archbishop of York, Edgar the Atheling and Edwin and Morcar surrendered to the Duke.

Statue of William the Conqueror, Falaise, Normandy

The Anglo-Saxon chronicle:
"They gave him hostages and swore oaths of allegiance, and the Duke promised to be a gracious lord to them".

King William I of England

On Christmas day 1066 Duke William of Normandy was crowned King of England in the newly built abbey of Westminster. He was anointed with the holy oil and at the very moment that the crown was placed upon his head, the guards outside mistook the acclamations in English for rebellion. Fearing that the Duke had been killed they immediately set upon the crowd, massacring everyone in the vicinity and burning down most of the surrounding buildings. The day ended with the bodies of the innocent littering the blood stained streets of London and the thatched roofed houses burning brightly into the night time sky. As dawn broke on the 26th of December 1066 a new period in British history began, Anglo-Saxon England was gone forever. The Normans and King William the Conqueror were here to stay.

Faced with a hostile Saxon population, King William needed to assert his authority over the country. The answer to this problem was the construction of hundreds of Motte and Bailey castles. They were built on strategic sites all up and down the Kingdom. Some were on important river bends or by river crossings. Others were built on natural defensive positions and some were even constructed in the middle of existing Anglo-Saxon settlements. They were designed to shock and awe the local inhabitants, making it clear to them that the Normans were in charge and here to stay.

In March 1067 William felt confident enough to return to Normandy. He left his half brother Odo in control of the south and close friend William Fitz Osbern in charge of the north. As a counter measure against rebellion, William took back with him Edgar the Atheling, Edwin and Morcar, Archbishop Stigand and Waltheof the Earl of Huntingdon and Northampton. During his absence the "rapes of the south" (Odo De Bayeux, Robert De Mortain, Robert Comte d'Eu and William Fitz Osbern) as they became known were insensitive and heavy handed in their treatment of the English.

Ordericus Vitalis wrote:

"The petty lords" who were guarding the newly built castles oppressed all the inhabitants of higher and lower degree, and heaped shameful burdens upon them"

The first revolt against Norman rule erupted in the west of the country on the border with Wales. An local Anglo-Saxon lord called Edric the wild, in league with the Welsh Princes of Gwynedd and Powys ravaged the borderland and attacked the Norman castle at Hereford. The Castle garrison held out, but Edric remained at large in the region causing havoc for the Normans until he disappears from the records in the early 1070s. Then a rising took place in Kent. The English laid siege to Dover castle and invited Eustace of Boulogne, who had been dissatisfied with his share of the spoils after Hastings to join the rebellion. Although the town and taken by the rebels, the castle held out until Eustace withdrew and Norman reinforcements arrived. William returned in the winter of 1067 and started to restore order. His first target was to suppress a rebellion in Devon. The rebels were led by King Harold's mother Gytha. For 18 days they held off the Norman forces of the King and William Fitz Osbern at the siege of Exeter. When the city capitulated William honoured the terms of surrender, but the Godwins escaped his clutches and fled to Ireland.

The remains of Rougemont castle built after the siege of 1068

After crushing the rebellion in the south west William returned to London. His wife the Duchess Matilda was brought over from Normandy to be crowned Queen of England. Trouble fermented in the summer of 1068 when the English hostages who had been at the King's court returned to their estates. In the Midlands, Edwin of Mercia raised a revolt. The Robin Hood like figure of Edric the Wild emerged from Wales and raided the English-Welsh Marches. They destroyed some of the small Norman castles and settlements on the border before assaulting Shrewsbury. After destroying the town they moved on, joining up with the disaffected men of Staffordshire and Cheshire.

The current Earl of Northumbria Gospatric, who had only just purchased the Earldom from King William changed sides and joined the revolt. William used the same tactic he had used to intimidate the English back in 1066 after Hastings. His army weaved its ways north into the Midlands, building castles as it went, and terrorising the population. At Warwick the fickle English Earls Edwin and Morcar, surrendered to the King. William then advanced to Nottingham and with the help of Archbishop Aldred captured York without a fight. Edgar the Atheling and the remaining northern rebels fled north into the Kingdom of Scotland seeking refuge with his brother in-law Malcolm III.

The Harrying of the north 1069-1070

William sent Robert De Comines, a Frenchman, to replace the disgraced Gospatric as Earl of Northumbria. In January 1069 the English besieged Robert and his 900 men in the city of Durham. On the 31st of January they broke through the city gates and went on the rampage. Most of Normans were massacred in the streets, Robert and a few soldiers managed to retreat to the Bishops house where they barricaded themselves inside. The English promptly set the building alit, burning the Earl alive. Only two Norman soldiers out of 900 managed to escape the carnage.

The magnificent splendour of Durham's Norman castle and cathedral

The rebellion gathered pace, Edgar the Atheling came down from Scotland and was welcomed by the population as the new Alfred the Great. At York the rebels murdered the castle garrison including its commander Robert Fitz Richard. In a lighting strike William surprised and dispersed the rebels at York. Edgar the Atheling returned to Scotland and left his people to face the wrath of the King. William was in no mood to be lenient and sacked the city because of its disloyalty. He left William de Malet in command while he headed south to quell the last sparks of resistance which included a failed invasion by the sons of Harold in the west.

The Norman Motte and Bailey Castle at York (Clifford's tower)

No sooner that his back was turned the north erupted in violence yet again. This time the English were assisted by a Viking fleet sent by King Swein of Denmark. Edgar the Atheling claimed the English throne and the Anglo-Danish alliance marched on York. On the 20th of September 1069 they arrived outside the city. The Norman constable William de Malet sent an urgent message to the King urging him to come north before everything was lost.

The English entered the city and went on the rampage, but this time the Normans set fire to the whole area within the ancient roman walls including the Minster. In the burning streets of the city the battle raged on for two days.

In a Norse ballad Waltheof the Earl of Huntingdon is mentioned

"He killed many Normans in the Battle of York, cutting off their heads as they entered the gate with his huge two handed axe"

The two newly constructed Norman Motte and Bailey castles were destroyed and burnt to the ground. The only Normans to survive the battle were William de Malet, his family and Gilbert De Ghent. They were kept hostage by the rebels until sometime in 1070.

William gathered together a mighty host to punish the rebels once and for all. He forced the Danes who were held up on the isle of Axholme back into Yorkshire. The King then headed across the country and defeated the western rebels at the battle of Stafford. With Edric the Wild and the Welsh defeated, the King had secured the Midlands against counterattack.

He now commenced his dreaded campaign "The harrying of the North". The King's army marched north destroying every village, town and city as they went. In an unparalleled act of brutality William carried out a scored earth policy of systemically wasting the land. The crops and food supplies were burned; salt was shattered in the fields to stop anything from growing. Men, women and children were slain, and those who were left were faced with famine. Over 100,000 people lost their lives in the destructive campaign

Ordericus Vitalis commented in a chilling account;

"He cut down many in his vengeance; destroyed the settlements of others; harried the land, and burnt homes to ashes. Nowhere else had William shown such cruelty ... In his anger he ordered that all the crops, herds, cattles and food of every kind should be rounded up and burned to ashes with consuming fire, so that the whole region north of the Humber might be stripped of all means of sustenance. In consequence so serious a scarcity was felt in England, and so terrible a famine fell upon the humble and defenseless people, that more than 100,000 Christian folk of both sexes, young and old, perished of hunger".

Even 17 years after the event much of the land was still classed as "waste" and only about a quarter of the original population were left inhabiting the region. William reached York by Christmastime 1069. The Normans celebrated Christmas in the ruins of the Minister. The campaign continued throughout the harsh cold winter and the land from York to Durham was completely wasted

The last Anglo-Saxon hero

Under the oppression of Norman rule, Anglo-Saxon England found a new hero. His name was Hereward the Wake. He was possibly a son of Leofric (The Old Saxon Earl of Mercia). Hereward had been outlawed during the reign of King Edward and after the Norman Conquest, he returned home back to England. On his return he found out that his family had been dispossessed of their lands by the new Norman lord. Worst still, the Normans had recently killed his brother, who's head hung above the door of the family house. Hereward driven by vengeance attacked a band of drunken Norman soldier's massacring them all. It is said that afterwards he replaced his brother's head with the sculls of the dead Normans. Hereward's legend grew day by day, attracting more disaffected Saxons towards his cause. He joined up with the Danes, who instead of leaving England after being paid off by King William, decided to attack the rich lands of Lincolnshire. In the heart of the fenland the rebels held out on the island of Ely. William, determined to crush the last resistance to his rule, marched north into the treacherous Fens (Marshes of eastern England) At Ely he attempted to build a causeway across the marshes. The first attempt failed when the wooden causeway collapsed under the weight of his men trying to gain access on the Isle. Many soldiers drowned in the watery marshes due to the weight of their heavy chain mail armour. William, not deterred, built siege towers and catapults. He bombarded the island for over a week with fire and stone, but the rebels refused to yield. William acquired the services of a witch and from a platform built for her she cursed them chanting day and night. Hereward set fire to the Fenland rush, in the blaze that followed the Norman siege machines were destroyed and the witch fell from her platform breaking her neck. With the help of some monks who could suffer no more hardship, the island was betrayed. They led the Normans through the marshes, on to the island, via a secret path. The rebels were taken by surprise and annihilated. Hereward escaped, and like Edric the Wild, disappears from the annals of history. Morcar, the former English Earl of Northumberland, was captured and imprisoned for the rest of his life. His brother Edwin was killed by his own men while trying to flee to Scotland.

The Magnificent Norman Cathedral of Ely

A conquest complete 1070-1087

With the English now relatively pacified, William turned his attention to re-organising the Kingdom and its laws. The Normans re-introduced an Old Danish law called the "Murdrum fine". When the body of an unknown person was found, the local villagers had to prove he was not a Norman. If they could not, the village would be fined a substantial sum of money.

Hugh d'Avranche's castle at Chester

The frontier with Wales was secured with the creation of three new Earldoms. Roger De Montgomery became the Earl of Shrewsbury, Hugh de Avaranches became the Earl of Chester and William Fitz Osbern became the Earl of Hereford. It seems William had no real intention of conquering Wales. Apart from a direct intervention in 1081, when many of the Welsh Princes acknowledged him as overlord of Wales, he was content to play one side off against the other avoiding any change in the status quo.

Scotland, on the other hand, had been a thorn in the side of the King since the Conquest. Time upon time again, it had harboured the various Anglo-Saxon rebels including Edgar the Atheling. Although Scotland was in its own right an independent Kingdom it was much poorer than its southern neighbour.

Malcolm III had come to power by defeating Macbeth of Shakespearian flame and had ruled Scotland for over 30 years. His intrigues in supporting Edgar now put his Kingdom in mortal danger from William and the Normans.

In 1072 William invaded Scotland in a two pronged attack by land and sea. The Normans devastated the Scottish lowlands before crossing the river Forth into the Highlands. No army had come this far north since the days of the Romans. The Norman war machine moved so swiftly that Malcolm III feared any resistance against them would be futile.

The Royal Arms of Scotland

At Abernethy, in the middle of the Cairngorm Mountains, he came before King William and signed the treaty of Abernethy. Malcolm III acknowledged William and his overlord and the Kingdom of Scotland became a vassal state of the English Kings. For his good behaviour William also requested that Malcolm III hand over his son Duncan as a hostage and exile Edgar the Atheling from his country.

Over the next 14 years William would have to put down rebellions not from the English, but from his own nobles and foreign powers eager to destroy the power of the new Anglo-Norman Empire. In 1073 the King returned to Normandy to deal with a rebellion in Maine, south of the Norman Border. In a lighting raid, William's army, which included many Englishmen, took the rebels by surprise and captured Le Mans. The King of France, who was concerned at the growing power of Normandy, tried to use Edgar the Atheling as a means of stirring up trouble against King William, but Edgar, no more than a puppet came to terms with the King.

The Anglo-Saxon Chronicler stated:

"King William received Edgar with great ceremony and he remained at the Kings court accepting great privileges bestowed upon him".

The revolt of the Earls 1075

A more serious plot came about in 1075 while William was in Normandy. During a marriage ceremony, Ralph de Gael (Earl of Norfolk), Roger de Breteuil the 2nd Earl of Hereford (the son of William Fitz Osbern) and the old English Earl of Huntington Waltheof conspired together to bring about the downfall of the King. In a bizarre conspiracy with no clear objectives, William was to be distracted by minor revolts in Brittany while the English rebels would join forces and offer King Canute IV (of Denmark) the crown. The coup d'etat was doomed from the start when William's loyal supporters in England got wind of the plan. Waltheof lost heart a revealed the conspiracy to Lanfranc the Archbishop of Canterbury. Roger de Breteuil was checked and stopped from crossing the river Severn by the English Fryd under the command of Walter De Lacy and Bishop Wulfstan. Ralph De Gael faired no better in Norfolk, and was forced to flee the Kingdom. When William returned to England in the winter of 1075, the revolt had being extinguished. Earl Roger was put in prison and the unfortunate Waltheof was executed.

An English poem wrote about the rebellion states;

> "Some of them were blinded
> Some were banished
> All traitors to William were laid low"

The Domesday Book

England was ruled well and efficiently under the iron fist of William the Conqueror and one of the greatest sources for information on Norman rule is the Domesday Book. Written over 900 years ago in 1086 the book is perhaps the oldest public record book in Western Europe. In simplified terms, it is a gigantic land survey of England and its resources. In 1085, a dangerous threat arose from across the North Sea. King Cnut IV of Denmark along with the hostile Count of Flanders planned an invasion of England. King William raised the Danegeld to pay for mercenaries from Normandy and France. In the winter of 1085, the Curia Regis (the King's court) convened at Gloucester. The royal council decided to institute a thorough survey of England to decide what each man owned and more importantly what each man should pay. The findings would be collated together and recorded in a book that would be known as Domesday. In early 1086 royal commissioners were sent out to the shires of England to collect and record all the information.

The country was split into 7 regions with 4 commissioners being assigned to each region. When they arrived in every village they asked a series of questions to the local Lord and representatives of the village

An example of the information in the Domesday Book:

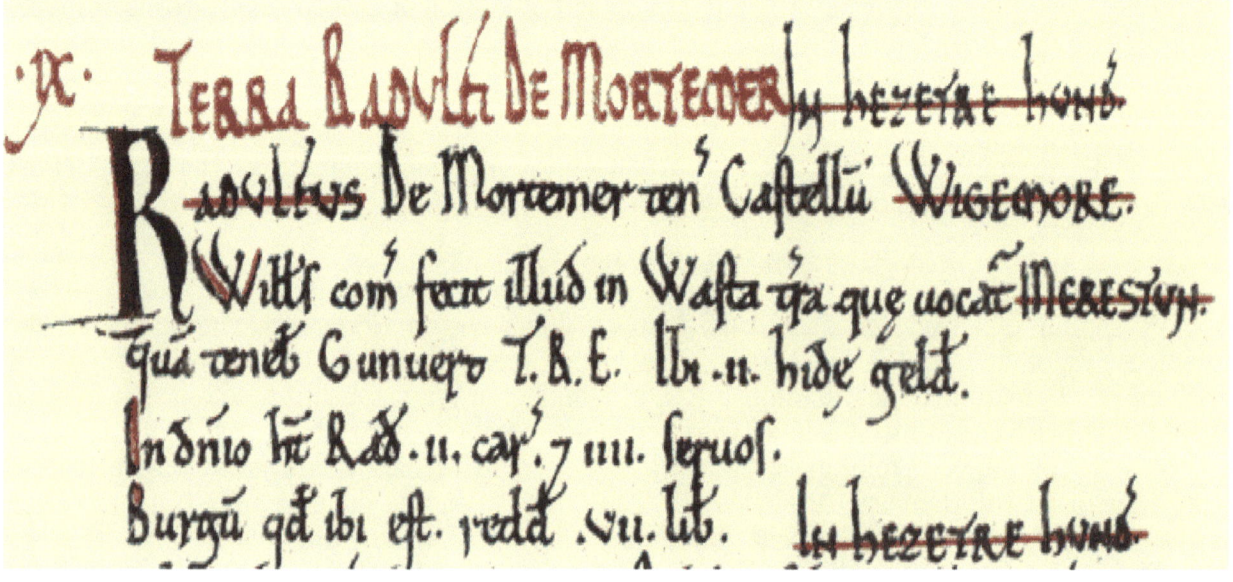

Wigmore = the Hundred of Hezrtre

County = Herefordshire

"Ranulph Mortimer holds Wigmore Castle, which Earl William built on wasteland that was called Merestun, which Gunfrid held before 1066"

There were two hides (cows) that paid tax, two ploughs in lordship and four slaves. The borough of Wigmore is recorded to have paid £ 7 - "*bergu qd ibi est redd vii lib*".

When all the information was collected, it was written down in Latin and compiled into the great and little Domesday books. The survey enabled William to squeeze every penny out of his subjects to fund the Norman campaigns in both England and France.

An observer reported;

"There was no single hide, nor a yard of land, nor indeed one ox, nor one cow, nor one pig which was left out".

The Domesday books Great Domesday and Little Domesday

The results of the Domesday Book are startling and reveal how much England had changed since the Conquest. In 1086 just over 50% of the land was in the hands of the new Norman aristocracy, the Church held 26%, King William controlled 17% and the remaining native English lords and nobles held only about 4%.

The Norman Legacy

For over 500 years, since the end of the Roman Empire England had looked north towards Scandinavia and Germany for its cultural identity. Its language and people were by nature Teutonic. One day in 1066 changed all of that. The Normans psychical legacy can still be seen up and down the country in the form of their mighty building projects.

The great cathedrals of England, York Minster, Ely, Durham, Lincoln, Canterbury, Winchester and Westminster are all Norman constructions. The Normans built with a grandeur that was unrivalled in England since the days of the Romans. In the twenty years since the conquest, England had become a Norman Fortress. The new Norman lords ruled their estates from the guise of their mighty castles and fortresses. The timber Motte and Bailey castles were slowly replaced with great Keeps of stone. William the Conqueror's castle "The Tower of London" dominated the City, and for many years it remained the tallest building in London. Caen stone was even imported from Normandy for the construction.

The transformation of the English language

The Norman Conquerors only made up a small proportion of the population of England (10,000 out of a population of between one and two million people in 1066). The vast majority continued to speak English but Norman French now became the language of power. It was spoken in the courts, castles and centres of administration. Latin remained the language of the clergy and English was in effect downgraded to the peasant patois spoken by the Anglo-Saxon masses.

The English language began to transform, it lost its genders and inflections and it increased its vocabulary from the new Norman ruling class. In the castle kitchens and on the working land, Doublets developed.

In the fields, where the Anglo-Saxons worked, the names of the animals were in English, but by the time they reached the dinner table they became Norman-French.

The White Tower (The Norman Keep of the Tower of London)

Examples:

English / Anglo-Saxon	Norman French
Sheep	Mutton
Cow/Ox	Boeuf =Beef
Calf	Veal
Pig	Porc = Pork
Chicken	Poultry
Start	Commence
Meet	Encounter
Withdraw	Disengage

Nearly 30% (80,000 words) of all words in the modern English language have a French origin. As the Normans and English started to inter-marry, so the language evolved. The children spoke English learnt from their mothers and wet nurses added together with the new Norman words. In just over 100 years after the conquest, the Treasurer of King Henry II (Richard Fitz Neal) wrote;

"The English and Normans having dwelt together, marrying and being given in marriage, for many years, the two nations have become so mixed that it is scarcely possible to tell who is of English, and who of Norman blood."

Many of the old Anglo-Saxon names simply disappeared; they were replaced by the new Norman French alternatives Roger, Richard, Henry and Robert. William became the most popular name even amongst the peasants and is still one of the most popular names in England and Wales today.

The Only area where the Norman invasion did not change was in place names, most towns and villages kept they original spellings / pronunciations. In the end, it was Norman French that faded and the language of the conquered that survived. The loss of Normandy in 1204 accelerated the process, and by the time of the English expulsion from France in 1453, English became dominant language once again but with its enlarged Norman vocabulary. Without the Norman influence, English would not be the world's most widely spoken language that it is today. The Normans reorganised England's institutions, keeping the best bits from the Anglo-Saxon era, and introducing new continental ideas. The key to the Norman success was in their ability to assimilate into the people they conquered. They created a new chapter in the history of the British isles for better or for worst and laid the foundations of a new superpower in Europe. According to Orderic on his deathbed, King William is supposed to have said;

"I have persecuted the natives people of England beyond all reason, whether nobles or commons. I have cruelly oppressed them and unjustly disinherited them, killed innumerable multitudes by famine or the sword and become the barbarous murderer of many thousands both young and old of that fine race of people."

Chapter 5: **Wales**

Into the Dragons lair
The Norman Conquest of Wales and the Marches

Wales was the first of the Celtic Kingdoms of the British Isles to face the Norman assault and invasion. Following the downfall of Anglo-Saxon England, William the Conqueror secured the frontier with Wales by establishing the Marcher Earldoms of Chester, Hereford and Shrewsbury. By 1088 the reins of the hated Norman Marcher lords had been effectively cut, allowing them to spearhead the conquest of Wales, which would take 200 years. The Welsh heirs of King Arthur were up against a cruel and cunning enemy, intent on destroying their way of life, identity and culture. The final showdown and reckoning would take place at the end of the 13th century when England's most ruthless warrior King Edward I invaded Wales.

Cymru (Wales) 410 – 1066 A.D

In the fifth century A.D the last Roman troops left Britain to defend the frontiers of the crumbling empire. The Island now entered the period of history known as the "Dark Ages". The departure of the regular Roman field armies left Britannia virtually defenceless. In the north, the Picts overran Hadrian's Wall and raided the fertile lands of the south as far as London. Scottish tribes from Ireland also attacked the province from the west. By the middle of the century the Britons made a final appeal to Rome for assistance, in the form of a letter that became known as the "Groan of the Britons".

Gildas wrote:

"The barbarians drive us to the sea; the sea drives us to the barbarians; between these two methods of death we are either massacred or drowned"

Their pleas fell on deaf ears, as Rome was in no position to send troops or resources to help the Britons. The Romano-British leadership divided Britannia into three sectors; "Dux Britanniarum" commanded northern Britain from York and the remaining garrisons of Hadrian's Wall, "Comes Litoris Saxonici" commanded the south and the Saxon shore forts, and a mobile field army was placed under the command of the "Comes Britanniarum". The Britons used the Roman tactic of recruiting barbarians to fight barbarians. They employed Saxon mercenaries to help them defeat the Picts and Scots, but the newcomers realising the weakness of their paymasters revolted after the victory. The Saxon Warlords, Hengest and Horsa, defeated the British high KingVortigern and the Britons in two pitched battles. Although Horsa was killed, the Anglo-Saxons had established a foothold on the Island.

The White Horse Stone, The believed burial Place of the Saxon leader, Horsa

King Arthur and the British fight back

The Germanic Angles, Saxons and Jutes slowly subjugated and pushed the native Romano-Britons west towards Wales and the western fringes of the country. The early Brythonic (British) Kingdoms of Powys, Gwynedd, Caerwent/Gwent, Dyfed and Brycheiniog emerged from the collapse of Roman Britain. Between 490 and 550 A.D the shadowy hero figure of Celtic Britain, King Arthur halted the invaders. The real King Arthur was certainly part of the remaining Romano-British aristocracy. He may even have been Owain Ddantgwyn, the 5th century warlord of Powys. Owain's nickname was the bear (Arth / Arthur is also the Welsh name for the bear). His father also had the name "the terrible Dragon's head, which translates into Welsh as "Uthr Pen Dragon", King Arthur's father. According to the Welsh monk, Nennius, Arthur defeated the invaders in twelve battles. If this is true, Arthur may have been in command of a Roman/Sarmatian style cavalry cohort enabling him to cover the long distances to surprise and defeat the Germanic invaders who fought mainly on foot. At the Battle of "Mons Badonicus" the invaders were decisively defeated.

The Roman ruins of Wroxeter (capital of the Romano-British Kingdom of Powys)

The Principality of Wales

Arthur had checked the invaders advance, but by the late 6th century the Saxons were on the move westward again. The Anglo-Saxons referred to the Britons as Welisc, (Welsh) from a Germanic word meaning 'foreigner'. As they pushed into the modern day border area with Wales, resistance stiffened. King Offa of Mercia decided to define the border by constructing a mighty fortified earthwork known as Offa's Dyke. This Dyke defined the geographical area of the Principality of Celtic Wales. During the 9th ad 10th centuries the increased Viking attacks on England curtailed any Saxon ambitions on the Welsh, and eased the pressure on her eastern border with Mercia. From time to time a Welsh Prince or warlord would assert his power and authority over the other dominions within the Principality, such as Rhodri the Great and Hywel the Good, but any cohesion would vanish as soon as he died. Welsh law also hindered the forming of any long term power blocks and centralisation. When a Prince or family head died, the land was divided into equal shares between his sons.

The First Normans (Pre-conquest) 1051

The first Normans to arrive on the Welsh border did not come with William the Conqueror in 1066. Some 15 years earlier, in 1051, King Edward the Confessor established a Norman colony in Herefordshire to defend the frontier against the Welsh. Ralph De Mantes became the first pre-conquest Norman Earl of Hereford. He and a small band of Norman adventurers built the first Motte and Bailey castles in Britain. The English and Welsh had never seen anything like it before.

The strange timber framed constructions were built on the huge earth worked Motte. Five castles were built, including Burghill and Richard's Castle near Ludlow.

The Anglo-Saxon chronicle recorded that:

"In September 1051, the French had built a castle"

In 1052 Norman and Celtic cultures clashed for the first time. The Welsh Prince, Gruffydd ap Llywelyn had successfully united most of Wales under his rule. He turned his attention towards raiding the English countryside. The Welsh advanced into Herefordshire and near Leominster they joined battle against a hastily unprepared force of Englishmen and Normans. The Welsh warriors using their spears and longbows decimated and put flight to the Anglo-Norman force. It was first blood to the Welsh, who returned with their booty back over the border.

In the following year, Gruffydd inflicted a second defeat upon the Anglo-Normans in Herefordshire.

The remains of Ewyas Harold Castle (Pre-Conquest Norman castle)

According to the Anglo-Saxon chronicle, the Anglo-Norman knights led by Ralph De Mantes were routed before the battle commenced. The Welsh then sacked and burned Hereford to the ground. The situation became so serious that Ralph was relieved of his command and replaced with Earl Harold Godwinson (the future King of England). In a series of devastating campaigns Harold defeated Gruffrydd and forced him to retreat into the mountains of Snowdonia. In 1063 the Prince of Wales met his end; Gruffrydd's own men murdered him, his head was cut off and sent to Harold as an act of submission.

1066 The New World Order

The Welsh feared the coming of the Normans in 1066. The foreign invaders had systematically destroyed Anglo-Saxon England within five years after the Battle of Hastings with ruthless efficiency. Although King William inherited the overlordship of Wales from his Anglo-Saxon predecessors, he probably never realistically contemplated the conquest of Wales.

William entrusted the defence of the Welsh border to his close companions, Hugh of Avranches, Earl of Chester, Roger Montgomery, Earl of Shrewsbury and William Fitz Osbern, Earl of Hereford. The first lords of the March had been given considerable freedom to enforce Norman control over the borderlands.

The medieval city of Hereford

William Fitz Osbern constructed a network of defences along the southern Marches of Wales. He built Norman castles at Monmouth, Clifford and Wigmore to protect the approaches from Wales. His masterpiece was the construction of the mighty castle of Chepstow. It was one of the first stone built castles in Britain.

Chepstow castle, strategically positioned on the river Wye

The First Incursions and the invasion of the Marcher Lords

The ancient Celtic Kingdom of Caerwent/Gwent was the first region to fall to the Normans under William Fitz Osbern. The Norman war machine that entered Wales was very much different to the Anglo-Norman force that had been utterly beaten by the Welsh in 1052. The private army of Earl William routed the combined Welsh forces of Cadwgan ap Meurig and Maredudd Ab Owain (King of Deheubarth). It was a shattering defeat for the Celtic warriors who were up against the chain clad armoured knights, who used the new tactics of combining infantry, cavalry and archers. The Royal policy worked well, as long as loyal lieutenants controlled the frontier, but after the death of Fitz Osbern in 1071 the Earldom passed to his son Roger who rebelled against the King in 1075 (the revolt of the Earls). This revolt altered King William's border strategy. In 1081 William paid a visit to St David's Church in Southwestern Wales. There he accepted the homage of Prince Rhys ap Tewdwr. This was an important development, for William hoped by promoting Rhys he could counter balance the power of the Marcher Lords. By playing one side off against the other, neither one could become too powerful. The Norman raids into Wales ceased, but when William the Conqueror died in 1087 his iron fist was removed from the sensitive border area.

The new King of England William II "Rufus" tried to continue the same policy of his father, but when a baronial revolt broke out in 1088 he was forced to offer concessions towards the Marcher lords. In return for their support he gave them a free hand to carve out an empire for themselves in the buffer states of Wales. Although they were restricted from directly attacking Rhys ap Tewdwr's Kingdom of Deheubarth, the adjoining state of Brycheiniog was classed as fair game.

Rhys ap Tewdwr came to the assistance of Bleddyn ap Maenarch, the beleaguered Lord of Brycheiniog. Together they marched out of the hills and confronted Bernard De Neufmarche who was constructing a castle near Brecon. The Welsh charged uphill against the Normans, but were cut to pieces by the mounted Norman knights. Rhys was killed in the vicious fighting and with him died the agreement made with King William.

The Normans crossed the border and overran most of Wales. In the north, Hugh de Avranches and his deputy Robert De Rhuddlan advanced up the Dee valley and captured Gwynedd and the Island of Anglesey. Roger De Montgomery was responsible for the massive territorial gains in the middle March and in south Wales; His armies wiped out Welsh resistance in the south, Pembrokeshire and Glamogan became so populated with Normans and English that the Welsh tongue virtually disappeared. Pembrokeshire became known and still is to this day called "little England beyond Wales".

The death of Rhys ap Tewdwr at the hands of De Neufmarche and his knights

The Prince of Gwynedd, Gruffydd ap Cynan

The invasion lost its momentum when Earl Roger died in 1094. The Welsh on the other hand gained a figurehead in the form of Gruffydd ap Cynan. Gruffydd, "Prince of Gwynedd", had languished in the rotting prison cells of the hated Norman Marcher Lord Hugh De Avranches "Hugh the Wolf" for over 10 years. One day in 1094 a Welsh merchant by the name of Cynwric spotted the Prince of Gwynedd enchained outside the newly Norman built castle in Chester. The once proud man had been reduced to an object of derision. The crowd gathered around him, jeering and insulting him. In the evening Cynwric plied the guards with liquor and set the Prince free.

Like the Scottish hero Braveheart, Gruffrydd championed the fight back against the Norman invaders. The rebellion spread rapidly and within a year all of Wales was in revolt. The Normans could scarcely leave the safety of their castles for fear of being ambushed.

Gruffrydd's guerilla war helped the Welsh regain much of Wales lost to the Normans. He chose to avoid pitched battles where the Normans could use their superior tactics and cavalry. Instead he attacked them in the woodland and mountainous terrain of the country. The Normans were also forced to change their strategy; they started an intense construction of new castles. These castles were built in strategic positions, guarding the entrances to the Welsh uplands. The Normans sort to control the fertile valleys, leaving the Welsh in control of the pastoral uplands.

Pembroke Castle, Wales

In 1098 the Normans chased Prince Gruffydd onto the Island of Anglesey. The Prince retreated and took safe passage to Ireland. Anglesey suffered the full fury of the Normans. The Holy church of Llandyfrydog was desecrated, and used as a kennel for the hunting dogs of the Earl of Shrewsbury. Even the clergy was not exempt from retribution: an elderly priest was mutilated and anyone believed to be a rebel was executed on the spot.. The Normans were surprised by a Viking raiding fleet of King Magnus of Norway. The dragon-head ships arrived off the Coast of Puffin Island. In the battle that ensued, the two armies fought each other to a standstill, but the Normans retreated when Earl Hugh De Montgomery was shot and killed by a stray Viking arrow.

Gwenllian, the Warrior Princess

In the south, the Welsh were led by Gwenllian, the daughter of Gruffydd. This brave warrior Princess resisted the Normans with a burning hatred. The end came when she was betrayed by a fellow countryman, to the Marcher Lord, Maurice de Londres. Near Kidwelly Castle she made a last desperate stand against overwhelming odds. She fought gallantly with sword in hand until she was finally overwhelmed and taken prisoner. Gwenllian and her surviving son were both decapitated after the battle on the orders of Maurice De Londres. The battle site is still called Gwenllian's field. Legend has it that it took its name because Gwenllian's severed head never left the field. Gwenllian's death only encouraged others to rise up against the Normans. At the battle of Llwcher, they ambushed and defeated a Norman force commanded by Richard Fitz Gilbert.

The Norman castle of Kidwelly near Gwenllian's last stand

← **Overleaf: Henry D'Essex losing the royal banner to the Welsh**

Owain Gwynedd

Gwenllian's brothers, Owain Gwynedd and Cadwaladr, continued the rebellion against the Normans. They defeated them at the battle of Llwchwr and won a resounding victory just outside Cardigan at the Battle of Crug Mawr. The Normans were slaughtered in the bloody conflict, and are reported to have lost 3000 men. In the rout that followed the battle, they attempted to cross a wooden bridge over the river Teifi. The bridge collapsed into the river because of the sheer weight of soldiers trying to cross it. Many of the Norman knights and foot soldiers fell into the cold river and drowned. Within 20 years Owain was the master of most of Wales. His victories caught the attention of Henry Plantagenet, King of England and the most powerful monarch in Europe, with an Empire that stretched from the borders of Scotland to the Spanish frontier.

Arms of Owain Gwynedd

The King invaded Wales to put Owain back in his place and restore the balance of power between the Welsh and the Marcher lords. The Royal army ravaged the towns and villages along the north Wales coastline, burning down churches and settlements as they went. The Welsh, who had become masters of guerrilla warfare, ambushed the Normans in a wooded valley at Ewloe. As the Norman advanced guard passed into the valley, the Welsh who were waiting, suddenly started running down the slopes shouting the cry "Maes Gwenllian" in honour of their brave warrior Princess. Unable to use their heavy cavalry in the narrow gorge, the Normans were annihilated. As the fog descended from the hills above, a massacre followed. In the melee, the King only just avoided capture. His standard bearer, Henry D'Essex lost the royal banner to the Welsh. It was a catastrophic defeat for the proud Normans.

The Battle of Crogen 1165 A.D

Not deterred by the defeat, Henry returned again to Wales in 1165. He entered the interior of Wales to try and bring Owain to battle. In the dense wooded Ceiriog valley beneath the Berwyn mountains, disaster stuck again. The Norman foresters cut down the trees making way for Henry's massive army.

The clouds darkened and the rain lashed down on the Royal army, and then at Bron-y-garth Owain's men ambushed the Normans. They came out of the mist, hurling spears and using the deadly Welsh longbow to devastating effect.

Plaque commenerating the Battle of Crogen 1165 A.D

Henry was nearly killed, and was only saved by the bravery of Hugh De Saint Clare, who flung himself between the King and the Welsh tribesmen, being killed in the process. Many men were killed in the vicous hand to hand combat of the forest battlefield. Henry retreated, but in a callous act of vengeance, he ordered the eyes of Owain's two sons, who were his hostages, to be torn out.

The Marcher Lordships

Today the Welsh Marches are essentially the border areas with England, but in the middle ages over half of the present day Wales was a Marcher lordship. The Marcher lords ruled their newly conquered lands in Wales as they saw fit. In England they were subject to the King's law, but in the Marches they could build a castle without licence, raise private armies and had the right to exercise justice according to the law and customs of the March. Indeed each lordship had its own different customs, a mixture of Welsh and English law. When a Royal messenger arrived in the Marcher lordship of Walter De Clifford, he was forced to eat the Royal writ, parchment and even the wax seal. Another infamous Marcher lord was William De Braose: the De Braose name became a byword for treachery in Wales. When Milo Fitz Walter was killed by the native Welsh in 1175, his lands passed in the hands of his nephew William De Braose.

The Massacre of Abergavenny

William determined to avenge the death of his uncle, invited all the local Welsh chiefs and leaders to his castle at Abergavenny for the Christmas celebrations. As the Welsh nobility were feasting, William gave the signal to his Norman guards who went to work and murdered the Welsh in cold blood. The bloody events of that night became known as the "Massacre of Abergavenny". William even hunted down the seven year old son of Seisyll ap Dyfnwal (the Welsh lord of upper Gwent) and had him put to death. For these evil deeds the Welsh nicknamed him the "Ogre of Abergavenny". The massacre of Abergavenny was not an isolated event, another Welsh Prince called Trahaiarn was dragged through the streets of Brecon, tied to the tail of a horse, before being beheaded on the orders of William De Braose in the town's market square. The Welsh never forgot the cruel treatment of De Braose.

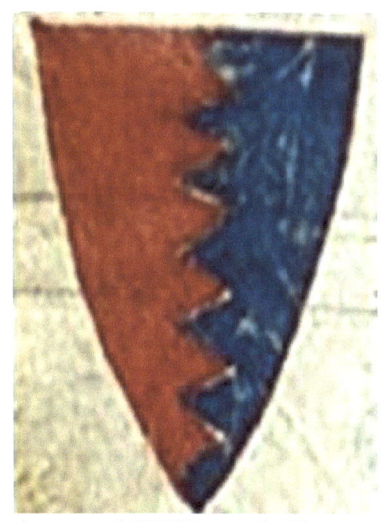

Arms of William de Braose

On several occasions they tried to kill the Marcher Lord and his henchmen. In a nighttime raid they gained access to Abergavenny Castle. The garrison was murdered and the castle was burned to the ground. Ranulf Poer (the sheriff of Herefordshire) who had actually committed some of the murders of the Welsh tribesmen and women after the massacre of Aberganenny, met his end at the hands of the vengeful Welsh in 1182. The Celtic warriors stormed the unfinished walls of the newly built stone castle of Dingestow in Monmouthshire. The Norman guards were overwhelmed and Ranulf was beheaded for his evil crimes against the native population. William De Braose escaped justice and survived all the attempts against his life. After an ambush by the Welsh, he was found hiding in a ditch. They dragged him out, but he was saved at the last minute by his bodyguard of mounted knights.

The De Mortimers "Earls of March"

One of the most famous and powerful families on the March was the House of Mortimer. The De Mortimers came from a small village in Normandy, France, called Mortemer sur Elaune. Even today the remains of their Motte and Bailly castle can still be seen. Ralph De Mortemer came over with William the Conqueror and was closely related to Earl Roger De Montgomery and William Fitz Osbern. It is possible that Ralph de Mortemer was part of William Fitz Osbern's retinue during the campaign against Edric the wild in 1067-1069. The Wigmore chronicle states that Ralph captured Edric

"After a long struggle Edric was captured and handed over to the King for life imprisonment, afterwards some of his lands became part of the abbey of Wigmore."

By 1086 Ralph was the established lord of the small village of Wigmore on the border with Wales

The Domesday book records;

"Ralph de Mortemer holds WIGEMORE castle. Earl William built it on wasteland which is called MERESTUN, which Gunfrid held before 1066. Ralph has 2 ploughs in lordship and 2 hides which pay tax, and 4 slaves. The Borough which is there pays £ 7."

Slowly but surely the Mortimers rose in power from their family seat of Wigmore castle. Like the De Braoses they were ruthless in their attitudes towards the native Welsh.

They had no compulsion in committing acts of great cruelty. A Welsh chronicler wrote that when Prince Rhys ap Howel was

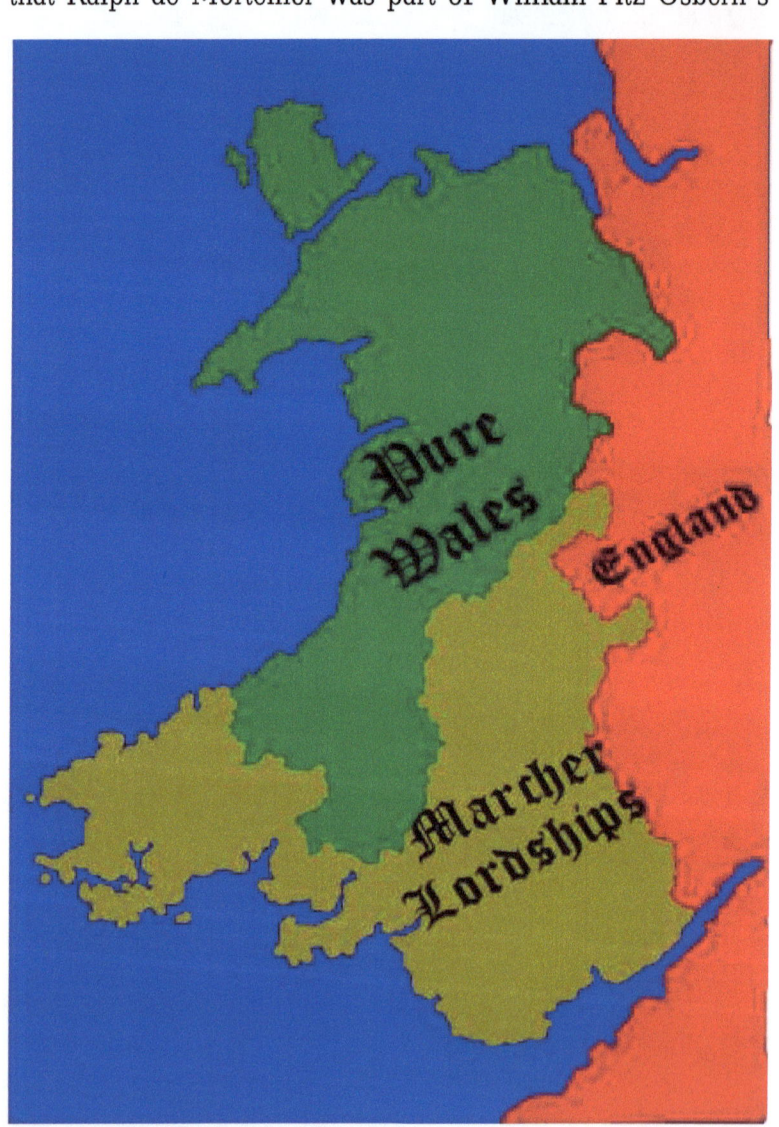

Map of Wales and the Marches 1250 A.D

Ralph de Mortemer, Lord of Wigmore

captured by Hugh De Mortimer the late 1140s, his eyes were put out and he and his son were later put to death. The Mortimers would use any means necessary to gain control and enlarge their Marcher lands in Wales.

The ruins of Wigmore castle, (The Mortimer family seat and powerbase for over 200 years)

In 1179 Hugh II was implicated in another treacherous act: Prince Cadwallon ap Magog was murdered whilst travelling in the March under the safe conduct of the King.

Llywelyn Fawr (the Great)

Llywelyn Fawr followed in the footsteps of his great grandfather (Owain Gwynedd) and led the resurgence against the Normans. Ironically he modeled himself on Henry Plantagenet, King of England, and united all of Pure Wales under his just rule. He was probably born at Dolwyddelan castle, in the heart of Snowdonia in 1173. By 1200 he was the undisputed Prince of Gwynedd. He further consolidated his power by annexing Eifionydd and Llyn. In 1201 his territorial gains were recognised by King John in return for Llywelyn's oath of fealty and vassalage. He married Joan Plantagenet (the illegitimate daughter of King John) in 1205, thus strengthening the ties with England. When Gwenwynwyn of Powys fell foul of the King in 1208, Llywelyn invaded southern Powys and occupied his lands. In 1209 he was summoned by his overlord King John, and accompanied the King in a campaign to overawe the Scots. The following year Prince Llywelyn fell from grace, and his relationship with the King deteriorated.

His alliance with the infamous De Braose family may have contributed to this factor, or it may just have been that the King thought Llywelyn was becoming too big for his boots and decided to check the Prince's power. The first campaign led by the Earl of Chester ended in failure. Llywelyn used the same guerrilla tactics as his grandfather and forced the Normans to retreat back to England. The King decided to lead the army himself and invaded Wales in the summer of 1211. Gwynedd was devastated by the Normans, and Banger was burned to the ground.

Prince Llywelyn had no choice but to come to the King and submit. He was forced to accept the harsh terms: all the land east of the river Conway (known as the four Cantrefs) was to be surrendered, and the Prince was heavily fined for his disloyalty. Only the pleading of his wife Joan to her father allowed Llywelyn to keep his title and the remaining territory of Gwynedd.

Arms of Llywelyn the Great

The Recovery

Prince Llywelyn was able to take full advantage of the baron's growing dispute with King John. By 1216 he had recovered the Four Cantrefs and had united most of Wales under his banner. In March 1218, the treaty of Worcester was concluded between the new King Henry III and Prince Llywelyn. In return for his homage to Henry, Llywelyn's recent conquests were ratified by the King. The Prince's power now started to encroach on the great Marcher family of the Marshals, who dominated South Wales. Sir William Marshall was the most respected and feared knight of the age. He had served some of the most powerful monarchs in Europe, Henry Plantagenet, Eleanor D'Aquitaine, Richard the Lionheart, King John and Henry III. In 1190, he had married Isabelle De Clare (the daughter of the Norman Conqueror of Ireland, Strongbow/Richard de Clare). This marriage made him the most extensive Norman landowner in south Wales.

Prince Llywelyn did not attack the lands of the old warrior until after his death in 1219. While the new Earl of Pembroke (William Marshal the younger) was restoring Norman rule in Ireland, Llywelyn seized his chance and invaded the Marshal lordships, capturing the important castles of Carmarthen and Cardigan. In the spring of 1224, William Marshal returned from Ireland and re-captured most of the territory lost in the previous year.

Statue of Llywelyn Fawr, Conway

Under the influence of the Prince, a series of Welsh castles were refortified and constructed at Castell y Bere, Criccieth, Dolbadarn and Dolwyddelan, defending Wales against the Norman threat. The tit for tat warfare continued in Wales for the rest of the Prince's reign. Both sides would gain the upper hand before castles and prisoners were exchanged in the treaties that followed.

In 1234 "the peace of Middle" treaty established an uneasy truce between the Normans and the Welsh. In 1240 at the age of 68 Llwelyn "Prince of north Wales and Lord of Snowdonia" died peacefully leaving the Principality of Wales stronger than it had been in a generation.

Dafydd and Gruffudd

Dafydd succeeded his father as Prince of Gwynedd in spite of the fact that he had an older brother Gruffudd. Gruffudd had been excluded from his inheritance because he was anti-English and his father knew that if Gruffudd succeeded him, it would have meant continued warfare with England, which in the long run the Welsh could not hope to win. Dafydd on the other hand had married Isabella De Braose and with this union Llywelyn hoped that the ties with England would strengthen the position of a semi-independent Wales.

Sarcophagus of Llywelyn the Great, St Grwst Church, Llanrwst.

The majestic setting of Criccieth castle, North Wales

When Dafydd became Prince, he imprisoned his brother Gruffudd. He was kept prisoner under close guard in the newly built Welsh castle of Criccieth. The situation with King Henry III deteriorated over the lands outside Gwynedd which both rulers claimed. In 1241 Henry III invaded Wales and forced Dafydd to sign the treaty of Gwerneigron. Dafydd agreed to relinquish the "Four Cantrefs" and also hand over his brother Gruffudd, whom Henry III hoped to use as a puppet in England if Dafydd had any visions of grandeur.

The Tower of London 1244

After three years of English captivity in the Tower of London, Gruffudd could take no more and decided to make his escape. On St David's Day 1244 he made a makeshift rope ladder out of tapestries, and started the abseil down the walls of the mighty White Tower. Suddenly, the rope snapped and Gruffudd fell to his death. The force of the fall was so great that it is said his head was pushed between his shoulders.

Back in Wales Dafydd used the martyr-like death of his brother and rival, to galvanise the Welsh people and rid themselves of the Normans once and for all. Disillusioned with the way Henry had treated him, he decided to take the war to the Normans. The Welsh harried the lands of the "Four Cantrefs". Henry III retaliated and invaded Gwyenedd. The King was frustrated at being unable to bring Dafydd to battle, and ordered some Welsh prisoners who had been captured during a raid on a shipwrecked Irish supply boat, to be beheaded on the beach. Dafydd in turn executed the Normans he had captured in the campaign, and threw their bodies into the river Conwy. Both armies retired with the onset of winter, preparing themselves for the decisive campaign due in 1246. Henry implemented an economic embargo on all trade between Wales and England, hoping to break the will of the Welsh people and force them to submit to their eastern neighbour.

The death of Gruffud, 1244 A.D

The final showdown was not meant to be, as Dafydd died early in 1246 leaving Gwyenedd to be divided between his family members. He was buried alongside his father at the abbey of Aberconwy with the epitaph

'Tarian Cymru' - The shield of Wales, Llywelyn the Last

In 1246 Prince Dafydd died childless; he was succeeded by his nephew Llywelyn ap Gruffudd, the son of the unfortunate Gruffudd who fell to his death at the tower of London. Llywelyn and his brother Owain begrudgingly acknowledged King Henry III as their overlord and were forced to cede the disputed area of the "Four Cantrefs" to him at the treaty of Woodstock in 1247.

The King intended to limit the powers of Llywelyn by breaking up the already small principality of Gwynedd. When Llywelyn's brother Dafydd came of age, the King in his office as overlord offered him some territory in Gwynedd. Llywelyn was outraged and refused to comply. In 1255 he went to war against his brothers and decisively beat them at the battle of Byrn Derwin. As the undisputed Prince of Gwynedd, Llywelyn decided to take the offensive and free his fellow Welshmen and women who were being oppressed by the Normans in the "Four Cantrefs". The Perfeddwlad, as it was called, had been given by the King to his son Prince Edward Plantagenet. Edward had visited his fief in 1256, but had treated his Welsh subjects with contempt and had failed to address the grievances they had regarding the oppressive rule. Disillusioned with their Norman lord, the Welsh begged Llywelyn for help. In the winter of 1256 he crossed the river Conwy and quickly overran the entire region. Only the castles of Deganwy and Dyserth held out. When the news reached the royal court in England, Prince Edward was furious and hell-bent on returning the Wales to punish Llywelyn.

Prince Edward Plantagenet

Matthew Paris commented;

"Edward was determined to punish the Welsh and exterminate those who dared challenge his authority"

Winter storms forced Edward to abandon any hopes he had to recapturing the "Four Cantrefs". Llywelyn now master of most of north Wales turned south and took Powys, and then Deheubarth. All across Wales the people flocked to his banner and ousted the hated Marcher lords. The rising even reached the Norman stronghold of the Gower lordship, Kidwelly town was ransacked and burned to the ground. The Norman Castilian De Chatsworth was besieged in the castle, but managed to hold out.

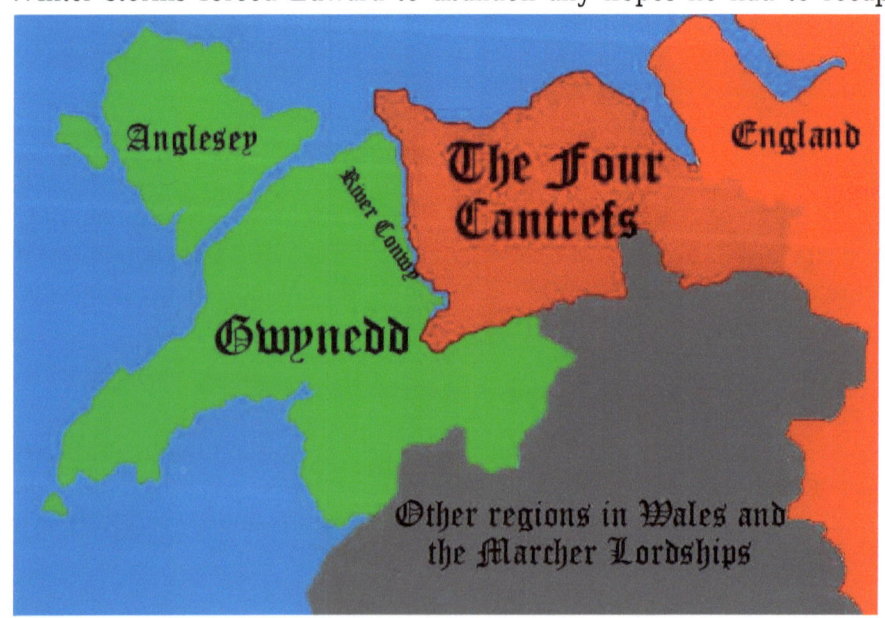

The Battle of Coed Llathen / Cadfan

A Norman counterattack led by Sir Stephan Bacon / Bauzon from Carmarthen was wiped out at the battle of Cadfan. In the thick wooded and boggy terrain the Norman knights were ambushed and killed. Sir Stephan was pulled from his horse and hacked to pieces in the stream at Pentrefelin. A small bridge "Pont Steffan" was named after him. The disaster sent shockwaves back to England. King Henry III was left with no choice but to lead the army with his son Prince Edward into Wales to put down the rebellion. From Chester the royal army advanced along the north Wales coastline as so many armies had done before it. They retook the "Four Cantrefs" and forced the Welsh back over the river Conwy, but with supplies running low the King abandoned the campaign and returned to England. The failure of the campaign of 1257 left Llywelyn in an extremely favourable position. He once again crossed the river Conwy and re-occupied the "Four Cantrefs". While England was slipping into civil war between the King and the barons led by Simon De Montfort, Llywelyn extended his gains in Wales and the Marches. Another one of Prince Edward's castles, Builth was captured by Llywelyn's forces in 1260.

The Battle of Evesham 1265

Llywelyn even sent Welsh troops off to help Simon De Montfort in his struggle against the monarchy. On the 4th of August 1265 Simon and his Welsh allies were trapped at Evesham. When the royalist forces came into view Simon is reported to have said;

"May the Lord have mercy upon our souls, as our bodies are theirs"

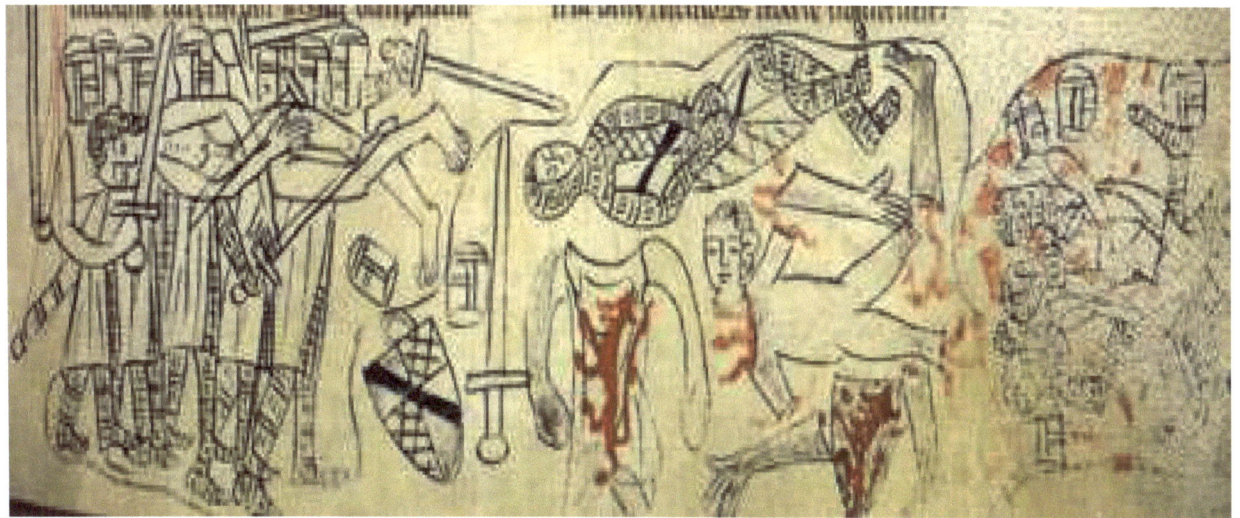

The aftermath of the battle of Evesham: Simon De Montfort being mutilated

The only escape route, the Bengeworth Bridge, had been captured by tenacious Marcher lord Roger De Mortimer. Simon De Montfort had no choice but to try and fight his way out against overwhelming numbers. Prince Edward who commanded the Royal forces ordered that no quarter would be given. As the battle commenced, a thunder storm from the heavens above lashed rain and lightning down on the two opposing armies. Simon and his men fought valiantly: he hacked his way deep into the Royalist ranks, trying to force a way through. His son Henry spattered with blood and mud was cut down and put to death, then Roger De Mortimer charged straight at Simon and killed him with his lance. The brave warrior was set upon and mutilated beyond recognition, his head, hands, feet and testicles were cut off. Simon's head was sent back to Wigmore castle as a trophy of war by the victorious Roger De Mortimer. The unfortunate Welsh archers and infantry who survived were also executed, or forced into the services of the Marcher lords.

The Treaty of Montgomery 1267

In 1267 King Henry and Prince Edward travelled to the Welsh border to broker a peace deal with the Welsh. The outcome of the treaty was a masterstroke for Llywelyn: he was officially acknowledged by Henry as the Prince of Wales. This was the first and only time an English King bestowed the title of Prince of Wales on a native Welshman. All the other Welsh nobles now gave homage to Llywelyn instead of Henry. The Four Cantrefs were surrendered including Prince Edward's castle of Builth. The Lordship of Brecon was also handed over to the Prince. It was the pinnacle of Llywelyn's career. He had achieved more than any other Welsh leader could have hoped for, the right to rule his country and people as an independent ruler.

The Marcher Lord
Roger De Mortimer at the Battle of Evesham
1265

Llywelyn knelt before King Henry III and performed the ceremony of homage, ratifying the treaty. The only snag with the Treaty of Montgomery was that it came at a price: Llywelyn would have to pay over 20,000 marks for his title and the agreement, but his annual income was probably only about 5,000 marks a year in total. The other problem was the Norman Marcher lords who controlled most of the fertile southern part of Wales. Llywelyn's title would be his downfall, for he did not have enough money to pay the annual payments to the King and fund the re-organisation and defence of the Principality against the Norman Marcher lords.

Caerphilly 1268

Within little more than a year into the agreement, trouble was already brewing in the Marches of Wales. Many of the castles in the lordship of Brecon which had been ceded over to Llywelyn were still in Norman hands. The Norman Marcher lords found a loophole within the Treaty: the lordship was Llywelyn's by right, but it had never been clarified who owned the castles within it.

Caerphilly Castle, Gilbert De Clare's masterpiece

Llywelyn's pressure for land and revenue encroached on Gilbert De Clare's lordship of Glamorgan in south Wales. The Earl of Gloucester's response was a massive castle building program on the lordships frontier. In 1268 he constructed a castle at Caerphilly, protecting the road to Cardiff and the lowland plains. Llywelyn attacked the first castle in 1270 and burned it to the ground. The confrontation had become a test of will and power between the Norman Earl and Welsh Prince. Gilbert, who was one of the richest men in England, decided to re-construct the castle at Caerphilly on a grand scale. No expense was spared on the mighty fortress. Caerphilly castle is the largest castle in Wales covering 30 acres and it was also the first concentric castle in Britain. It was so well defended that Llywelyn dared not attack it. King Henry III died in late 1272 and with Prince Edward in the Holy Land on Crusade all control over the Marcher lords evaporated. The private wars continued in Wales and the Marches until Edward's return in 1274. Llywelyn's position amongst the Welsh nobility was also deteriorating. Unable to defend the Principality from the raids of the Marcher lords, the Welsh conspired behind the Prince's back to overthrow him and replace him with his brother Dafydd. The plot to assassinate Llywelyn was uncovered and the Prince sent his guards to arrest Dafydd and the other conspirators, alas he was too late as the fugitives escaped across the border and took refuge in England.

The Reckoning 1274- 1282

Representatives from Prince Edward arrived at the court of Prince Llywelyn in Wales requesting him to appear before Edward to undertake the obligation of homage, which was required with the accession of a new Monarch. When the royal ambassadors arrived on the English-Welsh border Llywelyn did not show. Edward then sent out an invitation for his coronation, but the Welsh Prince declined the offer and refused to attend. In 1275 the new King travelled to Chester where Llywelyn was ordered to come and renew the oath of fealty. Once again Llywelyn did not turn up; he did however send King Edward a letter explaining that he refused to travel to England where Dafydd and the Welsh rebels were being harboured as he feared for his safety.

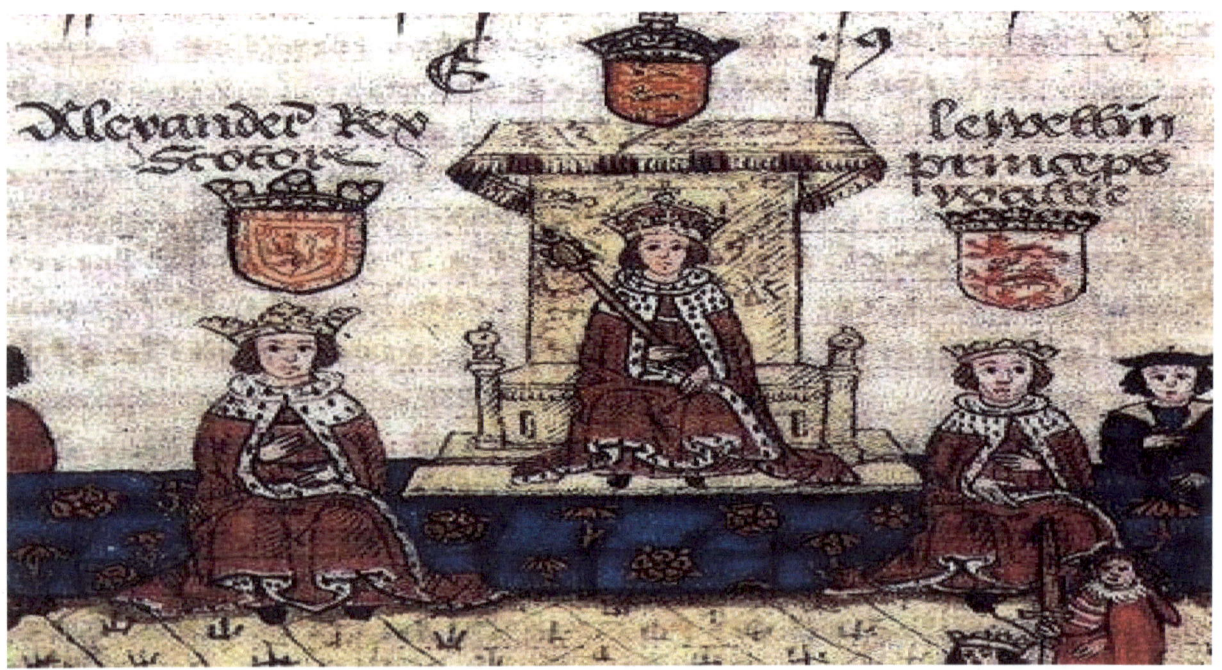

The hierarchy of the Kingdom of Britain: King Edward at the top and flanking him on the left King Alexander of Scotland and Prince Llywelyn seated on the right.

Edward's patience was now running out. He had offered the Prince safe conduct and his word he would not be harmed. After waiting several weeks, the King left Chester and headed back to London in a violent rage. Llywelyn received a stark letter instructing him to come to Westminster within a month or face the consequences

In late 1275 Edward found out that Llywelyn had been secretly negotiating to marry the daughter of his dead arch enemy, Simon de Montfort. Eleanor De Montfort's ship was intercepted on its journey from France to Wales by the King's men. For the King this was virtually a declaration for war. Edward may have wondered if Llywelyn was trying to drum up support with the old diehard De Montfort supporters in England and cause a civil war. His valuable prisoner was sent to the capital and placed under armed guard. In vengence after the discovery of the De Montfort coup d'etat, Edward ordered the Marcher lords to attack Llywelyn's lands at will. The Prince had misjudged his man, for King Edward Plantagenet was to become the most ruthless King to sit on the throne of England.

On the 12th of November 1276 at the King's parliament, Llywelyn "Prince of Wales" was declared an outlaw and disturber of the peace. The King's War council convened and discussed the plan for the forecoming campaign in

King Edward I of England

Wales. During the winter, the Prince sent letters requesting peace, but also with conditions attached to them. The time for negotiating had passed, Llywelyn had opened Pandora's Box and the lion now entered the dragon's lair.

The Invasion of Wales 1277

While the King made the preparations of mustering the royal army, his commanders on the March were tasked with breaking the Welsh resistance along the frontier. In the south, Payn De Chatsworth subdued the southern Welsh nobility into submission. William De Beauchamp (the Earl of Warwick), Henry De Lacy (the Earl of Lincoln) along with Llywelyn's rebellious brother Dafydd advanced into north Wales and besieged the defenders of the ancient hillfort castle of Dinas Bran. In the middle March Roger De Mortimer raided deep into Montgomeryshire along the Clun valley from his base at Wigmore castle. His objective was the Prince's castle of Dolforwyn. By the onset of summer 1277 the castles of both Dinas Bran and Dolforwyn had surrendered to the Anglo-Normans. Llywelyn's united Wales had fallen within a few months of the campaign; the Welsh nobles were disappearing from his court and changing sides at an alarming rate. In Worcester the King's younger brother, Edmund, was given command of the reserve forces that were tasked with strangling off Gwynedd from any help from the south. The King mustered his forces at Chester, Edward's army was the largest raised by an English King since the Norman invasion. Over 1000 armoured Knights and up to 15,000 infantry marched into Wales that summer. His strategy was very different to that of his predecessors. As the Norman war machine marched along the north Wales coastline it cleared and cut down the trees and bushes in its path, building a wide road through the densely wooded valleys that had been the defeat of so many armies before it. The King's men also constructed network of new castles to act as safe havens for his men and break the spirit of Llywelyn's Welsh. The new castles were founded at Flint, Rhuddlan and Aberystwyth. They rose up out of the ground to terrorise the native population into submission. They were built by the sea allowing them to be re-supplied in case they were besieged by the hostile native population.

Rhuddlan castle, in the "Four Cantrefs" modern day Flintshire

The King's fleet sent from the "Cinque Ports" of southern England struck the final hammer blow against Prince Llywelyn. In September they transported 3000 soldiers commanded by Otto De Grandson across the Menai straights onto the island of Anglesey. Within a few days, Otto and the Anglo-Normans had captured the Island, and more importantly, the gain harvest which was vital for Llywelyn. The grain helped maintain Edward's army in the field and forced the Prince who was now surrounded in the "Siege of Snowdon" to surrender. In early November 1277, Prince Llywelyn came out of the mist and fog of the Snowdonia Mountains where he had been hiding and surrendered himself to the officials of the King. The once proud and great man had brought shame and destruction upon himself and Wales by defying the King.

The Prince was forced to accept the humiliating terms of the treaty of Conwy which were harsh but not as harsh as they could have been. Firstly two of the "Four Cantrefs" would remain in English hands; the other two were given to Llywelyn's traitorous brother Dafydd. He then lost his right as overlord over the other Welsh Princes, who now paid homage to King Edward himself. Finally he was fined an enormous sum of over 50,000 marks for damages against the Crown. He was however allowed to keep the empty title of "Prince of Wales" and rule over the remainder of Gwynedd. Llywelyn was escorted to Rhuddlan castle where he met Edward face to face. The King forgave Llywelyn for his defiance and wavered the 50,000 mark fine, but this was not the end of the matter as far as Edward was concerned. Already humbled by the treaty Llywelyn was to be made an example of. Edward arranged for the Prince to be taken with him back to London to undertake the ceremony of fealty. At Christmas 1277 Llywelyn was paraded through the streets of London and at Westminster before all the nobles of the land he knelt before King Edward I and completed the ritual of homage.

Mathew Paris commented;

"Who does not know that the Prince of Wales is a petit Vassal of the King of England"

Magnanimous in victory, Edward even gave permission and paid for the wedding between Llywelyn and Eleanor De Montfort.

The couple was married in Worcester Cathedral on the 13th of October 1278. As the year ended it seemed that Llywelyn had survived the storm, and averted the total subjugation of his country by the Anglo-Norman King of England.

Worcester, the setting of Prince Llywelyn's marriage in 1278

The Great Rebellion

Apart from Gwynedd which was still directly ruled by Prince Llywelyn, most of Wales was suffering under the oppressive heel of Norman rule. The new Norman lords and administrators exercised contempt towards the native Welsh population who they believed to be inferior to them. Even in the Welsh governed part of the "Four Cantrefs", Dafydd was treated no more than a second class citizen by the Norman officials in Chester. By 1282 the Welsh could take no more and the country exploded in flames. A secret council of Welsh tribal leaders gathered at Denbigh and declared war against the Normans. The rebellion was scheduled to coincide with the Holy celebrations of Easter.

Dafydd launched a daring raid on the Normans at Hawarden castle, close to the English border. The nighttime festivities covered the approach of Dafydd and his Welsh tribesmen.

Then out of the darkness the full fury of the Welsh was unleashed upon the castle. The skillful Welsh bowmen dispatched the sentries while Dafydd's men scaled the walls and overran the castle. All in the castle were put to the sword and slaughtered; only Roger De Clifford, the Bailli of the castle, was taken hostage. The Norman Motte and Bailey castle was then ransacked and raised to the ground. Dafydd's act at Hawarden had lit the fire of rebellion that ignited the whole of Wales. Welshmen and women all over the country joined the revolt, attacking the settlements and castles of the Normans. On the west coast Aberystwyth castle fell, in the south Llandovery and the formidable Carreg Cennen fortress also fell into Welsh hands. The violence was not just restricted to Wales. The great border towns of England including Chester and Oswestry were also attacked. Dafydd laid siege to the symbols of Norman power in the "Four Cantrefs" (the castles of Flint and Rhuddlan).

The remains of Hawarden castle

Prince Llywelyn seems to have had no prior knowledge of the revolt. He was as surprised as the Normans when the news reached his court in Gwynedd. For the time being he refused to join the rebellion; he would wait to see how events unfolded before committing himself. When King Edward heard the news he was extremely disappointed. He became angry and vowed to punish the Welsh for their insolence.

He stated of the Welsh:

"They are a faithless people, their leaders are nothing more than a family of traitors, and it is time to put an end to their malice"

In May 1282 Edward arrived in Worcester. Gilbert De Clare (the Earl of Gloucester) was to take command of the southern forces and quell the rebellion in south Wales. Roger De Mortimer was recalled out of retirement and given the task of stabilising the Middle March. The King meanwhile carried on north to Chester to mobilise the invasion force. As the main army began its assault in north Wales, disastrous news arrived from the south. Gilbert's forces in Carmarthenshire had been wiped out. After retaking the castle of Carreg Cennen, they were ambushed in the wooded valleys of Carmarthenshire. The King's own nephew, William De Valance, lost his life in the debacle. Edward relieved Gilbert of his command and sent the dead boy's father another William De Valance to avenge his son's death and restore Norman rule in south Wales.

The Last throw of the Dice

Llywelyn who had been sitting on the fence, now made his move. A personal tragedy probably influenced his decision: in June his wife Eleanor De Montfort, who was heavily pregnant, died in childbirth. Their baby survived, but it was not a boy as Llywelyn had hoped for.

The Prince was by now an old man and Eleanor's death spelt the end of his dreams for the future. Grief-stricken and now with nothing to lose, Llywelyn threw his lot in with his brother Dafydd and his Welsh countrymen. The final showdown was at hand, where the winner would take it all. Edward's plan was to capture Anglesey, depriving the Welsh of the important grain reserves, just as he had done in the 1277 campaign. Luc de Tany (the seneschal of Gascony) launched an amphibious assault and secured the Island and the harvest. The main army of the King advanced towards the river Conwy at a slow pace to avoid being ambushed. William De Valance had subdued the south and retook the coastal town and castle of Aberystwyth. The pincers were now closing in on Snowdonia. Reginald De Grey and the Earl of Surrey marched up the Clwyd valley forcing Dafydd to retreat into the mountains.

Carreg Cennen Castle, Carmarthenshire Wales

The Battle of Moel-y-don

The King planned to construct a pontoon bridge from Anglesey to the mainland which would allow the Normans to attack the Welsh heartland of Snowdonia from two directions. By September the pontoon bridge was complete, but the King's force opposite the river Conwy was not ready to make its attack. By November the impatient Luc De Tany disobeyed the King's orders and decided to launch his attack on Snowdonia alone.
Walter of Guisborough commented:

"The English knights and armed men crossed the bridge at low tide eager for glory and renown."

On the 6th of November 1282 the Anglo Norman knights crossed the pontoon bridge to the mainland. Before the entire army was able to cross, Llywelyn's warriors descended from the mountains and fell upon De Tany's meager force.

"When they had reached the foot of the mountain and, after a time, came to a place at some distance from the bridge, the tide came in with a great flow, so that they were unable to get back to the bridge for the depth of water. The Welsh came from the high mountains and attacked them, and in fear and trepidation, for the great number of the enemy, our men preferred to face the sea than the enemy. They went into the sea but, heavily laden with arms, they were instantly drowned."

Luc De Tany was among the casualties on that fateful day. Sixteen knights were lost and over 300 infantry died on the shores of Snowdonia. The only notable survivor was Otto De Grandson: he tried his luck and swam to the safety of the other side, rather than face capture by the enemy.

The Menai Straight between Anglesey and mainland Snowdonia

The End of Llywelyn the Last, Irfon Bridge 1282

In the same month the old warrior Roger De Mortimer died of natural causes. His death sent the Middle March into chaos. Llywelyn fresh from his victory at the Battle of Moel-y-don, decided the time was right to open up a second front in the Middle March. Leaving Dafydd to hold Snowdonia, Llywelyn headed south to raise rebellion and support for his cause.
On the 11th of December 1282 in the hills near Builth, Llywelyn's force of several thousand Welshmen collided with the Norman Marcher coalition commanded by the Mortimer brothers Edmund and Roger, John Giffard and Roger l'Estrange. It seems that Llywelyn was not with the main army when battle was joined. At Irfon Bridge the Welsh spearmen protected the river crossing and their hilltop position against the Normans, but the Normans were told of a second crossing further downstream. The Norman archers rained countless volleys of deadly arrows onto the tightly packed Welsh Schiltrons, inflicting heavy casualties and depleting their numbers. The slaughter began when the Anglo-Norman cavalry arrived behind the Welsh positions. Now realising they had been outflanked some spearmen panicked and tried to flee, others held their ground and continued to fight to the death.

At the end of the day over 3000 Welshmen lay dead on the battlefield. In the vicinity of Climeri, Llywelyn and a party of knights were ambushed by the Marcher forces. Some say he was returning to the battle, others say he was secretly lured by the Mortimer brothers to discuss the possibility of an alliance. Whatever to truth may be, the Prince was killed in the skirmish by a humble knight Stephen De Frankton. After his body was identified, his head was cut off and sent to King Edward at Rhuddlan castle. Llywelyn's head was then taken to London where it was paraded through the streets. An ivy crown was placed upon it, as a symbol that Llywelyn was nothing more than a Prince of traitors. It was held high so all the crowd could see what happened to anyone who defied the King, before being displayed on London Bridge for the next 20 years.

Memorial in Welsh to Llywelyn the Last, Cilmery, Wales "Near this spot was killed our leader Llywelyn 1282"

Dafydd ap Gruffydd 1282-1283

The death of Prince Llywelyn broke the spirit of the Welsh. His brother Dafydd now proclaimed himself Prince of Wales, but his reputation for double dealing and changing sides was noy forgotten by his fellow countrymen. Edward's armies swept across Wales eliminating all resistance in its way.

Overleaf the death of Llywelyn the Last, Cilmery, Mid Wales →

Dafydd was a hunted man, fleeing from place to place escaping the clutches of the Anglo-Normans on several occasions. He was finally captured in the summer of 1283 by his fellow countrymen at the foot of Wales's highest mountain (Snowdon).

Royal letters recorded:

"Dafydd ap Gruffydd, last of a treacherous line has been captured, he was handed over by men of his own tongue"

This was the end for the native Princes of Wales, Llywelyn had fallen in battle, but a more gruesome spectacle awaited Dafydd in England. He was taken under armed guard across the border to Shrewsbury. In a showcase trial he was condemned to death for treason.

Arms of Dafydd ap Gruffydd

Firstly he was tied to the tail of a horse and dragged through the streets towards his place of execution. He was then hanged by the neck, disemboweled and had his entrails burned in front of his eyes, no doubt to the jeers and jubilation of the watching crowd. Finally he was beheaded and quartered. His head was sent to London to rest beside Llywelyn's, the rest of his body parts were distributed to the far flung corners of the Kingdom as a warning to the fate of any would-be traitors.

The Iron Ring

To complete to conquest of Wales, Edward put into motion "The Ring of Iron", a shock and awe policy of castle building on a monumental scale. The castles of Conwy, Caernarfon, Harlech and finally Beaumaris were designed and constructed by the greatest military architect of the time (Master James of St George). The new castles towered over and dominated the defeated Welsh. Caernarfon was built according to an ancient Welsh legend. It was the place, where Magnus Maximus (the father of Constantine, Romes first Christian Emperor) had been buried. When his bones were dug up in 1283, Edward drew upon the symbolism, and commissioned the castle towers to be polygonal instead of cylindrical, copying walls of Constantinople. The finished result is probably the finest medieval castle in Europe. There were further uprisings in 1287 and more seriously in 1294. The King and his retinue were forced to take refuge in the mighty castle of Conway which was besieged by Madog ap Llywelyn. By 1295 the last rebellion against the Normans had been put down with the defeat of Madog at the Battle of Maes Moydog. Legend has it that Edward placated the Welsh by promising them a Prince born in Wales who could speak no English. Tradition has it that the prophesy was fore filled when Queen Eleanor gave birth to the future Edward II at Caernafron castle. Edward placed the baby on his shield and presented him to the people of Wales. It had taken the Normans 200 years to complete the conquest of Celtic Wales, and was by far the most difficult campaign they had ever undertaken. The conquest did not mean the end of Wales, or its proud people. The Normans were only interested in the lowland and fertile valleys of the Principality. In the mountains and upland regions the Welsh were left in relative peace and harmony. Their language continued to survive and flourishes to this day. Llywelyn the Last is ultimately responsible for the downfall of his Kingdom by defying England's most ruthless warrior King Edward I

After the last great revolt by Owain Glyndwr in the 15th century the Welsh wars were finally over. Edward had also gained a secret weapon from his wars in Wales. The Welsh longbow would be used to defeat the Scots of William Wallace (Braveheart) and Robert the Bruce. It also allowed the Kings of England to regain the Duchy of Normandy, and inflict crushing defeats against the French in the 100 hundred years war. The Norman hunger for more land and conquest did not stop at the shores of Wales. Across the sea lay the Island of Eire. On the very edge of the known world, the Normans embarked on the conquest of Gallic Ireland. The Irish struggle for liberty against the Anglo-Normans would leave a scare that is only just starting to heal after 750 years of bitter oppression.

Caernarfon Castle, North Wales

Chapter 6: **Ireland**

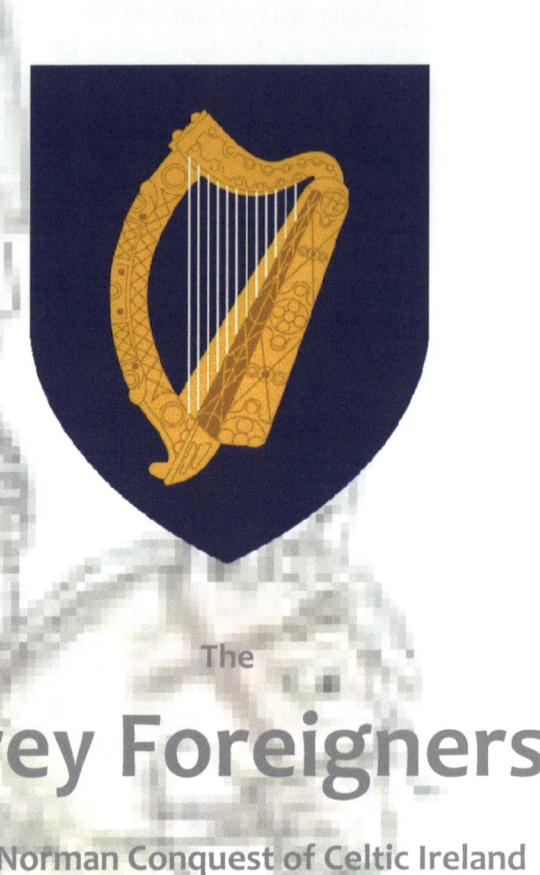

The

Grey Foreigners

The Norman Conquest of Celtic Ireland

Even today Ireland "the emerald isle" has a mystical Celtic allure about it. Back in the 12th century Ireland was on the very edge of the known world. Only the Vikings knew what lay beyond the sea of Europe's last outpost. In 1169 A.D Norman knights and soldiers landed on the shores of Eire. The first Celtic-Irish who saw these strange mounted warriors covered from head to toe in steel, called them "the Grey Foreigners" (the Normans). The Norman invasion of Ireland had begun. In an epic struggle that would last throughout the medieval period and beyond, the Celtic-Irish fought for their liberty against the Grey Foreigners.

In the late 1st century A.D the Roman Governor of Britain Julius Agricola defeated the Caledonian tribes of modern day Scotland at the Battle of Mons Graupius. His victory left only the island of Hibernia (Ireland) outside Roman rule. Agricola planned to conquer and subdue Ireland but the Emperor Domitian grew jealous of his victories and recalled him back to Rome. As the age of Roman expansion grew to an end, the fear of invasion from the legionaries of Rome subsided. The Celtic peoples continued to live as they had done for 100s of years until Irish pirates brought back a slave called Patrick from a raid on Roman Britain. Some 20 years after the sack of Rome by Alaric's Visigoths in 410 A.D Pope Celestine sent Bishop Palladius to Ireland to preach Christianity to the Pagan Irish. Palladius may have been the first Christian missionary in Ireland but Patrick remains the most famous of the Christian preachers. The young Patrick worked as a shepherd for his new Irish master. After six years in captivity he managed to escape and returned home to Britain. In Patrick's dream he had a vision that it was his duty to return to Ireland and convert the Irish people to Christianity. Sure enough Patrick returned to Ireland not as a slave but as a missionary. He landed at Wicklow and proceeded to the court of Laoghaire O'Neil, where he was given permission the preach Christianity throughout the territory. By the time of his death Patrick and the other Christian missionaries had succeeded in establishing a Christian foothold in Eire.

While the former provinces of the Roman Empire entered a period known to us as the dark ages, Ireland entered a golden age in its history. Monks set up new churches and Sees. By the 8th century Ireland's reputation for scholarship and learning was so well renowned that many scholars travelled from Europe and Britain to study in Irish monastic schools. The famous book of Kells illustrates the high level of insular (Hiberno-Saxon) artwork being produced in the post-Roman British Isles.

Hiberno-Saxon artwork

The Irish Kingdoms and the coming of the Vikings

Ireland was divided up into numerous petty Kingdoms and Celtic clans known in Gaelic as the "Túatha / Tuath". There were probably more than 100 of these Túatha, varying in size and competing for power. The Ri Ruirech, or provincial King dominated the political scene on a regional level and sometimes was able to claim to be the High King of Ireland, associated with the important site of Tara. The main traditional provinces of Eire consisted of Munster, Connacht, Leinster, Meath and Ulster. Constant in-fighting between the provincial Kings inhibited Ireland from becoming a "United Kingdom" and allowed a cruel invader to take advantage of the fragmented situation. The first recorded Viking raid occurred in 795 A.D on the island of Lambay, (Co. Dublin). It was followed by further raids on Meath in 798 A.D and Connacht (Western Ireland in 806/807 A.D). As was the case all over Europe, the Norsemen raided the rich Abbeys and undefended villages, taking slaves and booty back to Scandinavia.

Most of the original invaders probably came down the western Viking routes via Shetland, Orkney and the Western Isles sailing down the Atlantic coast of Scotland before crossing the Irish Sea to attack Ireland. By the mid 9th century the Vikings were starting to winter and settle on the coastal estuaries and rivers. They built fortified bases called "Longports" where they encamped and stationed their dragon head longboats. One of these Longport's was Dublin which means "Black pool" in Norse. From the protection of the Longport's Viking armies penetrated deep into the heart of the country raiding and pillaging.

In 844 A.D, one such army commanded by Thorgest ravaged and terrorised the Northern part of the country. For nearly a year his campaign of terror wreaked havoc on the Gaelic Irish. Then in 845 A.D Thorgest met his end when he was captured by Màel Sechnail (the King of Mide, later High King of Ireland) and drowned in Loch Owel. The Gaelic fight back against the Norse continued. Two years later seven hundred Vikings were wiped out at Forach and in 848 AD they suffered several heavy defeats including the Battle of Sciath Nechtain and in the oak-wood of Dochonna's desert where 1200 were supposedly slain.

The Irish were on the verge of destroying the Viking menace when internal division allowed the Norsemen to recover. Some of the petty Kings formed an alliance with the invaders against Màel Sechnail and the country was plunged into civil war. Viking reinforcements arrived in 851 A.D but a power struggle between the Norse settlers and the newcomers evolved. The newcomers were called the Dubgaill (Dark Foreigners) and they defeated the Findgaill (Fair Foreigners) of Dublin and systematically enforced their rule upon all of the remaining Viking inhabitants. The war was brutal with both sides committing terrible atrocities. Màel Gualae the Petty King of Munster, fell into the hands of the Dublin Vikings who sacrificed him to the Pagan Gods. The High King Màel Sechnail died in 862 A.D, but the war continued for many years to come. The legendary son of Ragnar Lodbrok, Ivar "the Boneless" ruled over the Kingdom of Dublin with Olaf the White during the second half the the ninth century. Ivar's military campaingns forged a short lived Viking empire that included parts of Scandinavia, Scotland, Ireland and nearly all of Anglo-Saxon England, except the Kingdom of Wessex. . In 873 AD according to the Irish annals the most cruel and invincible Ivar "the Boneless" died a peaceful death in Dublin.

Annals of Ulster:
"873 AD Ivar, King of all the Northmen of all Ireland and Britain died"

Ivar's brother Halfdan, not content in just ruling the Kingdom of Jorvik (York, England) decided to claim Dublin as Ivar's heir apparent. Gathering together a large war band he crossed the Irish Sea and deceitfully murdered Eyestein (Olaf the White's son). After the murder of Eyestein, Halfdan sat uneasy on the throne of Dublin. At a banquet he survived an assassination attempt upon his life by some disgruntled Viking and Irish nobles. Unable to control or trust the waring factions Halfdan abandoned Dublin and returned to the Kingdom of Jorvik, where he recruited soldiers and mercenaries to punish the Viking rebels in Ireland. Once back on Irish soil Halfdan conducted a final vengeful campaign of terror. In 877 AD he fought against a coalition of rebel forces (some of whom included Eyestein relatives) near Strangford Lough, Northern Ireland (*Strangr-fjörðr*) meaning "strong sea-inlet" in Old Norse. In the vicious battle that ensured Halfdan was slain in the fighting.

The second Viking invasion

In 914 A.D Rögnvaldr, the Viking ruler of most of North Western Britain including the Shetland and Orkney Isles arrived in Waterford to reclaim the territories lost to the Gaelic Irish. Another fleet under the command of Sigtrygg (probably one of Rögnvaldr's relatives) arrived in Dublin and took the city by force. In 917 A.D the Irish tried to retake Dublin but were utterly annihilated by Sigtrygg's Vikings at the Battle of Confey, losing Augaire mac Ailella (the Ri Ruirech / King of Leinster) in the confrontation. By no means a total victory for the Norsemen, it did allow them to strengthen their position in the enclaves of Waterford, Limerick, Cork, Wexford and Dublin.

These settlements grew in prosperity, trading slaves and goods from all over the Viking world and beyond. Silks arrived from the Middle East, soapstone from Shetland, and walrus ivory from the frozen lands of the Artic were amongst some of the goods traded in the ports of Hiberno-Norse Ireland.

The High King Brian Boru "The taker of tributes"

Brian Boruma /Boru was the son of the petty King of Thomond in Munster (Southern Ireland). He was born in 943 A.D and grew up in the dark days of the Viking raids. In one such raid Brian's mother was killed by the Norse. After the attack Brian was sent to the relative safety of the monastery of Clonnacnoise in West Meath. There he was educated by the monks, where he learnt Latin and studied ancient history. When he reached adulthood Brian returned home to the family tribe and joined his elder brother in the war against the Vikings. The two men achieved a notable victory in 964 A.D when they captured "the Rock of Cashel" (one of Ireland's most important religious sites).

At the Battle of Sulcoit in 968 A.D Brian and his brother Mathgamain defeated the Vikings. The victory led the way to the Gaelic re-capture of Limerick. When Mathgamain was murdered, Brian took up the reigns of power and became King of Munster. In a swift campaign he forced the Ri Ruirech of Leinster to submit and pay homage to him as overlord. By the end of the century he was begrudgingly accepted as High King of Ireland.

The Rock of Cashel / St Patrick's Rock, South Tipperary

The Battle of Clontarf 1014 A.D

In 1013 A.D a formidable axis of Vikings and disgruntled Irish nobles declared war on the old King. Màel Morda the Ri Ruirech of Leinster joined forces with Sitric / Sigtrygg (leader of the Dublin Vikings). Sigtrygg also asked for support from Sigurd (the Viking Earl of Orkney and Brooir the warlord of Man (Isle of Man). Brian tried unsuccessfully to besiege Dublin but had to retreat in the winter of 1013 A.D. Both sides prepared themselves for the final confrontation.

In the spring of 1014 A.D Viking troops from Shetland, Orkney, Man, England and possibly even Normandy arrived in Dublin. Brian had also mustered a mighty army of Irish and mercenary warriors. One of his Viking mercenary commanders was Óspak, who was actually the brother of

Sigurd the Earl of Orkney, defending the Raven banner at the Battle of Clontarf 1014 AD

Brooir who fought on the opposite side. On the 23rd of April (Good Friday) 1014 A.D just outside Dublin at Clontarf the two armies clashed together. The war cry from the Vikings broke the silence of the tense atmosphere. They shouted out a challenge "Where's Domhnall," (Who was an Irish noble) the Irish replied "Over here you Snake". After the exchanging of insults, the vicious hand to hand combat ensued.

Legend says that the Sacred Viking Raven banner had a curse on it.

"The army that carries the banner before it shall have certain victory. But whoever bears the banner, only certain death waits".

The Viking Raven Banner

The prophecy came true; all who held the banner high were cut down. In the end only Sigurd the Earl of Orkney was brave enough to take the banner, but he too was run through by an Irish spear and hacked to pieces. With their main leader dead the Vikings began to flee the battlefield. Some of them headed for the safety of their Dragon ships but the incoming tide cut them off. Many were drowned or slaughtered in the rout. The Irish victory was complete, but towards the end of the battle Brooir's retreating Vikings fell upon Brian's tent. The Viking warlord recognising the King, immediately set upon Brian and beheaded him. Brooir was later captured and brutally killed. He was cut open and tied to an oak tree using his own intestines. The battle did not destroy the Viking menace, but slowly the Vikings of Ireland assimilated into the Irish populace. They intermarried and became the "Ostmen" of the emerging towns and cities of Ireland.

The Enemy at the gates: The Normans

Over the next 150 years the Irish fought each other instead of forming into a unified state. This disunity effectively opened the door to an invader who had already destroyed Anglo-Saxon England and had brutally carved up the Celtic Principality of Wales. The Normans were waiting for their chance to infiltrate and conquer Celtic Ireland. Soon enough an opportunity presented itself when the Ri Ruirech of Leinster (Dermot MacMurrough) was driven out of the country by the High King Roderic O'Connor. Dermot fled his homeland and crossed the Irish Sea to Wales. He rode to the court of Henry II Plantagenet, King of England, the most powerful Monarch in Europe. Probably in Normandy, Dermot asked the King to help restore him to power in exchange for acknowledging Henry as his overlord.

Dermot MacMurrough;

**"I have been cast out of my own Kingdom.
To you I come to make plaint, great Sire, in the presence of the nobles of your Empire.
Your liege-man I shall become
henceforth all the days of my life, if you help restore me to power"**

The King was reluctant to get involved directly, but he gave Dermot a letter authorising him to seek the support of his nobles. The obvious choice was the Norman Marcher Lords of South Wales, for they had direct access to Ireland from the Pembrokeshire ports.

Dermot managed to gain the support of Gilbert de Clare "Strongbow" (Earl of Striguil and Pembroke). Gilbert was one of the most powerful Norman barons in South Wales. In return for military assistance Dermot offered the Earl the hand of his daughter Aefe in marriage and also the title of King of Leinster. Dermot was hoping that with the support of the Normans he could make himself the High King of all Ireland. With the backing of a major power broker Dermot set off for the west coast recruiting a mercenary army as he went. There was plenty of Normans willing to join the expedition; Ireland offered the chance for many of the landless sons of the nobility to gain riches and land across the sea in the Celtic Kingdom.

Dermot negotiated with Rhys ap Gruffydd (Lord Rhys) for the release of Robert Fitz Stephen. Fitz Stephen was an experienced soldier who had been captured during the wars between Owain Gwynedd and Henry Plantagenet. Another

King Henry II of England

experienced warrior to join the adventure was Maurice Fitz Gerald; he had survived the Norman defeat to the Welsh at the Battle of Crug Mawr, but had gained important experience of how the Celtic people fought in battle which would be put to later use in Eire.

The Norman invasion, Dún Cormaic and Wexford

In 1167 A.D a small detachment of Norman knights under the command of Richard Fitz Godbert de Roche landed in Ireland. They may have been part of the advanced guard, reconnoitring the area to test the feasibility for the invasion. Then in 1169 A.D Dermot, Robert Fitz Stephen, 90 armoured knights / men at arms, and about 300/400 archers and foot soldiers set sail for Ireland. They landed on the shore near Bannow in county Wexford. A further force of bowmen arrived under the command of Maurice de Prendergast. The Norman invasion of Ireland had begun; "The Grey Foreigners" marched northeast and headed for the Viking stronghold of Wexford. On reaching the settlement of Dún Cormaic (Duncormick) the Normans were faced with their first opposition. The local Hiberno-Norse population had decided to challenge the invaders by blocking off the ford, and the way to Wexford. The Irish warriors beat their shields with their huge Scandinavian battle axes and formed a shield wall. Undeterred by the wild axe wielding Irishmen that confronted them, the Norman war machine went to work. Firstly the Normans probably used their archers to break up the Irish shield wall. Then the Norman shock cavalry burst into action. At full charge, the very ground trembled as the Norman knights smashed straight into the disintegrating Irish shield wall. The Irish had never seen anything like it before, and within a short time the river run red with the blood of the slain. The first battle /skirmish ended in annihilation for the Hiberno-Norse and total victory for the Normans who continued their march towards Wexford. The citizens of Wexford also made a stand against the invaders, but when they realised that they were up against a professional army of combined infantry, cavalry and archers, they set fire to the suburbs and retired to the safety of the town walls. The attack on Wexford commenced with the Norman/Welsh archers firing volley after volley of arrows, pinning the defenders down while the armoured Knights and foot soldiers scaled the walls. Robert de Barri/Barry a fearless young knight from South Wales was one of the first men to reach the top of the battlements. De Barri killed all in his way and was gaining a foothold on the wall until he was struck straight in the face by a huge stone, covered in blood he fell backwards into the ditch below. Miraculously he survived the encounter being dragged to safety by his men. The battle raged on until nightfall, but the Normans were unable to breach the defences. During the evening representatives from the Irish Clergy entered the Norman camp and negotiated the surrender of the town. Dermot granted Wexford to Fitz Stephen, thus establishing the town as the first real Norman foothold in Ireland.

The Conquest of Ossory 1169 A.D

Together with troops loyal to Dermot, the Normans set out on a reign of terror towards Ossory. Duvenald / Giolla Pádraig (the Irish lord of Ossory) was a bitter enemy of Dermot, for this reason and also to terrorise the Irish into accepting that resistance was futile, the Normans destroyed everything in their wake. Giolla Pádraig fought back and used guerrilla warfare tactics against the Normans. In the woods and boggy terrain, where they could not use their cavalry they were

Depiction of the first Normans in Ireland, Dublinia Viking Museum

vulnerable and could be defeated. But at the Pass of Bealach Gabhráin the Irish were enticed into attacking the enemy on open ground. The classic Norman ruse of the "feinted flight" which had been used to deadly effect so many times before, (including at the Battle of Hastings 1066 A.D) was used for the first time against the native Gaelic Irish. The Irish chased after the fleeing Norman knights, when on the grassy plains the knights wheeled around and charged directly at the isolated Irish warriors who were cut down with ease.

The Giraldus Cambrensis states that;

"The enemy was pursued onto the open plains; the horsemen of Fitz Stephen attacked them and defeated them with great slaughter. They slew them with their lances and those who survived the charge were decapitated by the following foot soldiers"

The land and people were devastated by the "Grey Foreigners". When they returned to their camp they gave Dermot 200 heads as a present. Dermot picked up one of the severed heads and tore its nose off with his teeth. This savage form of disfigurement seems to have been common in Ireland, probably linked to the country's Celtic routes. Meanwhile the High King of Ireland (Roderic O'Connor) had marshaled his army and marched into Ossory to confront the invaders. Had he attacked Dermot and the Normans in their fortified camp near Ferns Irish history may have been very different. But instead he restored Dermot as King of Leinster on the condition that Dermot send his allies back to Britain. Even if Dermot had agreed, he had already opened Pandora's Box. Like the story of the Normans in Southern Italy, once they had been invited into the country, they were very hard to get rid of afterwards.

The second Norman invasion and The Battle of Baginbun / Dundonnell 1170 A.D

In 1170 A.D a second wave of Norman reinforcements was sent over by the Earl of Pembroke. Raymond le Gros (Fitz Gerald) 10 Knights and some 70 archers landed at Baginbun on the Hook Head peninsula (County Wexford). Raymond was the Earl's right hand man and had been tasked with pacifying the region before the arrival of his master Gilbert de Clare. Herve de Monte Marisco (Strongbow's Uncle) arrived at the Norman camp and brought disturbing news that the Irish from Waterford were amassing a large force to crush the invaders once and for all. The Normans quickly constructed makeshift ditches and a wooden palisade in the ruins of an old fort on the peninsular. They also rounded up herds of cattle to be used as provisions.

Raymond marched out with a detachment of Norman knights hoping to give battle to the approaching Irish forces, but when he saw the size of the army opposing him (some 3000 strong) he immediately retreated back to the fortified camp. The Ostmen of Waterford, high with confidence charged the Norman camp before the barricade was closed. On the verge of being overrun, the Normans started to panic and only the quick thinking of Raymond himself saved the day. The Normans counter attacked by driving the captured herds of cattle straight into the Irish centre. The sheer brute force of the enraged cows steamrollered over the Irish infantry, trampling and killing hundreds in the process. They were followed up by the Normans knights' eager the finish off the Irish who were now in total disarray. The battle turned into a rout as the Irish broke ranks and tried to escape the bloody field with loses of over 1000 men. After the battle the Normans committed a terrible atrocity, 70 unlucky Irish prisoners were handed over to Alice de Abergavenny who had lost her husband during the encounter. Her anger was uncontrollable and in a fit of rage she personally beheaded all 70 men, throwing their headless corpses off the cliff into the sea below.

Extract from "The Song of Dermot and the Earl";

"Of the Irish there were taken
quite as many as seventy.
But the noble knights
had them beheaded.
To a wench they gave
an axe of tempered steel,
and she beheaded them all

and threw their bodies over the cliff,
because she had that day
lost her lover in the combat.
Alice of Abergavenny was her name
who served the Irish thus."

On the 23rd of August 1170 A.D "Strongbow" Richard de Clare finally arrived in Ireland. He brought with him a formidable force of over 1000 men, including 200 mounted knights. Together with the existing troops, the Normans broke out of their defensive bridgehead and marched on the Viking port of Waterford.

Waterford was one of the greatest and prosperous towns in medieval Ireland. Its strategic position was vital for the Normans, who could not allow the port to remain in enemy hands. In the late summer of 1170 A.D the Earl's men arrived on the outskirts of Waterford and besieged the town. The Normans tried to take the town by force, but were beaten back by defenders on two separate occasions. Raymond le Gros spotted a weakness in the town's defences; a small structure on a wooden post was attached to the outside of the wall. Raymond ordered his men to cut down the post under cover from the legendary archers of Gwent (Wales). The Norman foot soldiers hacked down the wooden foundations of the support. Then the whole structure came crashing down, bringing a section of the wall with it.

Seizing their chance, the Normans rushed forward into the dust cloud and through the breach in the wall. In the custom of the time, any town / city that refused to surrender was at risk from the dreaded sack. Waterford was no exception; The Earls men rampaged through the streets killing anyone in their way. The Hiberno-Norse population was slaughtered and the once mighty town was reduced to a smouldering heap of rumble. Dermot arrived in Waterford, and in the ruins of the Cathedral the marriage between Richard de Clare "Strongbow" and Aefe took place.

The capture of Dublin

Earl Richard left a garrison in Waterford while he and Dermot marched on to the greatest prize of all: Dublin. The Gaelic chieftains of Ireland were summoned by the High King Roderic O'Connor to help defend Dublin. The Irish had learned their lesson from the defeat at the "Pass of Bealach Gabhráin" and had blocked off most of the routes towards Dublin, with armed troops waiting in the woods and boggy terrain to ambush the Normans. The Normans fearing such tactics switched routes and crossed over the ridges of Glendalough and the Wicklow Mountains, thus avoiding the area where Irish hoped to ambush them.

Reginald's tower, Waterford, Ireland

Panic gripped the citizens of Dublin when news reached them that the Normans had descended out of the mists of the Wicklow Mountains unharmed, and were heading straight for the city. Negotiations between the Normans and the Viking hierarchy of Dublin started, but Earl Richard fearing that Asculf MacTorkil (the Viking warlord of Dublin) was playing for time, (hoping for the arrival of King Roderic O'Connor's army) decided to launch a pre-emptive strike against the city. On the 21st of September 1170 the Normans attacked Dublin from several directions and caught the Norse defenders by surprise. Asculf and the leading Norse nobles managed to escape and took ship to the Viking safe haven of the Isle of Man.

The Irish fight back

The Normans and their Irish allies raided the county of Meath during the winter of 1170, burning down churches and pillaging the land. In retaliation King Roderic O'Connor ordered Dermot's son who was his hostage to be executed. The political alliance was sent into freefall when Dermot died in the spring of 1171 A.D. Immediately Earl Richard de Clare declared himself King of Leinster, but

De Clare, coat of arms

Richard de Clare "Strongbow"
Earl of Pembroke

many Irish nobles who had been loyal to Dermot found it hard to stomach a foreigner on the throne. Most of the Gaelic "Túatha" tribes of Leinster rose up in rebellion and attacked the Normans. The Ostmen of Wexford even captured Fitz Stephen, who was barricaded up in an early Norman Motte and Bailey castle. There was further trouble when Asculf returned to Ireland in order to reclaim his throne. Asculf's Viking army commanded by John "the mad" landed near Dublin and confronted the Norman outside the East gate. The Norman governor Milo de Cogan charged out of the gates with a company of mounted knights, hacking his way deep into the Viking ranks. The battle was vicious and one of the Norman knights had his leg cut clean off by a single stroke from a Scandinavian battle axe. Then just as the Norsemen were gaining the advantage a second force of Norman cavalry commanded by Milo's Brother Richard arrived and attacked the Norse from behind. The Vikings were slaughtered including John "the mad" their leader. Asculf was captured fleeing in the direction of his ships, and after a brief showcase trail he was executed. No sooner had the Normans defeated the Norsemen, they had to contend with another threat from the Gaelic Irish who laid siege to Dublin. Earl Richard hatched a plan to eliminate some of the Irish nobility by luring them to a peace conference, then having them murdered. The conference was attended by Giolla Pádraig (the pretty King of Ossory), but just before the assassins launched their attack Maurice de Prendergast intervened in a chivalrous act and foiled the ghastly plan. For his deed he became known by the Irish as "the faithful Norman". The situation in Ireland was becoming desperate, although the Normans defeated King Roderic's army outside Dublin and had recovered Waterford and most of the lost towns; supplies had all but dried up from across the sea. Word of Strongbow's conquest had reached the court of King Henry II Plantagenet. Henry was concerned that the Norman Marcher Lords were attempting to create a new Norman state without his authority. As a result Henry forbade any re-supplement from Wales/England until he arrived in Eire to restore order.

The arrival of King Henry II

On the 18th of October 1171 A.D King Henry II landed at Waterford. This was the first time in history that an English monarch had come to Ireland. Henry brought with him a massive army of 10,000 men. His objective was a "shock and awe policy" into showing both the Gaelic Irish and the Norman adventurers his power. The Irish realised that resistance against such odds was futile, and one by one the Celtic chieftains came before the King and paid homage. Although Henry had no right to the Overlord ship of Ireland, the actions of the Túatha affirmed this by submitting to him. First Henry was met by the men of Wexford, who handed over their hostage, the Norman Fitz Stephen. The King then began a tour of the country stopping at the Rock of Cashel where the O'Brian lords of Limerick submitted to him. When he reached Dublin he invited all the Kings of Ireland to come to his court and spend Christmas with him. Strongbow also submitted to the King and handed over his conquests. Henry pardoned the Earl and restored his title and lands minus Dublin, Waterford and Wexford which he intended to keep for himself. Henry intended to govern Ireland much in the same way as Wales. He protected the Irish by stopping the Norman Marcher Lords from extending their conquests, thus intern creating a balance of power where no side could extinguish the other. Hugh de Lacy and John de Courcy were left in charge as the King's representatives with instructions to keep the peace. Before leaving Henry also reformed the Catholic Church of Ireland. At the Synod of Cashel the Irish bishops agreed to bring the church into line, following the guidelines sent from Pope Alexander III in Rome.

The descent into chaos

As soon as the King left the trouble resumed, the original Norman conquerors ignored the orders from the Kings Viceroy's and restarted their conquests against the Irish. Even Hugh de Lacy was drawn into the conflict. During a peace conference with the former Irish Lord of Meath a dispute broke out, the one eyed O'Roric tried to kill de Lacy but was cut down in the process. Afterwards his head was impaled on the gate of Dublin castle, before being sent to King Henry in England. To further his control over Meath De Lacy built a series of Norman castles, including the mighty fortress of Trim which is the biggest castle in Ireland.

Trim castle, County Meath

In 1174 Strongbow launched a raid deep into Munster (South West Ireland) but at the battle of Thurles his men were ambushed by the O'Brian Gaels from Limerick. According to the annals of Tighernach, the Normans lost 1700 men during the battle. The Earl fled the battlefield and headed to Waterford. All over the country the Irish rose up in rebellion, Strongbow was besieged in

Waterford until Raymond le Gros arrived from Wales with 500 troops and rescued his Lord. The Normans counter attacked and rallied to the banner of Raymond who was regarded by the rank and file soldiers as an inspirational leader. In 1175 he avenged the defeat at Thurles by attacking the Hiberno-Norse stronghold of Limerick. In a daring attack on the town the Norman cavalry forced a crossing through the cold fast running waters of the river Shannon and stormed Limerick. No quarter was given and the Norman troops ransacked the settlement.

The Treaty of Windsor 1175

Had the Gaelic Irish continued their attacks on the Norman garrisons they might have well drove the invaders into the sea, but local politics intervened and they started to fight one another again. This restbite gave the Normans colonists' time to recover and strengthen their position. The old High King Roderic O'Connor sent the Bishop of Dublin (Lorcán Ua Tuathail/ Laurence O'Toole) to England to negotiate with King Henry. The outcome of the negotiations was the Treaty of Windsor. The terms stated that Roderic was to be acknowledged as the King of Ireland and be allowed to govern the lands outside Norman control according to Gaelic laws and customs. He had to however recognise Henry as his Overlord and accept that Ireland was nominally a country within the yoke of the Angevin Empire.

In 1176 A.D the leader of the Norman invasion of Ireland "Strongbow" died. The Earl was laid to rest in the cathedral of Christchurch in Dublin, where his effigy can still be seen today. Raymond le Gros was left in charge until Fitz Aldlem de Burgo arrived from England to take up the reins of power in the name of the King's son, John whom Henry had given the title "Lord of Ireland".

Tomb of Richard de Clare "STONGBOW" Christchurch Cathedral, Dublin

Invasion of the North 1177 A.D

The Gaelic Princes of Ulster (Northern Ireland) had never sworn allegiance to King Henry, thus were even more exposed to the advances of the land grabbing Norman Marcher Lords than their southern Irish neighbours. One such Marcher Lord was John de Courcy, in 1177 A.D he gathered together an army of about 350 men and set out to conquer Northern Ireland. Within three days the Normans arrived at the town of Downpatrick and captured it by complete surprise. Half starved and cold from the winter weather they pillaged the town, stripping it of everything they could lay their hands on. Ruaidrí Mac Duinn Sléibe (The petty King of Ulaid) assembled a massive native army comprised of wild men from the north and marched towards the Norman position. Few in number, Courcy decided their best option was to meet the Irish in open battle rather than risk a lengthy siege. The two armies clashed together, but the desperate situation of the Normans only made them more determined to gain victory from the jaws of defeat. John de Courcy led by example and was seen lobbing off the heads and arms of the Irish who confronted him. The battle raged on and hung in the balance, until the Normans broke the spirit of the Ulidians who fled the field. Some of the Irish survivors headed for the shore but were swallowed up by the treacherous quicksands. De Courcy succeeded in defeating the northerners in another two battles, but at Ferly he suffered a rare defeat. This time the Irish used the terrain to their advantage and ambushed De Courcy in the narrow pass. Nearly all of his army was annihilated and De Courcy only managed to escape the carnage with 11 knights. The Irish pursued him across the harsh landscape for 30 miles. De Courcy was forced to retreat on foot, hiding and evading the Gaelic trackers sent to capture or kill him. After two days in the wilderness, the remaining Normans reached the safety of a nearby friendly castle. The energetic Norman Baron continued the struggle against the Irish and eventually became the Lord of most of Eastern Ulster. King Roderic O'Connor halted Norman aggression when Miles de Cogan broke the Treaty of

John de Courcy statue, Carrickfergus castle

Windsor and ravaged the region around Thormond. On returning from their raid the Normans were ambushed by the banks of the river Shannon. The wild Irish warriors appeared in great numbers from out of the surrounding woods and forced Milo's men to retreat towards Dublin. Hugh de Lacy met an unfortunate end when he was inspecting the construction of one of his castles. As he stooped down, to check the workmanship, an Irish workman came behind him and looped his head clean off before escaping into the countryside.

Prince John in Ireland

Over the next few years both sides scored victories over one another. In 1185 A.D renewed hope reached the shores of Ireland when it was announced that Prince John was being sent over by his father King Henry II to restore order to Eire.

Dromore Motte and Bailey built by John de Courcy, County Down

Hope soon evaporated when the impetuous 18 year old Prince set foot in Ireland. The Chronicler Gerald of Wales, who was actually in the Royal party at the time, describes what happened.

"John being himself, young and little more than a boy treated the Irish Chieftains with contempt, he and his friends laughed at their Shaggy beards and made fun of them. He rebuffed the good and discreet men, treating them as though they were foreigners of no worth at all."

After a few months in the country John returned home to England a failure. The Irish and the Norman colonists continued their private wars against one another during the last days of Henry II and well into the reign of Richard I "the Lionheart". Richard I was to busy fighting in the Third Crusade and France to be concerned about the situation in Ireland.

Sir William Marshal in Ireland

Sir William Marshal was one of the greatest knights of his age. The victor of over 500 tournaments had faithfully

Arms of William Marshal

served Eleanor De Aquitaine, Henry II and Richard the Lionheart. He fell foul of King John after the loss of Normandy in 1204 A.D when he made a deal with the French King Philip Augustus, securing his lands in France and accepting Philip as his overlord on the continent. William had married Isabelle de Clare (Strongbow's daughter) thus inheriting the title as Earl of Pembroke and Leinster in Ireland. With relations at an all-time low between himself and the King, William decided to visit his vast estates in Ireland. When he arrived, he commenced a massive castle building program. Kilkenny, Carlow, Lea and Ferns were all constructed using the most up-to-date techniques of castle building. Marshal intended to secure his Fief of Leinster from the resurgent Gaelic Irish and also from the Kings henchmen in Eire. William's behaviour towards some of his Irish vassals seems to have been one of disdain. On one occasion he took control and dispossessed two manors that belonged to the Irish Bishop of Ferns. Unable to take back the manors by force, the Bishop excommunicated William. It is said he also laid a curse on the Earl, forecasting that all of William's male heirs would die childless. Curiously all five of his sons did die childless and within a generation only his daughters were left to carry on the Marshal seeds.

Kilkenny Castle built by Sir William Marshal in the early 13th century

In 1210 A.D King John returned to Ireland; after the loss of Normandy to the French. John was determined assert Royal authority over the last remnants of the crumbling Angevin Empire. The country had been a relative safe haven to some of the Kings troublesome barons including William Marshal and William de Broase. De Broase was Lord of Limerick, for which he had promised to pay John a fee of 5000 marks for the privilege. In a personal dispute with the King De Broase fled to Ireland, rumours circulated that De Broase knew the truth about the mysterious death of Arthur de Brittany (King John's nephew).

When the Kings men arrived to take hostages from the De Broase family, Matilda de Broase told them.

> **"I will not deliver my sons to your Lord, King John, for he foully murdered his nepthew Arthur de Brittany"**

John scoured the country looking for the fugitive William de Braose. In Dublin he accused Sir William Marshal of harbouring him, but Marshal challenged the King and offered to fight any man in single combat who called him a liar. Although he was nearly seventy years old, no one from John's entourage took up the challenge for Marshal's fearsome reputation preceded him wherever he went.

King John continued his vindictive reign of terror against the Norman colonists of Ireland. After defying the King's authority, Walter de Lacy was stripped of the County of Meath (including the important castle of Trim). Walter's Brother Hugh retreated to the north hoping to escape the clutches of the King.

In a lightening campaign against the remaining rebels, John outflanked the De Lacy defences in the Mountains of Mourne and launched a seaborne attack against Hugh's castle of Carrickfergus. Hugh de Lacy, Matilda de Broase and her children fled by sea to Scotland before the castle garrison surrendered to the King. Matilda and her children were handed over by the Scots to John who imprisoned them in Windsor castle. According to most of the chroniclers of the time, they were later transferred out of the way to Corfe castle, where they were starved to death.

The ruins of the Norman catle at Carlow

With Ireland submissive John began to reorganise the country. He received many oaths of fealty from the Gaelic Irish who were happy to see the King crush the power of the Norman Marcher lords. The Norman controlled parts of the country were reorganised into Shires just as in England. They included Kildare, Dublin, Meath, Louth, Carlow, Kilkenny, Wexford, Waterford, Cork, Kerry, Limerick and Tipperary. English/Norman law applied to these regions that became known as the "Pale", but in the far reaches of the country the Gaelic tribal system continued to survive. There were two forms of law in Ireland (Brehon/Gaelic and English). The Irish were at a disadvantage because English law only applied to the Norman colonists and to the settlers who lived in the towns of the "Pale". If an Irishman had a complaint against a Norman he had no redress. It was always in the self interest of the Norman Marcher Lords to keep this status–quo in place as they could commit crimes against the Gaelic Irish with little or no consequences. In Ireland John was known as "Good King John" and his campaign in Eire was certainly one of the most successful highlights of his career. The King returned to England in the summer of 1210 A.D leaving John de Grey in charge as Justiciar of Ireland

Tomb of King John, Worcester Cathedral, England

While England was descending into the chaos of the Second Barons war between King Henry III and Simon de Montfort, the free Gaelic Irish clans of Ulster and Connacht formed an alliance to try and force the Normans out of the country. The culmination of the campaign ended at the Battle of Druim Dearg (The Battle of Down) in 1260 A.D. Ironically most of the fighting was conducted between fellow Irishmen. The bulk of the Norman army was made up of mercenaries and Irish clans loyal to their Norman overlords. Irish hopes of a victory were dashed when their leader O'Neil was killed in the fighting. The Normans routed the remainder of the Irish and restored order in the north. During the next 50 years the endless private wars continued. It was not uncommon for the two parties to form alliances with each other to gain advantage over political rivals.

De Bermingham's feast

De Bermingham Arms

Norman notoriety and treachery was commonplace in the Celtic world's they tried to conquer. In Wales the De Broase Marcher Lords were loathed for the acts of treachery they committed against the native Welsh and Ireland was no exception; according to one of the "Kildare poems" the De Bermingham Lord of Tethmoy (Offaly) invited the Gaelic O'Connor clan to his castle at Carrick (near Edenderry) to celebrate the feast of St Trinity. Towards to the end of the night De Bermingham gave the signal to his men to attack his unarmed guests. In an act of unparalleled brutality all 30 of the O'Connors were slaughtered, including De Bermingham's own god-son, who was thrown from the keep into the ditch below. De Bermingham received 100 marks for the heads of the slain from the Norman Justiciar in Dublin.

Carrick castle (Edenderry) scene of the de Bermingham massacre

The pawn of Eire: the De Bruce war

Not for the last time in the country's history, Ireland was used as a pawn on the international chess board. At the end of the 13th century the Anglo-Norman King Edward I of England had decided to impose his rule over all of the Island of Britannia. First to fall was the Celtic Principality of Wales. In two ruthless campaigns Edward destroyed the Welsh, executing the last native Prince of Wales (Dafydd ap Gruffydd) in 1283 A.D. The subjugation of Wales left only the Kingdom of Scotland outside Edward's control. In 1286 A.D King Alexander III of Scotland (Edward's brother in-law) died followed by his heir Margaret "the Maid of Norway". These events plunged Scotland into a crisis of succession. The Scottish nobles asked Edward to act as arbitrator and choose the next King. Edward seized the chance to intervene and over the next 16 years he invaded and conquered Scotland. The legendary Scottish hero William Wallace "Braveheart" was captured and put to death and only Robert de Bruce resisted. In 1307 A.D Edward marched north to destroy De Bruce and finish the conquest of Scotland. However the old Plantagenet leopard died en route and his son Edward of Caernarfon aborted the campaign and returned south to London. By 1314 A.D King Robert de Bruce had reclaimed his Kingdom and defeated the Anglo-Normans at the battle of Bannockburn. Although defeated, he knew the English would return unless he could find a way of distracting their attention away from Scotland. De Bruce decided to use Ireland as a "second front" in his war against the Anglo-Normans. Some of the Gaelic chieftains of Ireland had been in contact with the Scots to try and form a "Celtic alliance" to help drive the Normans out of their homeland once and for all. In the spring of 1315 A.D Robert sent his brother Edward de Bruce and an army of 6000 men to Ireland. Edward landed near Olderfleet (Larne) in Northern Ireland. The Scots were welcomed by some of the local Irish Túatha as liberators. Edward read out a letter from his brother Robert to them;

Arms of Edward de Bruce

"To all the Kings and people of Ireland"

"Our two peoples have been free since ancient times; we share the same national ancestry, common language and custom. We sent over to you our beloved kinsmen to negotiate with you and help strengthen our special friendship. With Gods will, we will be able to recover our ancient liberty"

Together with the O'Neill clan and their subordinates, the O'Kane's, O'Hanlon's, and O'Hagan's the Scottish army set out on the great campaign to rid Ireland of the Normans. They attacked the major Norman settlement of Carrickfergus and defeated the Normans and their Irish allies under the command of Sir Thomas de Manderville. The town was captured, but the mighty castle proved too strong to take by force and remained in Norman hands.

Edward sacked and burnt Rathmore before moving on towards the Moiry pass (the gateway of Ulster). This strategic position was defended by a small force of Normans and Irishmen, although they halted the invaders for a while the sheer number of experienced Scottish troops forced them to abandon the pass and flee towards Dundalk. The De Verdun Norman castle of Castle Roche was destroyed before the Scots advanced on to Dundalk. Most of the local aristocracy gathered in the town and prepared the face the invaders. Scouts returned to the town after spying on the Scottish camp and reported that;

"They are nothing; they're only half a dinner"

Full of foolhardy confidence the garrison marched out of the town to do battle with the Scots. The Norman-Irish troops were completely routed in the fighting outside the town. The fleeing soldiers were chased by the Scots who managed to enter Dundalk before the gates were closed. Once inside the Scottish army went on the rampage, the entire population was put to the sword. The Scots wasted the surrounding area and committed a terrible atrocity at Ardee. The town was ransacked and the inhabitants were rounded up, locked in the Church and murdered when De Bruce's men set fire to it. The smell of death lingered in the air for days, but the shock waves galvanised the Norman Marcher Lords and the Justiciar (Edmund Butler) into action. Roger de Mortimer remained at Trim with the Norman rearguard while Richard de Burgh (the Earl of Ulster, called "the Red Earl") joined up with the Justiciar's forces near Inniskeen.

The de Verdun castle of Castle Roche (Louth)

They intended to give battle but De Bruce retreated north towards the safety of the O'Neill lands. After ravaging the town of Coleraine they destroyed the bridge over the river Bann, attempting the halt the Norman army who were closing in on them. Edward's plan worked, unable to ford the river the Normans hesitated on what to do next. The Red Earl retired to Antrim and the Justiciars force unable to remain in the field due to lack of provisions retreated back to Dublin. De Bruce used the age old tactic of double dealing to break down the fragile unity between the Red Earl and his Irish vassals. Edward offered Felim O'Connor, the Connacht region if he defected and joined the "Celtic alliance". He then gave military support to the O'Connor's rival Ruari Cathel if he too defected and joined him. Cathel left the Earl's camp and returned to Connacht and proclaimed himself King. O'Connor also left to counter the threat from Cathel and Connacht descended into civil war. With the Earls army vastly reduced, Edward decided to attack. In September the Battle of Connoyr was fought between the two armies near Ballymena. The Earl's men were either unaware of the presence of the Scottish army or were simply caught off guard, before they had time to organise their battle formation. The Scots had defeated the Anglo-Normans in such circumstances before at Stirling Bridge and Bannockburn. The Red Earl escaped the field but his brother William and many of the Norman Lords were captured by the victorious Scots.

Edward de Bruce headed south and at Kells, (County Meath) he fought another battle against the Normans under Roger de Mortimer. The Scots managed to set fire to the town causing panic amongst Mortimer's men. The outcome of the battle was decided when according to the annals of St Mary's church, Dublin;

"In the third hour, the De Lacy's turned their shields and fled"

Roger de Mortimer fought on but with his army disintegrating around him, he abandoned the field and fought a fighting withdrawal through the burning streets of Kells, just avoiding capture by the Scots.

The defeat caused general panic in Ireland with more of the Gaelic Túatha switching sides and joining De Bruce's "Celtic alliance".

The Last High King of Ireland

The first year of the campaign had been a total victory for Edward de Bruce. His reputation was so high that he had enough support from the Irish chieftains to be offered the title "High King of Ireland". In May 1316 A.D at Knocknemelan hill (near Dundalk) Edward was proclaimed King. Within a year Norman rule in Ireland had all but been wiped out. Only a few castles remained in Norman hands, but the "Grey foreigners" refused to give in. The "Red Earl" joined up with the forces of Richard de Clare and swore he would capture Edward de Bruce dead or alive. Roger de Mortimer was busy in England collecting men and material to take revenge on the Scots. The problem Edward de Bruce faced was that to keep his army in the field he needed vast resources of food and supplies. To sustain itself the Scottish army devastated the land and stripped the countryside of the meagre food that was available. This behaviour as well as the "Great Famine" of 1315-1317 A.D caused

Ardee Castle (Louth)

terrible suffering on the Irish who began to waver in their support for De Bruce. The campaign started well when De Bruce beat the Justiciar's men at Ardscull (the Battle of Skerries), but it was a shallow victory for the Scots suffered heavy casualties in the battle. The situation deteriorated when Edward's ally Felim O'Connor was slain by the Norman forces of the "Red Earl" at Athenry. In the pitched battle the leopard banner of Felim was trampled into the mud as the Normans knights of Richard de Bermingham hacked the rebel Prince to pieces. The great stronghold of Carrickfergus which had held out for over a year fell in September 1316 A.D. Legend says that the defenders has become so staved that they resorted to cannibalism before the castle surrendered.

Carrickfergus castle, besieged by the Scots 1315 - 1316 A.D

In early 1317 A.D Edward was joined by his brother King Robert de Bruce of Scotland. Robert hoped that with his personal presence they would be able to destroy the Normans in Ireland once and for all. Together the brothers marched on the Royal centre of power in Ireland; Dublin. When they reached the capital, the Dubliners burnt down the suburbs of the city, denying the Scots any material to make shelter or build siege machines. Unable to take Dublin by force the Scots decided on a campaign of terror against the Irish. They pillaged every village in their wake, hoping to force the undecided Irish to join them or face annihilation. In the spring Roger de Mortimer returned from England with troops and also a letter from the King of England (Edward II). The letter was a last chance by the Normans to gain Irish support by overturning the old laws of discrimination between the two communities. English law was to be introduced for all in Ireland. The terror tactic of the De Bruce brothers had failed, and with the arrival of the Mortimer troops in the south the Scots retreated north. The Normans did not follow De Bruce north; instead they pacified Southern and Central Ireland before readying themselves for the final showdown with Edward de Bruce and the Scots.

In the West, the Norman forces of Richard de Clare were battling the O'Brian Gaelic Irish for the control of the ancient independent Kingdom of Thomond (Brian Buro's heartland). The Normans ventured outside the "Pale" in three columns but were ambushed and annihilated at the battle of Dysert O'Dea (County Clare). Both Richard and his son Thomas were slain in the battle. When the panic stricken survivors reached the Norman castle of Bunratty De Clare's wife ordered both the castle and town to be burnt down to stop it from falling into enemy hands. Thomond was never captured by the Normans and remained outside English control until the 16th century.

14th century medieval Irish tomb effigy

The final reckoning; the Battle of Faughart

Although events in County Clare caused concern to the Norman Government in Dublin it did not distract them from prosecuting the war against De Bruce. Roger de Mortimer was recalled to England, but he assigned his deputies Edmund Butler and John de Bermingham with the task of finishing the campaign against De Bruce. King Robert returned to Scotland to raise more troops, but Edward instead of waiting for the reinforcements decided to confront the Normans, who were advancing towards Dundalk. Against the advice of his Irish allies and most of his captains De Bruce formed up his army into three divisions on the rising ground at Faughart near Dundalk. On the 14th of October 1318 A.D the Norman army arrived on the field. On seeing the great distance between the Scottish divisions De Bermingham took the initiative and attacked the Scottish vanguard, before the Scottish centre had time to come to the rescue. Although the Scottish schiltron formations formed an impregnable wall against the Norman shock cavalry, they were extremely vulnerable to the Anglo-Norman longbowmen. The archers let loose volley after volley of arrows into the dense Scottish formations, inflicting heavy loses upon them. Weakened by the archers, gaps started to appear in the Scottish ranks. De Bermingham's knights charged in, cutting down the Scottish Gall-oglach warriors and lightly armoured Irish kerns. Heavily outnumbered and too far apart from one another, the Scottish divisions were annihilated by the Normans who surrounded the remaining groups of warriors and slaughtered them to the last man. Apparently before the battle King Edward de Bruce had given his coat of arms to his squire, Gilbert Harper to avoid being a target of the Normans. The ruse did not work as both master and servant were cut down by an Anglo-Irish Knight (John de Maupas) from Drogheda. Spotting the King's standard, Maupas charged in and cut through the ranks of the royal household. He killed both Edward de Bruce and Gilbert Harper before being slain by De Bruce's personal bodyguard. The death of the last "High King of Ireland" (Edward de Bruce)

Overleaf: The death of King Edward De Bruce at the Battle of Faughart 1318 AD →

ended the battle. Now leaderless the remnants of the Scottish invasion force retreated north and returned to Scotland. The Irish showed little sorrow for the death of De Bruce. Three years of bloody warfare had caused great suffering to the whole of Eire.

The Annals of Loch Cé reported:

"No better deed was performed since the beginning of the world, than the slaying of Edward Bruce. The destroyer of all of Eire, in general both English and Irish. For in this Bruce's time, for three years, falsehood, famine and murder filled the country, and all men were destroyed in Ireland."

The end of the conquest and the Gaelic resurgence

The De Bruce war signalled the end of the Norman conquest of Ireland. By the mid 14th century many of the major Norman nobility in Ireland were "absentee landlords". They saw their fiefs in Ireland only as a source of revenue and were not interested in the day to day running of the baronies/Earldoms. The Normans themselves were becoming Irish. In order to survive and hold on to their lands in a hostile country they had little choice but to marry into the Irish aristocracy and adopt Gaelic dress and customs. The petty wars continued between Irish, Norman and fellow Irish, hindering any form of unity. In 1329 John de Bermingham (the victorious Norman commander at the Battle of Faughart) was lured into a trap by the Savages and Gernons and mercilessly slain in cold blood. Three communities developed in Ireland, in the west and fringes of the country were the independent Gaelic Kingdoms, the Normans controlled the east known as the "Pale" and between the two was the Irish Marches (the borderlands) whose nobility were a mixture of Gaelic and Norman, with their own laws and customs similar to that of Wales.

King Richard II of England

The continued resurgence of the Gaelic Irish and loyalty of the ancestors of the original Norman conquerors worried the English government so much so that in 1367 A.D they introduced the statues of Kilkenny. The Statues decreed that in the "land of peace" ("the Pale" / Norman/English controlled shires) the Irish language was banned, intermarrying and the wearing of Irish cloths were forbidden, and the employment of Irish bards was not allowed. In effect it was an apatite system designed to relegate everything Irish to second class status. Even today in many Irish towns and cities there are many areas still called "English town and Irish town" symbolising the forced segregation between the two peoples.

King Richard II

The Statues of Kilkenny had little effect outside Dublin and the Gaelic resurgence continued. By 1384 A.D King Richard II of England decided to embark on a campaign in Ireland to restore order, just as King Henry II and King John had done before him. The King arrived and spent Christmas in Dublin castle where nearly every Gaelic King and Anglo-Irish noble came before him and paid homage. Had he addressed the discrimination of the statues of Kilkenny, Ireland may well have entered into the fold of English domination more comfortably. Instead as soon as he left in the spring of 1395 A.D Eire descended into the customary anarchy.

The King left Roger de Mortimer (the heir presumptive) in charge. He was given the title of Lord Lieutenant of Ireland along with his heraldic title, the Earl of Ulster, but Roger seems to have been fallen under the spell of the Celtic charm. After three years in Ireland he had adopted Irish dress which led to his murder in 1398. On the 20th of July 1398 A.D the Anglo-Normans forces of Mortimer met the O'Brien's and O'Toole's in the battle of Kenlis (near Carlow).

The Wigmore Chronicler stated that:

"On the banks on the "King's river" Roger at the head of his army, unattended and wearing Irish dress was slain. Those who struck him down did not realise who they had killed".

Norman warrior carving, Kilfane Church

When the news reached England, Richard II decided to return to Ireland and punish the rebels once and for all. In June 1399 the King landed at Waterford, and then moved on to secure Kilkenny. Faced with the might of the Anglo-Norman army the Irish under the command of Art Mór Mac Murchadha Caomhánach retreated into the bogs and inhospitable terrain of County Carlow. The King unable to bring them to battle returned to England, where he lost his crown and life to the usurper of Henry Bolingbroke (later King Henry IV). The conquest of Celtic Ireland proved to be a bridge too far for the Normans. There were many reasons why they were not able to fully complete the conquest. The Power balance created by King Henry II curtailed the ambitions of the land hungry Norman Marcher Lords and the war of Edward Bruce devastated Ireland economically and also politically. Perhaps the greatest reason was the Irish themselves, after the initial shock of the invasion the Gaelic Irish adapted their tactics, only fighting the Normans where their superior arms and armour could not be used to their advantage. By the 15th century the Normans had assimilated into the Anglo-Irish, but colonial domination from England would cast a shadow over Eire for over 750 years until Ireland became a Republic in 1949.

Chapter 7: **Scotland**

INTO THE LION'S DEN

The Norman infiltration of Scotland

In 1072 A.D William the Conqueror (King of England / Duke of Normandy) and the Norman war machine invaded Scotland and forced the Scottish King Malcolm III to sign the Treaty of Abernethy. In the Treaty, Malcolm acknowledged William as his overlord and the Kingdom of Scotland became a vassal state of the Norman Kings of England. Over the next 200 years the Normans infiltrated Scotland. The final showdown took place at the end of the 13th century when the nation-breaking Anglo-Norman King Edward I "Longshanks" entered the Lion's den to do battle with the Scottish heroes William Wallace "Braveheart" and Robert de Bruce.

SCOTLAND 84 -1066 AD

In 84 A.D the Celtic peoples of modern day Scotland united for the first time to fight a foreign invader, the Romans. After 40 years since the invasion by the Emperor Claudius, the Roman Legions had pacified most of the Southern half of the Island of Britannia. Only the wild mountainous region of Caledonia lay outside the Roman world. Julius Agricola (the Roman governor of Britain) had been given the task of completing the conquest and subduing the northern tribes once and for all. After seven years of hard campaigning Agricola was able to bring the Caledonians to battle in the Highlands of Scotland.

Mons Graupius 84 A.D

Roman Legions (Trajan's Column)

The Celtic war leader Calgacus had united the Caledonian tribes and gathered thirty thousand men to fight the Roman invaders. Somewhere between Inverness and Aberdeen, the Caledonians took up a defensive position at Mons Graupius. At the edge of the known world the Celtic Caledonian army of wild painted men and war chariots squared up against the most efficient war machine the world had ever seen, the Roman Legions. Although heavily outnumbered, Agricola ordered his auxiliary troops to attack the Caledonian lines. Once the Romans had scattered the Celtic chariots and cavalry, the tightly packed auxiliary infantry squadrons begin the close combat and vicious hand to hand fighting. At close quarters the Caledonians were no match for the disciplined Roman soldiers who began to inflict devastating casualties upon them. Instead of staying on the slope, Calgacus ordered the whole Caledonian army down the hill to try and encircle the Romans.

Agricola seeing the danger sent in his auxiliary cavalry units to attack the Caledonian flanks. . By nightfall the Caledonian army had been slaughtered. Over ten thousand "Picti" (the Roman word for the Caledonians, meaning painted men) lay dead on the battlefield. By contrast Agricola had only lost a few hundred men and had not even had to use his crack Roman legionary troops which he held in reserve.

With the Caledonians destroyed, Caledonia/Scotland could have been brought into the Roman Empire, but a jealous Emperor (Domitian) recalled Agricola and abandoned the subjugation of Caledonia. By the 2nd century A.D Roman rule in Northern Britain was under pressure from the resurgent Celtic Brigantes and Caledonians. The legend of the Ninth Legion "Hispania" who marched into Scotland and was wiped out may not be far from the truth. A Roman chronicler in the 3rd century wrote that:

"The Britons could not be kept under Roman control".

Reinforcements were sent to Britain and when the Emperor Hadrian visited the Province in 122 A.D he ordered the construction of a massive defensive wall to be erected to keep the Caledonians out of the Roman Britain. Subsequent Emperors invaded Caledonia in campaigns to contain the threat from the Picti. The Emperor Antoninius Pius built a new wall between the Firth of Forth and the Firth of Clyde, but after 20 years of occupation the Romans withdrew south to Hadrian's Wall. The Wall marked the border between the two worlds until the collapse of the Roman Empire in the 5th century A.D.

Hadrian's wall, the border between the Roman world and Caledonia

Dark Age Scotland

The Picts ruled most of modern day Scotland until the arrival of the Gaels from Ireland known as "Scoti" settled in the in Western Isles and Argyll. This new Celtic colony became known as the Dalriada (Dál Riata). Dark Age Scotland was divided up into several Kingdoms. Pictland consisted of most of the mainland north of the river Forth. To the south lay Strathclyde, Bernicia and in the west Dalriada, Galloway and Cumbria. Like most of the British Isles and Europe, Scotland was attacked by the Vikings. In 794 A.D the Norsemen raided the island monastery of Iona in the Hebrides. By the mid 9th century they had started to colonise the Orkney and Shetland Isles, the Hebrides, the Isle of Man and even some parts of the Scottish mainland. In 839 A.D the Vikings defeated the armies of the Scottish Kingdoms of Dalriata (Dál Riata) and the Picts. This defeat led to the rise of Scotland's first King. Kenneth MacAlpin is regarded as the founder of the medieval Kingdom of modern day Scotland. He brought about the uneasy unification of the Picts and Celtic Scots of Dál Riata and stopped the Vikings from taking over the entire country. In order to rule his newly founded Kingdom of Scotia, Kenneth made Dunkeld in Perthshire his royal headquarters. Some of the holy relics of St Colombia were transferred from Iona to Dunkeld to avoid them being stolen by the pagan Viking raiders. The "Stone of Destiny" which is an ancient coronation stone first used by the Celtic Gaels of Dál Riata was placed in the now ruined abbey of Scone where it was used to crown Scottish Kings until it was taken to England by the Anglo-Norman King Edward I "Longshanks" in the 13th century.

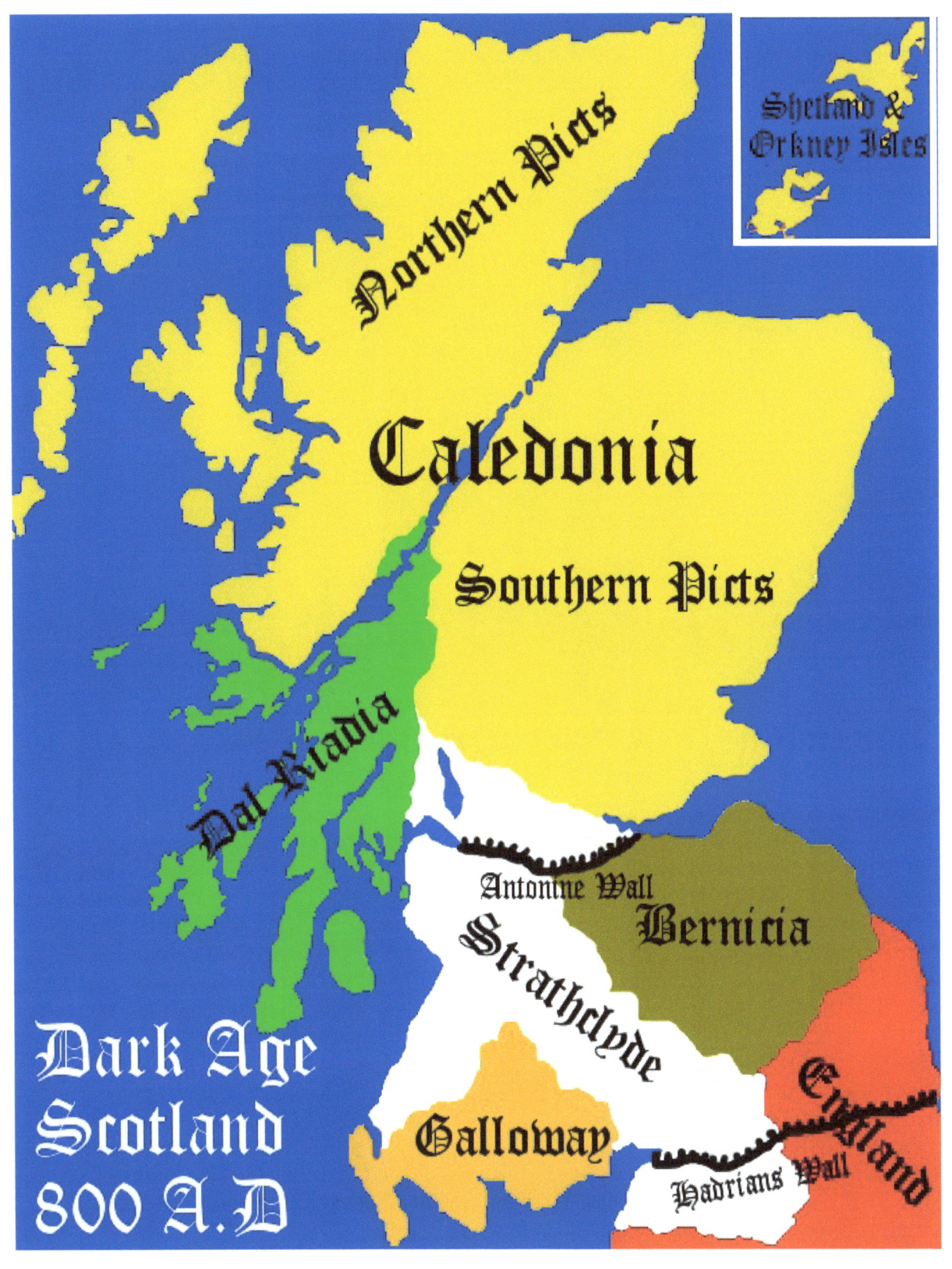

Kenneth MacAlpin's successors had to fight against ever increasing pressure from the Vikings who were now intent on a campaign of full scale invasion and settlement of the British Isles. In 870 the impregnable fortress of Dumbarton Rock (Strathclyde) fell to the Norse invaders after a lengthy siege.

Dumbarton Rock (West Dunbartonshire, Scotland)

Seven years later King Constantine I (Kenneth's son) was also killed by the Vikings. In 915 A.D Domnall (King of Strathclyde) died, King Constantine II intervened in the succession and supported the claim of Áed. Constantine II compelled Áed to recognise Scotland as the overlord Kingdom, thus bringing Strathclyde into his Kingdom as a vassal state. Constantine's growing empire then began to threaten Anglo-Saxon England to the south. King Athelstan of England had reconquered Northern England from the Vikings and in 927 A.D King Constantine II along with Owen of Strathclyde and Hywel Dda of Wales submitted to Athelstan, acknowledging him as overlord of all of Britain. In 934 A.D Athelstan invaded Scotland as far north as Aberdeen to punish Constantine's recent unfriendly behaviour towards his southern neighbour. The ravaging of his country by the Anglo-Saxons only encouraged Constantine to enter into a Celtic-Norse alliance against Athelstan. At Brunanburgh, the combined armies of Scotland, Strathclyde and the Viking King of Dublin were utterly defeated by Athelstan's Anglo-Saxons. The battle was remembered in England as "The Great Battle", but for Constantine it was a catastrophic defeat, for he also lost his son who was cut down in the melee. The old King abdicated the throne of Scotland in 942 A.D and retired to the monastery of St Andrews leaving his nephew Malcolm I as his successor. Over the next 100 years the Kingdom of Scotland suffered further Viking attacks and civil wars but remained intact until a cold October morning changed the fate of the British Isles.

1066 A.D "The Year of Destiny"

Although King Malcolm III "Canmore" of Scotland had given refuge to Tostig (the former Earl of Northumbria and also Harold Godwinson's brother), he did not directly support the ill-fated Viking invasion of England by King Harald Hardrada of Norway and Tostig in 1066 A.D. Harold Godwinson's victory over the Vikings and English rebels at Stamford Bridge near York was short lived for on October 14th 1066 A.D he too was killed fighting against a second invasion from Duke William of Normandy at the Battle of Hastings. Malcolm watched events unfold in England as the Normans systematically dismantled the Anglo-Saxon Kingdom with brutal force. In 1068 A.D important refugees from England arrived at the Scottish court seeking asylum. Edgar the Atheling (the heir to the House of Wessex), and his close family were taken in by Malcolm and given support to use Scotland as a base to attack Norman controlled England. Edgar invaded Northern England several times to stir up rebellion but unsuccessfully failed to unseat the Normans from power.

The Norman invasion 1072 A.D

After putting down the last sparks of resistance in the "Harrying of the North" campaign, William the Conqueror turned his attention towards Scotland. In 1072 he launched a major military campaign to bring Malcolm III to his knees. The Normans crossed the border and pillaged Southern and Central Scotland, burning down the villages and settlements in their wake. The lightning speed of the Norman attack compelled Malcolm to sign the Treaty of Abernethy, where he recognised William as his Overlord. For security in honouring the terms of the Treaty William required Malcolm to exile Edgar the Atheling and also hand over his son Duncan as a hostage. According to the Anglo-Saxon Chronicle;

"Malcolm became William's man"

Duncan the Norman-Scot and the disputed border

Prince Duncan was treated well by William the Conqueror and the Norman aristocracy. Slowly he became familiar with the Norman culture and even participated in some of the Conqueror's military campaigns on the continent. When William died in 1087 A.D, Robert Curthose (William's son and the new Duke of Normandy) released Duncan from the obligations of the Treaty of Abernethy. Duncan instead of returning to Scotland left Normandy and resided at the court of William II "Rufus".

Newcastle castle built by Robert Curthose in 1080 A.D

In 1080 A.D King Malcolm III raided Northumbria taking advantage of local disturbances in the Northern Province. William the Conqueror sent his son Robert Curthose north to stabilise the frontier and construct a castle on the banks of the river Tyne. This settlement became the great border city of Newcastle. The Kings of Scotland firmly believed that the Northern counties of England including

Northumberland and Cumberland were theirs by right and in 1091 A.D Malcolm III marshaled his army and invaded Northumberland. Edgar the Atheling negotiated a truce between William Rufus and Malcolm III, where the latter again acknowledged the over-lordship of the Norman King. Malcolm III came south to visit William's court at Gloucester in the summer of 1093 A.D to discuss the Normanisation of the Northern counties. William had recently fortified Carlisle which in theory was part of Cumbria/Cumberland belonging to the Kingdom of Scotland. William refused to negotiate and Malcolm returned frustrated to Scotland intent on retaking the North of England. According to the chronicler Simeon de Durham in the bleak winter of 1093 A.D the Scottish army invaded Northern England, east of the Cheviot Hills. Near Alnwick by the river Alne, at a place now called Malcolm's well, the Scottish invasion force was surprised and attacked by a smaller force of Norman knights under the command of Robert de Mowbray (the Earl of Northumbria). In the confrontation Malcolm and his son Edward were killed by the Normans in the melee. The death of the Scottish King plunged Scotland into civil war. Donald Bane (Malcolm's brother claimed the throne and forced Malcolm's sons Edgar, Alexander and David into exile in England.

Carlisle castle built by King William II "Rufus" in 1092 A.D

King Duncan II, Donald III Bane and Edgar

In England Prince Duncan gained Norman support and with the help of King William "Rufus" he invaded Scotland with an army of Norman mercenaries and Northumbrians. The invasion succeeded and Donald Bane was forced to flee. Duncan was crowned King Duncan II, but within six months he too was killed at the Battle of Mondyne in Aberdeenshire trying to eliminate resistance to his rule. Scotland was slipping into anarchy with supporters from the Gaelic North supporting Donald Bane and the pro-Norman South supporting the surviving sons of Malcolm III in England. Donald Bane resumed power but the Normans were already plotting his downfall south of the border. In 1097 A.D Edgar (Malcolm III son) invaded Scotland with Norman troops under the command of Edgar the Ætheling and defeated King Donald Bane in battle. The Scottish chronicler John of Fordun wrote that Edgar captured his uncle and to prevent him from causing any more trouble Donald was;

"Blinded, and sent to prison for the rest of his life"

For the next 10 years Edgar ruled Scotland without any major threat to topple him from power. In 1098 A.D he was forced to surrender some of the North-Western Isles to the Viking King Magnus Barefoot of Norway.

These Islands were already under Norse influence and without any realistic chance of being able to re-take the Islands Edgar handed over sovereignty. In 1107 Edgar died and was buried in the Abbey of Dunfermline. He was succeeded by his two brothers Alexander I and David I.

King Alexander I and David I

In accordance with the wishes of Edgar, Alexander was crowned King of Scotland and David was given the title "Prince of the Cumbrians". In effect David was given the old Kingdom of Strathclyde and Southern Scotland to rule in his brother's name. The situation worked well and relations with the new Norman King of England Henry I "Beauclerc" were strengthened when Alexander I joined Henry on campaign in Wales against Gruffudd, Prince of Gwynedd. Alexander led one of the King's detachments and fought bravely in the campaign which ended when Gruffudd was forced to surrender and pay homage to Henry.

Alexander I earned the nickname "the fierce" after putting down a rebellion by the men from Moray and Mearns in Northern Scotland. He

Copy of a 19th seal of King Alexander I of Scotland, he bears the arms and armour of a classic Norman knight

also introduced the Norman style Chancellor and sheriff / Baillie offices into the country. In the spring of 1124 A.D after 17 years on the throne Alexander I died at Stirling in central Scotland, the crown passed the David I   David had spent most of his childhood in England during the reign of his uncle Donald Bane. The chronicler William of Malmesbury stated that David had become fully Normanised during his years in England and Normandy;

"David had rubbed off all the tarnish of Scottish barbarity during his time and friendship with us"

He married the daughter of the Old Saxon Earl of Huntington (Waltheof), thus gaining land and title south of the border in Norman England. The family connections with England did not stop there as David's sister Matilda was the wife of King Henry I "Beauclerc".
This situation helped David become King of Scotland on his brother's death in 1124 A.D. The early years of David's reign were fraught with revolt and rebellion from his distant family and rebels who believed that the King was too pro-Norman.
It was during these years that many minor noble Norman knights came north and settled in Scotland. One such family was the De Brus (Bruce) who originated from a small village called Brix in the (La Manche) dept of Lower Normandy. The De Bruce's increased their land and power over the next 200 years. In 1135 King Henry I "Beauclerc" died, leaving his daughter (the Empress Matilda) as heir to the Anglo-Norman Empire. After the King's death some of the nobility backed the claim of Stephen De Blois who usurped the throne and declared himself King. The situation created a civil war in which David I declared for his niece Matilda and invaded Northern England on the pretext of her behalf.

In a devastating campaign David with the forces loyal to the Empress Matilda took the border castles of Carlisle, Alnwick, Norham, Wark and Newcastle. King Stephen marched north with the English Fryd and an army of Flemish mercenaries but instead of a pitched battle he offered concessions to David and the Scots. In return for the cessation of hostilities and the return of some of the border castles, Stephen granted David the great border fortress of Carlisle and re-granted the Earldom of Huntingdon to David's son Henry. The Scottish King refused to pay Homage to Stephen as he had already given his oath of fealty to Matilda. Instead his son Henry was sent in his place to concrete the Treaty of Durham. Prince Henry fought with Stephen at the siege of Ludlow and was saved by the King who cut off a grappling hook attached to Henry's armour in an attempt by the garrison to capture the Prince. It was a total victory for David who had gained

King David I investing a knight

Carlisle and also received the promise if the old Earldom of Northumbria were to be revived it would be given to his son Henry. Stephen had in effect given the far reaches of Northern England to David without a fight.

The Chronicler Gervase de Canterbury wrote of Stephen;

"The King started many endeavours with vigour, but brought few to a praiseworthy end"

The Battle of the Standard / Northallerton 1138 A.D

In early 1138 A.D David reneged on the Treaty of Durham and invaded England again, this time advancing further south into Yorkshire.
The Chronicler Richard d'Hexham wrote that;

"The Scottish army was savager than any race of heathens, yielding honour to neither God or man. They harried the province and slaughtered all the folk of either sex, of every age and condition, destroying, pillaging and burning the villages, churches and houses"

While the main Scottish army laid siege to Norham castle and ravaged the North, a contingent under the command of William Fitz Duncan (King Duncan II son) raided Lancashire, resulting in the Battle of Clithroe. King Stephen's forces were utterly defeated causing panic amongst the nobles of Northern England. The Normans were rallied by the 70 year old Archbishop of York (Thurstan de Bayeux). They gathered their forces in York and marched north to meet the Scots who had now entered "the land of St Cuthbert". At the head of the army, the Normans pulled along a strange wagon with a ship's mast mounted on it carrying the banners of St Cuthbert, St Peter, St Wilfred and St John. This seems to be the first time such a wagon was used in Britain and the idea may have been implemented by Thurstan who had seen similar masts used as battle rallying points in Italy.

Robert de Brus (Bruce) and Bernard de Bailliol who held lands in both England and Scotland were sent to King David as emissaries to try and urge the Scottish King to turn back. Their pleas fell on deaf ears as King David I overconfident from the victory at Clithroe continued his march south towards the capital of Northern England, York. Just outside Northallerton the road to the south was blocked by the Normans who formed up into battle array.

According to the English monk Aelred of Rievaulx one of the Norman commanders Walter Espec gave his troops a rousing speech before the battle was joined;

"Great nobles of England, Normans by birth, remember who you are, and against whom you fight, for then no one shall resist your prowess. Bold France has quacked beneath your valour, fierce England, led captive, has submitted to you; rich Apulia, on having you for her masters, has flourished once again; Jerusalem so famed, and great Antioch have bowed themselves before you; and now Scotland, which by right is a subject to you, attempts to show resistance, These people have no knowledge of military matters, no skill in fighting, no moderation in ruling. There is no room then left for fear, but rather for shame, that those whom we have always sought on their own soil and overcome have come flocking into our country."

In the early morning of the 22nd of August 1138 A.D the Scottish army formed up into battle formation. David intended to use his knights and armoured troops against the Norman men-at-arms but the Galwegians insisted they have the honour of leading the charge against the enemy. David against his better judgment relented and let them lead the army into battle.
Out of the mist charged the men from Galloway "the Galwegians" they considered themselves the finest troops in Scotland. Aelred of Rievaulx described these warriors as;

"The Galwegians were agile men, unclothed and remarkable for their baldness; armed with knives formidable to any armed men, having a hand most skillful at throwing spears and directing them from a great distance; raising their long lance as a standard when they advance into battle"

The wild warriors of South-Western Scotland shouted terrible war cries as they smashed into the Norman front line. It was pure carnage as the Galwegians thrust their 12 foot long spears at the dismounted Norman knights and spearmen. They fought with great courage and briefly broke through the Norman ranks, but their lack of armour and discipline exposed them to the deadly fire of arrows from the Norman archers. When the Galwegian commander was hit in the face and killed by a Norman arrow, his men started to panic and retreat. They had been so badly decimated by the Norman archery that one chronicler wrote that the dead Galwegians looked like hedgehogs bristling all over with arrows.

At the same time as the Galwegians were in full retreat Prince Henry (David's son) broke through the Norman lines and attacked the baggage train. The Normans quickly filled

Coat of arms of King Stephen

the gap and Prince Henry without any support was forced to flee the field to avoid capture.

King David watched in horror as his army disintegrated around him. The King tried to act as a rallying point and took off his helmet to show his men he was still alive, but it did not stop his panic stricken soldiers from abandoning the battlefield. David stood firm hoping to save the day but his close companions forced him to mount his horse and retreat before he was captured by the advancing Normans.

After 3 hours of bloody combat the battle was over. The Scottish are said to have lost as many as 10,000 men in the confrontation and although this figure seems exaggerated, they suffered heavy casualties compared to the Normans. It could have been much higher, but as most of the Norman knights and men-at-arms fought on foot they could not follow up their victory by launching a mounted assault on the fleeing Scots. King David retreated to Carlisle to regroup and although he had lost the battle in the second Treaty of Durham, he effectively won the war. Prince Henry was given the Earldom of Northumberland and the lordship of Doncaster. David retained Cumberland and expanded the Kingdom of Scotland to its greatest extent. For the next 20 years while England was torn apart by the civil war between Matilda and Stephen the Northern counties of England prospered under the control of King David.

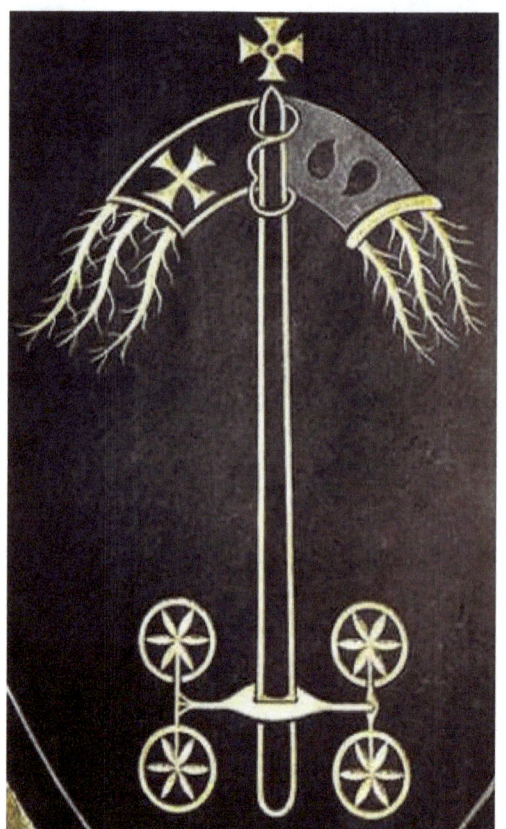

Battle of the Standard memorial stone

In 1152 Prince Henry (David's son) died. It was a terrible blow for the King who named his grandson Malcolm IV as his successor and heir. Within a year the old warrior King David also died, closely followed by King Stephen in 1154 A.D

The loss of the Northern Counties

Malcolm IV was only 11 years old when he was crowned King of Scots in 1154 A.D. The death of King Stephen signalled a new era south of the border in Norman England. Matilda's son Henry Plantagenet became King of England as well as Duke of Normandy, Aquitaine, Count of Anjou, Touraine and Overload of Brittany, Wales and more importantly for our story Scotland. With most of Western France under his control he was the most powerful monarch in Europe. In 1157 Malcolm travelled to England to pay homage to the King, Henry is reported to have said;

"The King of England should not be deprived of a greater part of his Kingdom"

Referring to the Northern counties lost to the Scots in the disastrous reign of King Stephen and the civil war. It was made clear to Malcolm that unless he handed over the Northern counties, Henry would invade and crush Scotland.

With little choice left open to him Malcolm returned Northumbria which was a fief under control of his brother William, and Cumbria which he had ruled over himself from the sandstone castle of Carlisle. Relations with Henry improved and Malcolm even joined the King on campaign in 1159 A.D against the Count of Toulouse in South-Western France where he was knighted by the King. The rest of Malcolm's reign was filled with minor rebellions from his subjects who thought he was too pro-Norman.

William I "the lion"

Coat of arms of King William the Lion

When King Malcolm IV died in 1165 A.D from natural causes the crown passed to his brother William I nicknamed "the lion" because of the lion he bore on his coat of arms and shield. William acknowledged Henry as his feudal overlord but petitioned the King to return Northumbria and the Northern counties to Scotland. Henry refused and William bided his time until a chance arose in 1174 A.D. In 1173 A.D Henry faced rebellion from his own family "the Devils Brood". The revolt quickly spread and included some of the great magnates of the Angevin Empire, supported by the King of France. William "the lion" believing that Henry would be toppled from power took his chance and invaded Northern England. His forces fell upon Newcastle, but the great border town and castle was too strongly fortified to be taken by direct assault. William returned back to Scotland to prepare for a second invasion in 1174 A.D. With his army strengthened with fresh troops and mercenaries from Flanders William crossed the border and attacked the frontier castles of Prudroe, Warkworth and Alnwick. The Scottish King besieged Alnwick while his army split up to raid the countryside and reduce the last remaining Norman castles. The Norman nobility gathered in Newcastle and decided to bring fire and sword to the Scottish invaders. William of Newburgh tells us that the Normans were purely cavalry as there was no time to muster the infantry foot soldiers. Commanded by Ralph de Glanville they arrived at Alnwick and spotted the Scottish King with a bodyguard of only 60 knights. As de Glanville and his knights came into view through the early morning fog, William leapt onto his horse and led a foolhardy charge. He shouted to his men;

"Now let us see who knows how to be a soldier"

The King charged straight into the fray with reckless courage. Within minutes he had his horse killed from under him and was quickly overwhelmed and captured along with his close retainers.
The prisoners were taken back to Newcastle and then on to Richmond Castle. When the Scottish army heard the dreadful news from Alnwick they abandoned the campaign and retreated back to Scotland. King Henry rejoiced at the victory and ordered William to be brought over to Normandy. On the 8th of December in the great Norman castle of Falaise William signed the humiliating Treaty of Falaise. The terms of the treaty were harsh; not only did Scotland become a feudal possession of the English King but William also lost the Earldom of Huntingdon (later returned) and was forced to hand over the Scottish castles of Edinburgh, Berwick, Roxborough, Jedburgh and Stirling.

Henry sent Norman troops to garrison these important strongholds to ensure William did not renege on the treaty and cause him any more trouble. William was allowed to return to his Kingdom but he was a broken man and virtually nothing was heard from him until 1189 A.D.

Alnwick castle, scene of the second battle of Alnwick 1174 A.D

William's luck changed in 1189 A.D when Henry died and Richard I "Coeur de Lion" came to the throne in England. Richard was desperate to raise money for "the Third Crusade" (the Holy war to re-capture Jerusalem back from the Saracens). He offered William the release from the conditions of the Treaty of Falaise for 10,000 marks of silver. In late 1189 A.D William signed the "Quit Claim of Canterbury" thus regaining Scottish independence from the Normans. The death of the Lionheart (Richard I of England) caused a crisis of succession in the Angevin Empire. William took advantage of the situation and raided the Anglo-Scottish frontier destroying the castle of Tweedmouth just south of Edinburgh. In 1200 A.D William paid homage to King John at Lincoln but again demanded the return of Northumberland and Cumbria. John, who was at the height of his power refused and William returned empty handed back to Scotland. By 1209 A.D the once mighty Angevin Empire had been reduced to Poitou and the Duchy of Aquitaine in France. John had lost Normandy and Anjou to the French King Philip Augustus and was determined to impose his authority on Norman control in the British Isles, (Wales, Ireland and independent Scotland). He invaded Scotland with a huge army that even included Llywelyn the Great (Prince of Gwynedd), Wales. Faced with the wrath of John's army William decided to negotiate rather than risk a pitched battle. At the Treaty of Norham John agreed not to rebuild Tweedmouth castle but William had to pay the Norman King 10/15,000 marks and hand over two of his daughters as hostages for his good behaviour.

In 1212 A.D Williams son Alexander travelled south to Norman England and was knighted by King John who supported Alexander's claim to the Scottish throne when William "the lion" died.

Most of Alexander II reign was filled with campaigns against internal revolts and rebellions from his own subjects. Indeed it must be remembered that large parts of Scotland were virtually independent from Royal rule during this period. In 1215 A.D Alexander joined the rebel barons of England in their struggle against King John. He crossed the border and ravaged the land but in the following year John took revenge on the "little red fox cub" (John's nickname for Alexander) and burnt Berwick-upon-Tweed to the ground. The Normans advanced up to Dunbar and pillaged most of lowland Scotland.

The monk Ralph of Coggeshall commented on John's soldiers;

"They made great slaughter and destruction, everywhere they went".

Alexander supported the French invasion of England by Prince Louis (the son of King Philip Augustus) hoping that the latter would grant him the disputed Northern counties. All Alexander's hopes came to nothing when King John died and the rebel Barons were either defeated or reconciled with the forces loyal to the boy King Henry III. The relationship with Norman England became reconciled when Alexander married Henry III sister Joan in 1221 A.D. By 1237 A.D Alexander abandoned his claims to the Northern counties at the Treaty of York. The modern-day border was drawn up and Alexander was given land and title in Northern England to be held in the name of the King (Henry III).

Statue of King Alexader III
St Giles, Edinburgh Cathedral

Alexander III and the Battle of Largs

In July 1249 A.D Alexander II died and his son Alexander III was crowned King of Scotland at Scone using the "Stone of Destiny". Relations continued to improve when Alexander married Margaret (the daughter of Henry III) in 1251 A.D. The ceremony took place in the great Norman Cathedral of York Minster. Henry attempted to persuade the young King to pay homage to him for Scotland but Alexander refused to be drawn on the issue. Instead of digging up the old issue of the Northern counties with Norman England, Alexander turned his attention towards regaining the Western Isles which had been lost to the Vikings during the previous centuries. Alexander's father had extended Royal power and authority into the Highlands, Galloway and Argyll. By 1262 A.D Alexander was ready to finish his fathers work. On hearing reports of Scottish attacks and attempts to conquer the Western Isles, the Norwegian King Hakon Hakonarsen decided to launch a pre-emptive strike against Scotland and put Alexander III firmly back in his place. King Hakon called upon the resources of his vast Scandinavian Empire which included Norway, Iceland, and Greenland, the Northern Isles of Shetland, Orkney and Faeroe. In 1263 A.D he embarked from

Norway with a fleet of over 200 ships and 20,000 men. After securing the Western Isles Hakon's fleet sailed into the Firth of Clyde. The Norwegian King sent sixty ships under the command of Dugal (the Viking ruler of the Isle of Man) into Loch Lomond to raid and pillage the region.

The Icelandic chronicles records that;

"The Norwegians burned all the buildings and wasted the land around the Lake" (Loch Lomond)

Faced with a mighty Viking army on his doorstep, Alexander opened negotiations hoping to buy time and raise his own army. Scotland's unpredictable weather played a part when on the 30th of September Atlantic storms battered the Viking fleet. Some of the Norse long ships ran aground and were beached at Larg's on the north Ayrshire coast. The Scots attacked the stranded Norwegian crews and King Hakon was forced into

Arms of King King Hakon Hakonarsen

sending reinforcements to stabilise the situation. The local Scottish militia pillaged some of the supplies and retreated under the cover of darkness. The next morning King Hakon arrived on the beach to supervise the salvage operation. In the meantime the Scottish had mustered a considerable force of 500 mounted knights and a substantial body of archers and infantry foot soldiers under the command of the Stewart of Scotland. They immediately advanced towards the Norwegian position on the high ground above the beach. The Norse commander on the mound Ogmund Krokidans made a tactical decision to abandon the hill and join the main Norwegian force on the beach rather than risk being cut off and surrounded by the larger Scottish force. The Norwegian ordered withdrawal from the mound turned into a rout as the Scottish vanguard attacked the retreating soldiers.

"The Pencil tower" built to commemorate the Battle of Largs

King Hakon, who was with the main force on the beach, was advised to return to the safety of his ship. Before long the Norwegians were in full retreat, fleeing towards their ships. The Norse commanders managed to rally them on the edge on the beach against the incoming waves before all was lost. Re-galvanised, they defended the beachhead, fighting around the makeshift barricades of the beached dragon head ships. One Scottish knight called Ferashled, led a reckless charge straight into the ranks of the Norse army. He was killed by a huge Viking battleaxe in his thigh, which cut deep through his armour, leg and into his saddle. The Norwegians stripped him of his Gold painted helmet, gem studded armour and belt. It was a small victory but did nothing to change the outcome of the battle. By nightfall both armies broke off the engagement. On the morning of the 3rd of October the Norse landed in force at Largs to collect their dead. Although neither side had won or lost the battle, it was too late in the season for King Hakon to continue the campaign. After sending raiding parties to pillage Lenox, he returned to the Western Isles and then onto Orkney to prepare for his next campaign against the Scots. It was not to be and during the cold winter of 1263 A.D King Hakon died from illness. By 1266 A.D hostilities ended when King Magnus VI of Norway and King Alexander III signed the Treaty of Perth. Magnus sold the Western Isles and the Isle of Man to Alexander for 4000 marks and a payment of 100 marks a year. In return Alexander acknowledged Norse sovereignty over the Northern Isles of Shetland and Orkney. The treaty was concreted when Alexander's daughter Margaret married Prince Eric (Magnus VI son).

King Edward I of England and Alexander III

In 1256 A.D Prince Edward travelled north to visit his sister Margaret and brother in law King Alexander III. Edward and his wife Eleanor enjoyed their state visit to Scotland and insisted that the Scottish King and Queen return with them to be entertained by the Anglo-Norman court in England. When the Baron's war broke out between Henry III and Simon de Montfort, Alexander supported the Royalist cause and even sent Scottish troops to fight alongside King Henry III and Prince Edward at the battle of Evesham.

In 1269 A.D Prince Edward set out on Crusade and many nobles from Scotland including members of the de Bruce and Bailliol families joined his retinue. After gaining experience in the holy land Edward returned to England. Whilst on the island of Sicily news reached him that his father Henry III had died. Alexander and Margaret attended Edward's coronation at Westminster in 1274 A.D.

The oath of homage seems to have been avoided as Edward was more concerned about the refusal of Llywelyn ap Gruffudd (the Prince of Wales) to attend his inauguration. Tragedy struck Alexander in 1275 A.D when his beloved wife Margaret died. Edward sent letters of condolence to his brother in law as a sign of mutual friendship and respect. Alexander watched events unfold as Edward brought down the full weight of Norman power and strength against Llywelyn and Wales in his devastating campaign of 1277. Llywelyn was quickly defeated and humiliated by Edward who had him brought to Westminster to perform the act of homage. Alexander was also obliged to perform the oath but only for his lands/fiefs in England. He is reported to have said;

> **"No one has a right to homage for my Kingdom of Scotland, save God himself, and I hold it only of God alone"**

Further bad luck hit the Scottish King when all his children died; David died in 1281 and was followed by Margaret in 1283 and Alexander in the following year. It was a hammer blow to the King who quickly remarried a young French Princess called

King Edward I "Longshanks"

Yolande De Dreux in 1285 A.D. to try and continue his line of succession. On a stormy night in March 1286 A.D, after attending the council of nobles at Edinburgh castle Alexander decided to return to his young wife in the evening. In atrocious weather conditions Alexander became separated from his close companions. In the darkness his horse stumbled and the King fell down a rocky embankment. When his attendants found him he was already dead, from a broken neck. Alexander's death left his three year old granddaughter Margaret "the maid of Norway" as the sole heir to the Scottish throne. Scotland was ruled over by a council of nobles until Margaret was old enough to be brought over from Norway. In 1289 A.D the guardians of Scotland, ambassadors from Norway and King Edward gathered in Salisbury to discuss the situation in Scotland. All parties agreed that Margaret would marry Edward's son (Edward of Caernafon). The guardians of Scotland returned north and summoned all the Scottish nobility to Bingham in Berwickshire. There they ratified the treaty and voted in favour of the union between the two Kingdoms under the strict understanding that Scotland would keep its current independence from Norman England. In the autumn of 1290 A.D Margaret set sail from Norway, but during the voyage she became ill and when the ship reached Orkney, the young Princess was dead. The Royal house of Dunkeld/Canmore was extinguished.

The First Interregnum and King John Bailliol

The question of who would be the next King was wide open with many nobles putting forward their claim. Unable to decide between themselves the Scottish nobility invited King Edward of England to assess the validity of the claimants and help choose the next King. In 1291 A.D Edward summoned the leading Scottish nobles to a meeting at Norham. Edward had purposely arranged for the meeting to take place on English soil and was slowly turning up the pressure on the Scots. On and off negotiations took place, but by June Edward had the Scots where he wanted them. The choice was simple, Scotland either faced immediate civil war in which the country would be ruined or accept Edward's terms which were extremely high handed. Edward would judge all the claimants and decide who would be the next King on the condition that the Scots acknowledge him as overlord. 104 auditors were appointed to assess the evidence from the major claimants which included Robert de Bruce, John Comyn and John Bailliol.

King John Bailliol

In November 1292 A.D a decision was reached, the Scottish auditors chose John Bailliol and submitted their findings to King Edward. Edward agreed hoping that John would be his man in Scotland and become a puppet-King for him. Edward had probably decided to subdue Scotland by 1292 A.D. The reasons for this may have been fourfold. Firstly after the death of Alexander and Margaret "the Maid of Norway" all family links had been effectively cut with the Northern Kingdom. In 1290 A.D Edward's wife Eleanor died and the King became less tolerant, bitter and dark in character. By 1291 A.D Edward's dream of returning to the Holy-land on Crusade evaporated when the last great Crusader State of Acre fell to the Muslims. And finally since the subjugation of Wales in 1283 A.D, Edward had a chance to unify the whole of the island of Britain under his sole rule.

With King John installed in Scotland Edward resumed his plan to re-conquer the Holy-land from the Muslims, but events in France forced the King to postpone the idea. A violent spat between French and Anglo-Gascon sailors developed into an international row between Edward and the French King Philip IV. Philip wanted Aquitaine (England's last province in France) and had duped Edward into handing over the Duchy in 1294 A.D with the promise that it would be immediately returned. The French King reneged on the deal and war was declared between the two countries. Edward had been undermining King John's position in Scotland and the final straw came when he demanded feudal service from John and the leading Scottish nobles to fight in France. King John refused and sent ambassadors to France to form an alliance against King Edward. The friendship pact became known as the "Auld Alliance". In 1296 A.D the Scots crossed the border and attacked Carlisle and Hexham. Some Scottish nobles including Robert de Bruce did not participate in the raid and remained loyal to Edward. King John had underestimated the resolve and capacity of King Edward's Anglo-Norman England. Longshanks was not a man to be crossed and he mustered the feudal nobility of England and marched north to destroy the Kingdom of Scotland.

Berwick to Dunbar 1296 A.D

In the spring of 1296 A.D the Anglo-Norman army advanced into Scotland and headed for the important Scottish port of Berwick. On the 29th of March Edward's army arrived outside Berwick and demanded its immediate surrender. The townsfolk full of foolhardy confidence shouted insults towards the English King and even showed their buttocks as a sign of defiance. As Edward arranged his army into battle formation, the fleet that was blockading the bay of the town launched an un-ordered pre-emptive attack on the port. Three ships ran aground and were attacked and burned by the Scottish garrison. When Edward saw the smoke rising into the air from the burning vessels he ordered an immediate assault on the town. The Anglo-Norman soldiers overrun and forced their way through the wooden palisade. Once into Berwick, they went on the rampage sacking the houses and murdering the inhabitants. Some of the town's Flemish merchants put up fierce resistance in a building called the "Red hall". Unable to gain access, the Anglo-Normans set fire to the building killing all inside.

One chronicler wrote that;

"The King's anger was like that of a Wild boar pursued by dogs. The people of Berwick fell like autumn leaves from a tree".

By nightfall Berwick was reduced to a burnt out shell of smouldering rumble. Thousands of men women and children lay dead in the streets. Only the castle held out but upon asking for terms from King Edward, Sir William Douglas surrendered the Keep. Edward's massacre of Berwick was an example to all other Scotsmen and women of what would happen to them if they defied his rule. After a few weeks of strengthening the garrison of Berwick Edward received word from King John who renounced his oath of fealty and homage. Edward sent John de Warenne (the Earl of Surrey) to besiege the castle of Dunbar. King John had mobilised the feudal host of Scotland and advanced on Dunbar to relieve the siege. On the 27th of April the Scottish army arrived and took up position on the high ground at Dunbar. As de Warenne's men crossed "Spots burn" the Scottish soldiers and knights charged down the slope. Inexperienced and undisciplined they were no match for the battle hardened veterans of Edward's Welsh wars.

Within a short time the battle turned into a slaughter with many Scottish nobles taken prisoner. The survivors fled in the direction of the Ettrick forest totally demoralised.

The subjugation of Scotland

With the destruction of the Scottish army at Dunbar, Edward consolidated his position by receiving the surrender of Roxburgh and Jedburgh before moving north to complete the subjugation of Scotland. Edinburgh surrendered and by the time Edward's army reached Stirling castle the garrison had already fled. King John, a fugitive in his own country was hunted down like a common criminal. In early July he was captured and brought to Edward where he was publicly humiliated. In front of the King and the Anglo-Norman commanders he had the Royal coat of arms torn from his surcoat/tunic. This is where he earned the nickname "Tuyme tabard" (meaning empty coat). With his enemies either in captivity or dead Edward set about the final phase of the campaign. Robert the Bruce hoped that he would be made the new King of Scotland but Edward is reported to have told him;

"Do you think we have nothing better to do than win Kingdoms for you?"

Scotland was to cease to be a Kingdom; Edward planned to reduce it to the status like that of Wales, a province of the English King. The Royal Scottish records, the Black rod relic and the stone of destiny were confiscated and taken south to London. Edward had a coronation chair constructed around the stone of destiny where it was used to crown the Kings and Queens of England until it was returned in 1996. Edward travelled south to Berwick and summoned the nobility of Scotland to swear allegiance to him and sign a document known as the "Ragman Roll". Within less than six months Scotland had been conquered and subjugated. Edward returned to England master of the British Isles, Celtic Wales, Ireland and now Scotland were now firmly under his iron rule. He is reported to have said about Scotland;

"Bon besoigne fait qy de merde delivrer "
("He who rids himself of shit does a good job").

William Wallace "Braveheart" and the Battle of Stirling Bridge

As soon as Edward left Scotland to prosecute the war with France over the Duchy of Aquitaine trouble started north of the border. Robert Wishart (the Bishop of Glasgow) and Andrew Murray were stirring up rebellion. Then in May 1297 a virtually unknown Scotsman by the name of William Wallace rose in revolt and murdered William Heselrig (the Anglo-Norman sheriff of Lanark). The Scottish writer "Blind Harry" wrote in the 15th century that Wallace rebelled because the Sheriff had cruelly murdered his wife in cold blood. Whatever the truth may be Wallace became a focal point for the rebellion in

William Wallace statue, Edinburgh castle

Southern Scotland. From the relative safe haven of the Selkirk/Ettrick forest Wallace's growing army struck terror into the hearts of the Anglo-Norman garrisons throughout Southern and Central Scotland. By August they crossed the river Forth and joined forces with Murray and the northern rebels. Further panic was caused when Wallace launched a bold raid on Scone, where he nearly captured William Ormsby (the Anglo-Norman Justiciar of Scotland). When Edward heard the news from Scotland he sent Sir Henry Percy and Robert Clifford north to restore order. In the summer of 1297 A.D the Scottish nobles including Robert de Bruce and Bishop Wishart fearing another Dunbar capitulated at Irivine to the Anglo-Norman force. The debacle at Irvine discredited the nobility and reinforced Wallace's position as leader of the rebellion. With Anglo-Norman control over Scotland disintegrating day by day Hugh de Cressingham (Edward's Treasurer in Scotland) sent urgent letters to England requesting help before all was lost. John de Warenne was dispatched north to put down the Scottish rebellion with 300 armoured knights and nearly 10,000 infantry. With the rebels in the north, Warenne headed for the gateway to Northern Scotland, Stirling. The town and castle of Stirling had a very important strategic position in medieval Scotland for it was one of the only places to cross the river Forth. When de Warenne arrived at Stirling the Scottish army of Wallace and Murray were already waiting for them on the other side of the banks of the river Forth. Most of the Scottish army was concealed in the woods of Abbey Craig waiting for the order to attack. De Warenne sent some local monks to parley with the Scots but they were sent back with the message from Wallace;

"Go back and tell them we have not come for the benefit of peace, we are prepared to fight and ready to free Scotland"

On the 11th of September Wallace and Murray left the Abbey Craig and formed up into battle array. De Warenne overconfident decided to cross the wooden bridge and give battle. Richard de Lundie, a Scottish knight (in De Warenne's army) objected as the bridge was only wide enough to carry two men at a time. Instead he offered to lead an outflanking column upstream and ford the river where it was wide enough to cross in force. De Lundie was overruled and Hugh de Cressingham led the vanguard across the bridge. As soon as the last of the vanguard reached the other side Wallace took the initiative and ordered the Scottish schiltrons (spearmen) to charge straight at the Anglo-Normans with their 12 foot long pikes. The Anglo-Norman vanguard was caught completely off guard by the attack, and any sort of organisation quickly evaporated when the Scots came crashing into their ranks. The Welsh infantry and archers bore the full brunt of the Scottish attack and were forced to flee towards the riverbank. Wallace's troops gained control of the bridgehead and cut off de Cressingham's men from any further help. The vanguard was pushed back into the loop of the river bend and slaughtered by the merciless Scots. De Cressingham was pulled from his horse and hacked to pieces by Wallace's men in a brutal manner. Marmaduke de Thweng (an Anglo-Norman knight from Yorkshire) galvanised the last few knights on the field and forced his way through the Scottish ranks towards the bridge. After saving a young relative he made it to the other side before the slaughter was complete. In complete shock and with panic running rife through the ranks of his army de Warenne ordered the bridge to be destroyed hoping to stop the Scots from following up their victory. The battle had cost the lives of the constable of Strirling castle, De Cressingham (the Treasurer of Scotland) and some 2000/3000 men.

Wallace celebrated the great victory by having the corpse of the hated De Cressingham flayed. Pieces of his skin were distributed amongst his men and according to the Lanercost Chronicle Wallace had a sword belt made out of the rest of his skin.

"William Wallace had a strip of his skin taken from his head to toe and made a baldrick for his sword"

Although only part of the Anglo-Norman army had been beaten, De Warenne panicked and instead of blocking off access to Southern Scotland he fled a hastily retreat first to Berwick and then on into England to report the disastrous news. A mere month after the battle Wallace and Murray wrote a letter to the merchant town of Lübeck (Germany) exclaiming that Scotland was free from oppressive Anglo-Norman domination and Scottish ports were open for business. Shortly afterwards in November Andrew Murray died from wounds received at the battle of Stirling. This left William Wallace as the sole commander of the rebellion. After retaking some of the last outposts of Anglo-Norman control in Scotland, Wallace decided the take the war to Edward and invaded Northern England. The destructive raid devastated Northumbria and Cumbria and earned Wallace a brutal reputation in England as a savage barbarian. Wallace returned back to Scotland and was knighted and made "Guardian of the realm of Scotland in the name of the absent King John". It was the crowning moment for Wallace, who within a year had risen from being regarded as a common thief to the protector of the free Kingdom of Scotland.

The Hammer of the Scots

King Edward had not been idle during the winter of 1297 A.D. After months of campaigning in Flanders he was able to secure a truce with the French King, allowing him time to turn his attention towards crushing the Scottish revolt. Edward returned to England in March to take personal command to the campaign. Troops were raised from all the counties of England, as well as soldiers from Wales and contingents from Gascony (Aquitaine) and Flanders. This was the biggest army to invade Scotland since the days of the Romans. Edward made York his capital and took with him the ancient banners of St Cuthbert and St John used by the Normans at the Battle of the Standard (Northallerton). In June the King marched north with some 20,000 men including virtually the entire Anglo-Norman nobility of England. As the Royal army entered Scotland, the Scots withdrew destroying the provisions, hoping to halt the advancing Anglo-Normans by using "a scorched earth policy". Edward's men cut a path of destruction right through Southern and Central Scotland. The castles of Dalhousie, Tantallon and Dirleton were captured and all the nearby settlements were burned to the ground. Wallace was nowhere to be found and disaster nearly struck Edward's army when a fight broke out between the Welsh and English soldiers. The Welsh got drunk from wine brought in from a supply ship and started brawling with their English counterparts. Edward had to send in his armoured knights to break up the disturbance, killing some 80 Welshmen. Rumours spread that the Welsh were planning to desert and join the Scots but Edward reacted with the comment;

"Let them join together for we shall destroy them both in a day"

The Battle of Falkirk 22 July 1298 A.D

Then on the 21st July the situation changed, Edward's scouts located Wallace and the Scottish army nearby at Falkirk. Wallace had been shadowing the King's army, hoping that when their supplies became low he could attack/ambush them on their return to England. His strategy had nearly worked, but Edward took the initiative and headed for the final showdown at Falkirk. During the night of the 21 of July Edward's army made camp at Linlithgow only a few miles away from Falkirk. The army was on full alert in case Wallace tried to launch a night time raid. Walter de Guisborough tells us that the Anglo-Norman soldiers and knights slept with their arms and armour, using their shields as makeshift pillows and blankets. The King's horse kicked him in the night causing minor confusion in the Royal camp. As morning broke Wallace's own spies brought the terrifying news that the King's army was marching on the Scottish positions. With no possibility to escape, Wallace formed up his army into four "Schiltron spearmen divisions", with the Scots archers between the formations and cavalry to the rear. The King urged caution, but his nobles eager to gain fame and glory persuaded him to let them take the field and engage the Scots. Wallace watched the chivalry of England commanded by the Earls of Lincoln, Hereford, Surrey, the Bishop of Durham, the Earl Marshall and the King himself charge towards his position.

Wallace shouted out to his men;

> **"I have brought you here; now let us see if you can dance"**

The charge of the armoured knights was halted by the boggy ground of the Westquarter Burn in front of Wallace's position. Instead the Knights were forced to wheel round and attack the Scottish flanks. They steamrollered over and routed the Scottish cavalry and archers. When the knights turned their attention to Wallace's "Schiltons" it was another story. The Scottish spearmen stood firm and posed an impregnable wall against the Anglo-Norman cavalry. After some reckless young knights were killed whilst trying to break through the Schiltron formation, Edward ordered his knights to break off the engagement and reform their ranks. The King had valuable knowledge from his wars in Wales of how to beat such stubborn resistance. In 1295 A.D the Earl of Warwick had beaten Welsh spearman and infantry at the Battle of Maes Moydog by using combined cavalry and archer tactics. Edward now used this tactic on a grand scale. He unleashed his secret weapon, the deadly longbow. The Welsh and English archers let loose volley after volley of deadly arrows into the Scottish Schiltrons. It was pure carnage as hundreds fell into the mud, dying in agony. Even the English infantry joined in, throwing stones into the Scottish ranks. As gaps started to appear, the Anglo-Norman knights charged in, finishing off the brave spearmen who refused to yield. One chronicler wrote that the Scots; "fell like ripen fruit from the trees in an orchard". Wallace and a lucky few managed to flee the slaughter and reach the safety of the Callander forest. By the end of the day the Scottish army had been completely annihilated. Edward had avenged the defeat of the Battle of Stirling Bridge, but the war was far from over. The reason why Falkirk was not the decisive battle of the war was because Wallace and most of the Scottish nobility still remained at large and free to stir up rebellion. Wallace's credibility had been badly damaged at Falkirk and shortly afterwards he resigned as guardian of Scotland. Robert de Bruce and John Comyn took up the role as joint protectors of the country and continued the struggle against King Edward and the Anglo-Normans. In 1299 A.D William Wallace travelled to France to seek French help in the war against King Edward I. Meanwhile Edward continued his ruthless subjugation of Scotland. In 1300 A.D Edward crossed into Scotland with an army of over 10,000 men. His objective was to pacify Southern Scotland before moved north over the river Forth. After a few days into the campaign the fortress of Caerlaverock fell and the King managed to bring the Scottish nobles to battle near Wigtown.

Hopelessly outnumbered, the Scots were again beaten and fled into the wilderness. From 1300-1304 A.D the war continued, French and Papal support put pressure on Edward and gave hope to the Scots, but by the end of 1304 A.D the subjugation of Scotland was nearly complete. France and the Pope abandoned their promises to the Scots, and Scotland was on her own. Even Robert de Bruce had changed sides and was fighting in the Anglo-Norman army. Only the patriot William Wallace refused to submit and continued to defy Longshanks.

The end of William Wallace

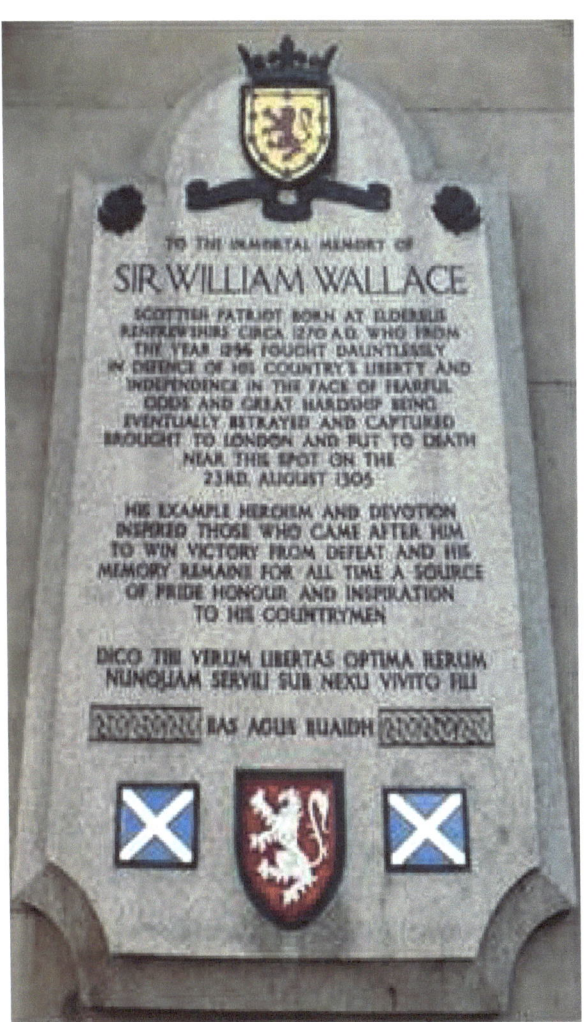

William Wallace plaque, London

In 1304 A.D Edward placed John de Brittany (the Earl of Richmond) as Lieutenant Governor of Scotland. His main priority was to capture William Wallace, now a shadowy bogeyman figure who continued to wage his campaign of terror against the Anglo-Normans. Wallace could not be bought off with land or title and for him there was no compromise, only a "free Scotland". On the 3rd of August 1305 A.D Wallace was captured near Glasgow by a fellow Scotsman (Sir John Menteith) who became nicknamed "false Menteith" for the traitorous act. Wallace was imprisoned in Dunbarton castle before being taken south to London to face the wrath of the King. During the showcase trial Wallace was accused of being a traitor, to whom he responded that he had never sworn allegiance to King Edward I in the first place. He was found guilty and sentenced to death. Wallace was dragged naked 4 miles through the streets of London tied to the back of an ox cart, where the people jeered and hurled abuse at him. When he arrived at Smithfield, he faced a cruel and horrible death. The executioners hanged him by the neck, then he was drawn, emasculated and had his bowels burnt before his very eyes before finally being quartered. His head was placed on London Bridge where some 20 years earlier the heads of Llwelyn and Daffydd (the last Princes of Wales) had once stood. The rest of his body parts were sent to Newcastle, Berwick, Perth and Stirling to serve as a warning to the fate of any more would be traitors.

The rise of Robert de Bruce

After the death of William Wallace one man decided to fight for his nation's freedom, he was Robert de Bruce. On the 10th of February 1306 A.D Robert de Bruce met with John Comyn (the two previous Guardians of Scotland and also political rivals) in the church of Dumfries. The

Robert De Bruce "King of Scots"

conversation between the two men developed into an argument and Robert de Bruce drew a dagger and stabbed John Comyn in cold blood. As Comyn lay dying in a pool of blood he was quickly finished off by De Bruce's followers. After meeting with the Bishop of Glasgow (Robert Wishart) and being absolved of his crime, De Bruce quickly travelled to Scone Abbey and proclaimed himself "King of Scotland". Edward was furious with rage; he dispatched Aymer de Valence north to bring de Bruce in dead or alive.

The Battle of Merthven

Aymer de Valence advanced into Scotland and joined forces with the Comyn's at Perth. De Bruce arrived and offered to do battle with the Anglo-Normans and their Scottish allies. Fearing a trap, Aymer declined and garrisoned his men behind the castle walls of Perth. Unable to take the castle by force Robert left and made camp nearby at Methven. Then on the 19th of June, Aymer de Valence made a daring dawn raid on the Scottish camp. The Norman cavalry thundered out of the mist burning down the tents and hacking down all in their way. Robert de Bruce managed to escape and flee with a few companions to Argyll. At a place called Dalrigh (meaning the King's field) near Tyndrum in Central Scotland De Bruce was forced to fight yet another battle against the MacDougall clan who were loyal to Edward I and the Comyn's. Outnumbered and still demoralised from the Battle of Methven, De Bruce suffered another defeat, but again managed to escape and flee into the wilderness. The unfortunate rebel prisoners who were captured in these two

Arms of Aymer de Valence

battles were sent to England where they were publicly executed. By the end of 1306 A.D the Scottish revolt had all but been crushed. The Anglo-Normans captured De Bruce's Queen Elisabeth, his daughter, his sisters and his brother Neil. Edward's treatment of the De Bruce family signaled a ruthless side of his temperament. Mary and Isabella (De Bruce's sisters) were imprisoned in specially constructed steel cages, hung up high in the castles of Berwick and Roxburgh. Neil de Bruce was taken to Berwick where he suffered a similar fate to that of William Wallace (Hung, drawn and quartered). Robert de Bruce remained at large and probably sought refuge in the Western Isles during the winter of 1306 A.D. This is where the popular legend of Robert De Bruce and the spider came from. According to legend, Robert hid in a cave on Rathlin Island where he saw a spider weaving a web. The rain from the cave roof broke the web time and time again, but the spider continued to weave until he succeeded in building his web. With such encouragement and determination Robert returned to the mainland early in 1307 A.D. The campaign started off badly when two more of Robert's brothers fell into the hands of Edward's men. Thomas and Alexander de Bruce were taken to Carlisle, where they were executed. Their heads were placed above the town gates facing towards Scotland.

The first victory, Loudoun Hill

Aymer de Valence marched into Ayrshire to capture "King Hobbe" the English nickname for Robert De Bruce. At Loudoun Hill De Bruce lured the Anglo-Normans into attacking him on a pre-prepared battle site. As the Normans knights advanced towards the Scottish position, they became funnelled and charged straight onto the Scottish spears. De Valence escaped the carnage, but the shock defeat caused the aged King Edward I "Longshanks" now 68 years old to raise an army and march north. The King was determined to destroy De Bruce once and for all, but on the 6th of July 1307 A.D at Burgh-by-Sands near the Scottish border he fell ill and died. Before "the hammer of the Scots" died he encouraged his son Edward of Caernarfon to continue the campaign and bring De Bruce to heel. His pleas fell on deaf ears as Edward II had none of his father's attributes. He disbanded the army and returned south to London leaving Robert de Bruce's rebellion to grow. By 1314 A.D the English suffered a catastrophic defeat at the Battle of Bannockburn; Robert de Bruce was the undisputed master of Scotland. After nearly 20 years of bloody warfare Scotland was free from Anglo-Norman aggression for the time being, until the reign of Edward III.

The Norman infiltration of Scotland by the De Bruce's, Bailliol's and other families helped the Canmore Kings forge a Kingdom that was regarded by Norman England as an equal sovereign nation. The Normans helped shape the identity of Scotland, expelling the Vikings from the Western Isles in the 13th century and finally securing independence from the Plantagenet Kings of England in the 14th century. From a Norman point of view they had succeeded in Scotland, for in 1306 A.D (recognised in 1328 A.D) their candidate Robert de Bruce became King of Scotland. As the 14th century dawned the age of Norman conquest and expansion was coming to an end. Their last conquest, almost forgotten by history would take them to the very edge of the known world. In 1402 A.D Norman adventurer's set sail on an epic journey to conquer the mystical volcanic Islands of the Canaries in the Atlantic Ocean.

Statue of King Robert De Bruce, Bannockburn battlefield

Chapter 8: The Canary Islands

The Forgotten Conquest
Jean de Béthencourt and the Norman Conquest of the Canary Islands

At the beginning of the 15th century Norman adventurers under the command of Sir Jean de Béthencourt and Gadifer de la Salle set sail on an epic journey to conquer the mystical volcanic islands of the Canaries at the very edge of the known world. Their conquest would secure a strategic base for the Spanish exploration and conquest of the New World (the Americas).

Norman origins: Jean de Béthencourt

The Béthencourt's come from a small village called Grainville-la-Teinturiére in the Seine Maritime (76) department of upper Normandy. The name "Grainville" like many towns and villages in Normandy is probably Viking in origin meaning "Grim's ville / domain. Grim may have been one of the followers of Hrolf / Rollo the Walker, the Viking warlord who created the Duchy of Normandy at the Treaty of St Clair sur Epte in 911 A.D. The Vikings assimilated into the Frankish majority and became "the Normans". Grainville is first mentioned in 1060 A.D during the reign of William the Conqueror (Duke of Normandy and later King of England). A simple wooden Motte and Bailey castle dominated the village, later replaced by a stone fortification in the 12/13th century.

The 100 years War; Normandy

Jean de Béthencourt was born in 1362 A.D during one of the most turbulent periods of French history "The Hundred year's war with England. The descendants of William the Conqueror "the Anglo-Norman Kings of England" had never forgotten the humiliating loss of Normandy by King John to the French King Philip Augustus in 1204 A.D. When the French King Charles IV died in 1328 A.D leaving only an infant daughter as heir to the Kingdom, the French nobility changed the rules of succession. They introduced the "Salic law" barring female heirs and their children from inheriting the crown. This decision frustrated Edward III of England, who had a right to the French crown through his mother Isabella de France (sister of Charles IV). This along with French pressure on trying to annex English controlled Gascony (Aquitaine) and interfering in Scotland and Flanders led to open warfare by 1340 A.D. Edward III assumed the title King of France and defeated the French fleet at the Battle of Sluys.

The motte of the old castle at Grainville-la-Teinturiére, replaced by a dovceote in the 1800s.

In July 1346 A.D Edward III invaded Normandy with an army of over 10,000 professional soldiers. The invasion force landed at St-Vaast la Hogue in the Contentin (Lower Normandy) and captured the port after brief resistance from the local militia. The English ravaged the region, cutting a vast swath of devastation on their march towards the great Norman city of Caen. Carentan, Saint Lo, Togini and Bayeux were amongst some of the towns sacked and burnt to the ground. When Edward's men arrived at Caen they attacked the city from several directions. Division within the French garrison allowed the English to first take the old-town and then gain access to the new town.

The Castle of Caen: Normandy, France

Once inside the English and Welsh soldiers went on the rampage and massacred the population. As dusk descended, Caen was a burnt out shell of its former glory. Edward III rode through the burning rubble of the city and entered the Cathedral of the Abbaye aux Hommes where he paid homage to the grave of his ancestor William the Conqueror. After resting a few days, Edward advanced up the Seine valley in the direction of Paris. The Norman capital of Rouen was too well defended to be taken by direct assault, but the English contented themselves by ravaging Central and Eastern Normandy from Lesiux to the great border town of Vernon. At the gates of Paris itself Edward tricked the French into thinking he was going to give battle before crossing the Seine and heading north to join his Flemish Allies. At the small village of Crécy in Northern France the French finally caught up with Edward's army. In the ensuing battle the French knights were utterly annihilated by Edward's secret weapon "the longbow". Ten years later Edward's son (the Black Prince) scored a great victory at Poitiers, where he destroyed the French army and captured the King of France (John II, Le Bon). By 1360 the English had gained the upper hand and at the Treaty of Brétigny they succeeded in gaining an enlarged Aquitaine and the end of the service of homage to the Kings of France.

In 1364 A.D Jean de Béthencourt's father (Jean III) was killed at the battle of Cocherel fighting for the French forces loyal to the new King of France Charles V. Jean de Béthencourt was only two years old when he inherited his father's Fief of Grainville-la-Teinturière under the orders of the legendary French commander Bertrand du Guesclin.

Tomb of Edward "The black Prince" Canterbury Cathedral

Sir Jean de Béthencourt

In war torn France the loyalties of the nobility changed with the wind and when Jean's grandmother Ysabeau de Saint Martin and her second husband, Mathieu de Braquemont threw in their lot with the rebel King of Navarre (Charles the Bad) they invoked the wrath of the King. Charles V sent his troops to ravage the De Braquemont and Béthencourt lands. Jean's family seat at Grainville-la-Teinturière was attacked and the castle of Grainville was destroyed. At the age of fifteen Jean entered the service of the King's brother, the Duke of Anjou. After many years of loyal service to the Duke, Jean gained promotion and joined the retinue as the Chamberlain to one of the new King's brothers, Louis de Valois (the future Duke of Orléans). Jean's rise to power enabled him to rebuild the castle at Grainville-la-Teinturière in 1387 A.D and also purchase a hotel in the Beaubourg area of Paris.

Arms of Louis II de Bourbon

The Barbary Crusade 1390 A.D

In the spring of 1389 A.D a truce between England and France was agreed. This rest bite allowed King Charles VI of France to launch a major military operation against the Barbary pirates of North Africa. Ambassadors from the Italian state of Genoa arrived at the court of King Charles and proposed a joint Crusade to capture the Barbary port of Mahdia (Tunisia). The Genoese had captured the island of Jerba in 1388 A.D and were eager to capture a port on the North African mainland, hoping to destroy the power to the Barbary pirates who had been terrorising western shipping and also to control the lucrative trade links with sub-Saharan Africa. Charles was reluctant to participate, but when the Genoese offered to provide naval support, provisions and several thousand soldiers including 1000 elite crossbowmen the king relented to the wishes of his nobility and agreed to the plan.

The King's uncle Louis de Bourbon was given command of the Crusader army. Louis, a veteran warrior of the Hundred year's war against England recruited the flower of French chivalry into his army. Some of the finest knights in Europe joined the ranks of the Crusader invasion force, including Philip d'Artois (the Constable of France), Enguerrand VII, de Coucy, John de Vienne, (Admiral of France), Geoffrey de Charny (the Younger), John Beaufort (The Earl of Derby) from England and two young knights eager to gain fame and fortune, Jean de Béthencourt and Gadifer de la Salle. Jean de Béthencourt left Normandy and made his way south to Marseilles where the Crusader army was mustering. In July the fleet set sail via Genoa towards its objective, Mahdia (south-east of modern day Tunis). Curiously Mahdia had been captured by the Norman Kingdom of Sicily back in 1148 A.D. Roger II's African Empire was short lived and during the reign of his son William I Mahdia was retaken by the Almohad Muslims. On the 22 of July the Crusaders landed on the shores of North Africa and besieged Mahdia. The port was too heavily fortified to by taken by direct assault, but the Crusaders quickly cut Mahdia off from both land and sea, hoping to stave the garrison into submission. Jean de Béthencourt may have been involved in a skirmish when the defenders tried the break the siege on the third day. The Muslim defenders were defeated in the confrontation and were forced to retreat back to the safety of the city walls. Over the next few weeks both sides tried to break the deadlock but a stalemate ensued.

Negotiations were opened between the Genoese and the Hafsid regime only to the distain of Louis de Bourbon who wanted to continue

Jean De Béthencourt and Gadifier de la Salle at the siege of Mahdia (Barbary Crusade)

to blockade the garrison into submission. In the finish the Crusade ended when the Hafsid Sultan Ahmed II agreed to pay the Genoese 10,000 ducats (a sum equivalent to fifteen years of revenue for Mahdia). The Crusaders returned home, where they were welcomed back as heroes. Jean de Béthencourt and Gadifier de la Salle returned to France, but the great cause upon which they had undertaken had evoked an inner spirit of adventure.

The Canary Islands

The Canary Islands lie nearly 2000 miles from the coast of Normandy and 50 miles from mainland Africa in the Atlantic Ocean. They were known to the Greeks and were recorded to have been visited by the Carthaginians. The actual name of the Canary Islands is derived from the Latin name "Canariae Insulae," meaning "Island of the Dogs" (Grand Canaria).

There are many legends about how this name came about. Some say that the Islands were home to a race of large dogs worshipped by the local tribes. It may also refer to a community of seals that once inhabited the Islands, who may have been mistaken for dogs from a distance. Whatever the truth may be the connection to dogs has lingered and can still be seen on the flag and coat of arms of the Canary Islands today.

In the 1st century A.D, the Roman Governor of Mauritania (Juba II) sent an expedition to the Canary Islands; they found a small stone temple at Juronia (the Roman name for La Palma) and later traded with the indigenous population, known as the "Guanches" (inhabitants of Tenerife). In the fifth century A.D the Roman Empire collapsed and any trade and communication between the Western World and the Islands was abruptly severed. Contact between the Islamic world only remained one of trade/slavery and there seems to have been no interest of conquest or colonisation by the Umayyad or Berber dynasties of Morocco.

Flag/Coat of arms of the Canary Islands

The Norman connection "The book of Roger"

Slowly over time the Canary Islands were forgotten about and became a place of only myth and legend, believed by many to be the lost world of Atlantis. In the 12th Century King Roger II (the Norman King of Sicily) commissioned the Arab geographer Al-Idrisi to create a map of the world. The map was called the Tabula Rogeriana "the book of Roger". On the furthest Western point of the map (see below), the Canary Islands can clearly be seen marked in red.

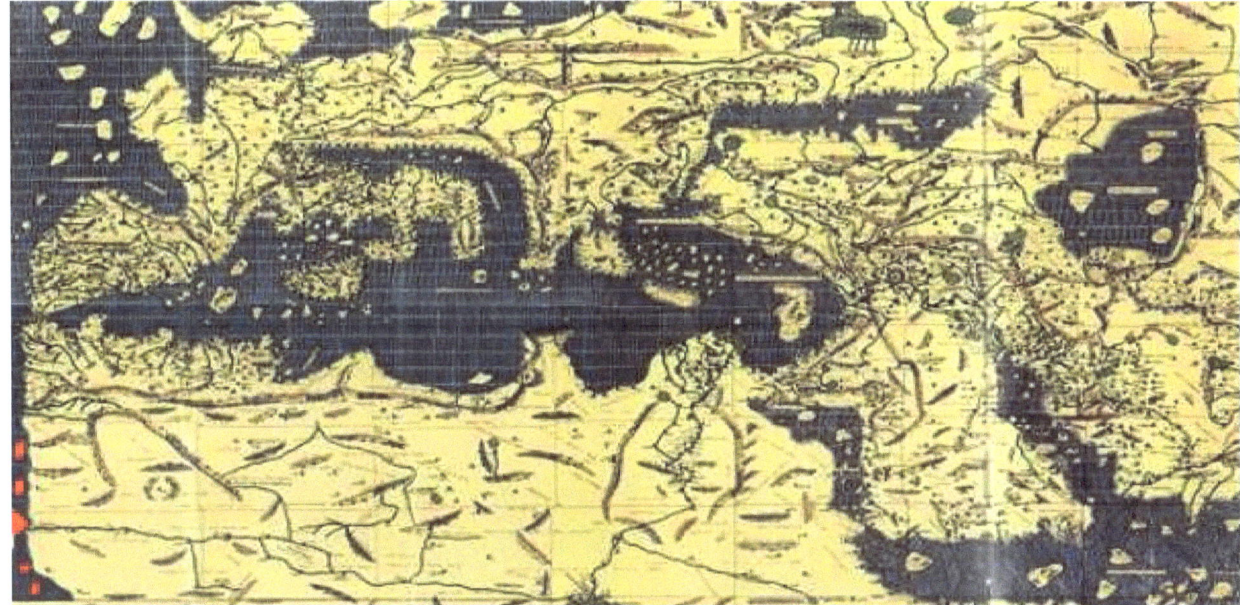

Canary Islands marked in red from "The book of Roger" King Roger II of Sicily

Lancelotto Malocello 1312 A.D

In 1312 A.D the famous Genoese navigator Lancelotto Malocello explored the Canary Islands and established a settlement on the island of Lanzarote (which may have been named after him). He built a small fortress near the modern-day town of Teguise, but within a generation the colony disappeared and may have being destroyed by an uprising or revolt of the Guanches. The castle / fortress was still in existence nearly a century later when the Normans arrived. The later fortification of Castillo Santa Barbara ou Castillo de Guanapay stands on the site of Malocello's castle.

The Norman Conquest 1402 A.D

In early spring 1402 A.D Jean de Béthencourt left Normandy with his retinue and headed for the Atlantic port of La Rochelle to rendezvous with his old comrade in arms Gadifer de la Salle.

On the 1st of May Béthencourt's expedition force set sail for the mysterious Canary Islands. On the voyage south at Corunna a strange incident took place in which Jean de Béthencourt's men were accused of committing an act of piracy against a Scottish ship. Béthencourt fled the scene but on arriving at Cadiz on the Southern tip of the Iberian peninsular he was arrested and taken to the King's court in Seville.

Castillo Santa Barbara ou Castillo de Guanapay

Béthencourt's royal connections back in France and also his reputation as a Crusader helped him secure vindication by the King's council and allowed him to return to his ship. During his time in Seville some 27 sailors deserted, reducing the expedition force to just over 50 men. Undeterred Béthencourt left Spain and headed into the unknown towards the Canaries. After 8 gruelling days at sea land was spotted, Béthencourt's Normans had reached their destination. Béthencourt landed and disembarked on the island of La Graciosa before moving onto Lanzarote. His first objective was to scout the island to try and make contact with the Guanches. Unable to track down the local inhabitants of the island Béthencourt's men returned to camp empty handed. It was agreed with Gadifer de la Salle to split up the expedition force into companies of men and spread out over the terrain. This was a risky strategy as they did not know if the Guanches would be friendly or attack them, but with the most up-to-date weapons from Europe including the fearsome longbow and Genoese crossbow, De Béthencourt took the risk and sent out his search parties. The decision paid dividends when the Normans encountered some of the natives coming down from the mountains to see the strange bearded foreigners. The native Guanches made an agreement with De Béthencourt to hold a meeting between himself and their King Guadaria.

The meeting of two worlds

King Guadaria of Lanzarote came down from the mountains with his entourage and entered the Norman camp. It must have been a strange meeting of two worlds with Béthencourt's Normans on the one side dressed in the finest clothes and armour from Europe and the near pre-historic indigenous Guanches on the other side. The two leaders talked to each other, although how much was understood can only be left to the imagination. Whether intimidated or generally interested by the Normans King Guadarfia agreed to friendly terms and allowed them to stay on the Island. After the meeting De Béthencourt started the construction of a castle (castle Rubicon) to act as a secure base to explore the strange volcanic islands.

The Port of La Graciosa where the Normans first landed in 1402 A.D

With the newly built Castle Rubicon securing a beachhead for the Normans, Jean de Béthencourt decided to return to Spain to organise reinforcements, fresh supplies and provisions. To stand any chance of holding onto the Islands De Béthencourt also needed to gain Royal permission from King Henry III of Spain to legitimise the conquest. He left his chaplain Jean le Verrier and Jean le Courtois in charge of Castle Rubicon during his absence.

Fuerteventura

Gadifer de la Salle was charged with exploring and conquering the adjacent Island of Fuerteventura. The Guanches of Lanzarote told Gadifier that the Fuerteventurians were unfriendly and were likely to attack his men if he landed on their island. With this intelligence Gadifer launched a daring nighttime assault on the beaches of Fuerteventura hoping to surprise the Fuerteventurians. When the sun rose on the next morning the Fuerteventurians could not be found.

The island seemed deserted, and after eight days with supplies running low Gadifer was forced to abandon the search and return to his ship. The Fuerteventurians had withdrawn to the other side of the island in fear of the Norman invaders. Gadifer held council with his senior officers on the Island of Lobos (a small safe haven between Lanzarote and Fuerteventura) where they had been hunting seals for meat and also using their skins to make shoes. It was agreed that they would return to Fuerteventura and not leave until they had conquered all the land and converted its inhabitants to Christianity.

Mutiny and betrayal

Gadifier signaled his ship to pick up his men and ferry them over to Fuerteventura, but the ship's Captain Robin le Brument refused. Some of the sailors were tired of the whole enterprise and wanted to return home to Europe. The mutiny was led by a Norman knight, Bertin de Berneval (from Northern Caux in upper Normandy). Gadifer was left stranded on Lobos while Bertin stirred up further mutiny on Lanzarote. When the Castilian ship the Tajamar docked at Graciosa, De Bertin hatched a plan with its Captain to capture as many of the native Guanches as possible and sell them off as slaves.

Statues of the Guanch Kings, Fuerteventura

The renegade Norman knight De Bertin tricked the Guanches into thinking that he had come to the village of Great Aldea to protect them against the Castilian slavers. After the evening feast, De Bertin and his men arrested 24 Guanches, including their King. The shocked natives were then taken to Graciosa to be transported onto the dreaded Tajamar. The Guanche King managed to free himself and escaped, but for the rest it was an evil betrayal by the Normans whom they had welcomed as friends. Before leaving the Canaries, De Bertin stripped castle Rubicon of it resources and left the Normans loyal to Gadifer and De Béthencourt for dead.

When a relief party from castle Rubicon arrived on the shores of Lobos they found Gadifer and his men in great distress from dehydration and thirst. De Bertin's mutinous act had not only nearly destroyed the expedition but it had damaged the good relationship between the Normans and native Guanches.

Quote from the Canarian Manuscript;

"The Guanches of Lanzarote were very much aggrieved at being betrayed and captured, and now believed that our faith and law was not as good and we had told them. Since we betrayed each other and were not consistent in our actions. At last their rage and terror became so great, that they turned against us and killed our people".

The situation for the remaining Normans was dire. De Bertin had taken with him most of the arms and artillery from Castle Rubicon, including the bow strings for the deadly longbows and crossbows which the Guanches feared so much. Without the superior technological advantage of these weapons the Normans were in extreme danger of being wiped out. Gadifer a veteran of the Hundred year's war, Italy and the Barbary Crusade had to use all his experience to avert disaster. So many times before the Normans had used the age old tactic of "divide and conquer" and the Canary Islands was not exception.

The first meeting of the Normans and Guanches 1402 AD

Gadifer exploited the Guanche social hierarchy by offering to depose the King and replace him with Asche (another member of the Royal family). Asche accepted, and this split in the Guanche unity allowed Gadifer to take the offensive. On the eve of St Catherine 1402 A.D Gadifer took 19 men and launched a covert nighttime raid on the village of Acatif where the Guanche leadership was meeting. The Normans charged out of the darkness and surrounded the house where the Guanche leaders were held up. The fighting was vicious but Gadifer managed to capture the King alive and return back to castle Rubicon.

On deciding that the current King could not be manipulated, Gadifer had him deposed and crowned Asche in his place on the condition that he convert to Christianity. The old King escaped from custody and upon returning to his people, fomented a revolt in which the traitorous Asche was stoned and burned to death. Gadifer was furious and decided to use pure terror against the Guanches.

Reconstruction of a Guanche settlement (Parque del Drago) Tenerife

Jean le Courtois brutally beheaded one of the high ranking Guanche prisoners and placed his head on a pike as a warning against disobeying Norman rule. Gadifer's reign of terror spread fear throughout the island. His plan was to kill all the male Guanches and have their wives and children converted to Christianity. The Canarien chronicle commented of the Normans:

"We took great abundance and killed their people and took their women and children. Those left hide in the caves and dared not face us in the open"

Jean de Béthencourt in Spain

Jean de Béthencourt had also been blighted by the threats from mutinous sailors on his voyage back to Spain. He managed to control the disturbances until he reached the port of Cadiz. Once safely on dry land he had the ringleaders of the mutiny arrested and thrown into prison. De Béthencourt then headed for Seville to organise an audience with the King of Castile. After some time in Seville De Béthencourt managed to gain access to King Henry III and tell him of his voyage and exploration of the Canary Islands. De Béthencourt is reported to have said:

"I have come to ask you for permission to conquer and bring into the Christian faith the Canary Islands".

The King was pleased that De Béthencourt had come to him, and accepted his homage and proposition. He gave Jean the Lordship of the Canaries and also provided him with money, soldiers and a ship to complete the conquest. With a Royal licence, Jean set about organising the supply ship to return to the Canaries. He had received word of the treachery of De Bertin and was concerned about the situation of the beleaguered Normans. Jean's wife Jeanne de Fayel had made the journey from Normandy to Seville to see her husband and was probably due to leave with him to visit the Canaries but the situation on the islands was too dangerous and Jean sent her back to Grainville la Teinturiere.

De Gafifer's exploration 1403 A.D

In July 1403 A.D the supply ship sent by Jean de Béthencourt arrived at Graciosa. Gadifer and the Norman garrison were overjoyed with relief. Apart for the much needed supplies King Henry III had sent 80 soldiers armed with crossbows and longbows. De Gadifer's mood changed when he read the letters from his partner Jean de Béthencourt. Jean informed him that he had done homage to King Henry III for the Canary Islands and the King had bestowed upon him the title of Lord/King of the Islands. Gadifer felt betrayed but calmed himself and embarked on the exploration of the remaining Islands.

Stained glass window of King Henry III

He had unfinished business on the adjacent Island of Fuerteventura, and landed there in force with the King's soldiers. Gadifer marched into the interior to search for the Fuerteventurians who had evaded him thus far. As they trekked into the mountains of the Island the Spanish soldiers refused to go any further and returned to the ship. De Gadifer was displeased but continued on with the twelve remaining men. At last in one of the fertile palm valleys of the island they caught up with the elusive Fuerteventians. After a brief skirmish in which Hammequin d'Auberbose was nearly killed, De Gadifer managed to capture four women before returning to the safety of the ship.

Grand Canaria

The Normans and Spanish then sailed on to the Island of Grand Canaria. As their vessel entered the bay between Feldes and Argonnez the Canarii (Guanches of Grand Canaria) came out in their boats and canoes to meet the newcomers. It was not the first time they had seen Europeans, according to the Canarien a group of Christians (probably sailors) had been killed some 12 years previous. Some of the Canarii came aboard the Castilian ship and exchanged goods with the Normans. Gadifer sent his translator (Pierre the Canarian) onto the Island to talk with the Canarii Chief, but Pierre never returned. He may have been killed or may have changed sides and explained that the white foreigners were intent on the Conquest and subjugation of the Canary Islands and their people.

When the Normans tried to land to take on water they were met with fierce resistance from the Canarii. Unable to disembark they sailed onto La Gomera where they set ashore a raiding party during the night and captured some of the Guanches. Such tactics did not please the Guanches who gathered on the beach in large numbers and refused to allow the Normans to land.

The rugged coastline of Fuerteventura (Canary Islands)

A huge Atlantic storm drove Gadifer's ship onto the shores of the distant island of El Hierro (called Ile de Fer, the iron island, by the Normans). Stranded on El Hierro while the ship's carpenters repaired the vessel; Gadifer explored the island on foot. He found few natives but a large number of animals such as pigs, goats and sheep in the Island's pine wooded interior. After nearly a month exploring El Hierro Gadifer departed and reached the island of La Palma before heading back to Castle Rubicon. After an absence of over a year, Jean de Béthencourt finally returned to the Canary Islands. As the ship anchored in the dock, Gadifer and the garrison of fort Rubicon cheered his arrival. Once ashore De Béthencourt discussed Gadifer's recent exploration of the other islands.

The intelligence that Gadifer had collected was invaluable for the future conquest. It was agreed that Lanzarote and the adjacent island of Fuerteventura must be totally subdued before embarking on the subjugation of the

La Gomera (Canary Islands)

larger islands of Grand Canaria and Tenerife. De Béthencourt and Gadifer launched a fresh campaign to capture King Guadaria. The King on realising that it would only be a matter of time before he would be captured or killed, gave himself up and requested an audience with the Norman invaders. On the 20th of February 1404 A.D King Guadafia yielded to Jean de Béthencourt and agreed to be baptised into Christianity, taking the name Louis. Once King Guadarfia/Louis submitted to the Normans resistance on Lanzarote evaporated and many of the Guanches also followed suit and converted to Christianity.

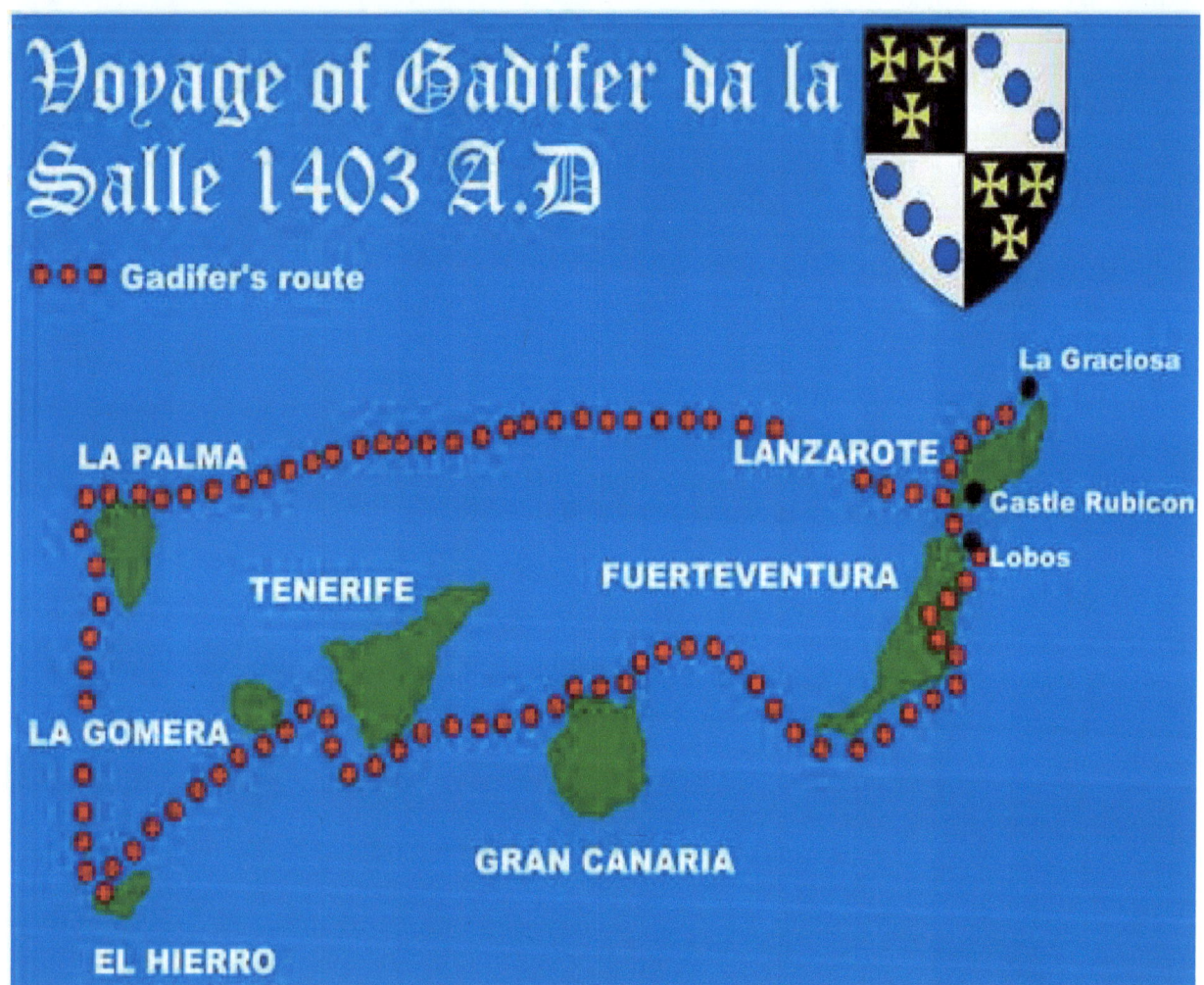

The return of Jean de Béthencourt

With the island of Lanzarote relatively subdued Gadifer was eager to reassess his partnership with De Béthencourt. In Gadifer's eyes he had been cheated out of the deal De Béthencourt had made with King Henry III of Castile. According to one version to the Canarian manuscript he is reported to have said;

"There is one thing that causes me great dissatisfaction, that you have already done homage for the Canary Islands to King Henry of Castile and that you call yourself Lord of them"

Gadifer asked Jean to give him the unconquered islands of Fuerteventura, Tenerife and La Gomera. De Béthencourt refused, relating that he could not give any of the Islands away until he had spoken to the King of Castile. For the time being Gadifer and De Béthencourt put their differences aside and embarked on the conquest of Fuerteventura. The campaign started well, during an early raid the Normans captured several highly ranking Guanches leaders, but King Fez of Fuerteventura evaded capture and united the Fuerteventurians to counterattack. The Normans constructed a new castle called Richeroque in order to launch raids across the island. After three months of campaigning on Fuerteventura Gadifer decided to abort the conquest. He had been fobbed off by De Béthencourt and sought to gain nothing for all his hard work and bravery. Gadifer and De Béthencourt both set sail in different vessels for Spain to put there cases to the King on who should govern the Canary Islands. Once in Seville Gadifer put his case to the King, but in the end the King agreed in favour of De Béthencourt and Gadifer had no choice but to return ruined and empty handed back to France. It was a sad end to the man that had explored all to the Canary Islands and held together dwindling fortunes to the Norman garrison during the early years of the conquest when de Béthencourt had been in Spain.

Sir Jean de Béthencourt

The subjugation of Fuerteventura 1404-1405 A.D

Jean de Béthencourt was anxious to return to the Canaries to complete the conquest of Fuerteventura. During his absence the Norman garrison of castle Richeroque had been besieged and hemmed in by the Fuerteventians. Even with the return of De Béthencourt and fresh troops the situation did not improve. Jean constructed a new fortress called Baltarhayz and garrisoned it with Hannibal (Gadifer's bastard son). The Fuerteventurians used their own guerilla tactics against the Normans. They secretly advanced around De Béthencourt's position and destroyed the half empty castle Richeroque before cutting off the supply lines and raiding the Norman port of Gardin on the coast. The desperate situation required a merciless reaction from Jean de Béthencourt.

Arms of Sir Jean de Béthencourt

He gathered all his remaining forces and took the offensive, destroying all the Guanche settlements that he came into contact with. When re-enforcements arrived from Lanzarote De Béthencourt hatched a plan to destroy the Fuerteventurians once and for all. He feinted a retreat back to castle Richeroque and sent William d'Andrac, Jean le Courtois and most of his men back to the ships to cast out to sea. His plan was to lure the Fuerteventurians into thinking that the Normans had left the island and only left a small garrison to hold castle Richeroque. De Béthencourt's plan worked, while the Guanche warriors attacked castle Richeroque, and unsuccessfully tried to break through its defences the Norman knights attacked the undefended Fuerteventurian villages, destroying their supplies and bases of refuge. Several more raids and counter raids followed before the Normans gained the upper hand over the Fuerteventurians. On the verge of total victory, divisions from within the Norman camp threatened to derail the entire campaign. An argument between Hanibal and the Gadifer supporters over the allocation of prisoners and the spoils of war nearly erupted into open conflict with those loyal to De Béthencourt. By 1405 A.D the Fuerteventurians laid down their arms and surrendered to the Normans. The petty King's of the Island came forward and like King Gaudarfia of Lanzarote they paid homage to De Béthencourt and converted to Christianity.

A Norman mounted attack on the Fuerteventurians

Return to Normandy 1405 A.D

By early 1405 A.D the Island of Fuerteventura had been pacified. Jean de Béthencourt decided to return to Normandy and recruit skilled tradesmen and women to help colonise the new Norman settlement of the Canary Islands. Within three weeks he arrived off the Norman coast and disembarked at the thriving Norman port of Harfleur.

Jean stayed two nights in Harfleur at the house of his relative Hector de Bracqueville before crossing the pays de Caux and heading home to Grainville-la-Teinturiére. When the news reached Grainville that Jean was returning his uncle Robert de Bracquemont rushed out of the castle and met his nephew on the old Roman road. The townsfolk and local nobility flocked to see the Conqueror of the distant Canary Islands who rode through the streets of Grainville. After a week of recuperation and festivities Jean announced that he would be returning to the Canary Islands. When word got around that he was recruiting for a new expedition Grainville was flooded with would-be suitors eager to leave the old world and set up a new life on the Canary Islands. On the 9th of May 1405 A.D an expedition force of over 100 knights, tradesmen and their dependants boarded De Béthencourt's three vessels and set sail for the Canaries.

The Medieval streets of Harfleur, Normandy

Return of the King Béthencourt and the expredition to Grand Canaria

When the Norman ships arrived off Lanzarote the native Guanches assembled on the beach along with the Norman garrison to welcome their lord and master, Jean de Béthencourt. They shouted out in their language **"Here is our King coming!"** Once ashore Jean was met by his trusted lieutenant Jean le Courtois and Gadifer's son Hannibal. De Béthencourt then traveled to

Fuerteventura to inspect the castle at Rricherocque and begin the colonisation of the island. Jean founded the church of Notre-Dame de Béthencourt (modern-day Betancuria) establishing a focal point for the Norman colonists and newly converted Christian Guanches.

With the expanding colonies of Lanzarote and Fuerteventura firmly under Norman control, De Béthencourt decided to embark on the conquest of the larger island of Grand Canaria. Before a full scale invasion of Gran Canaria could be launched De Béthencourt needed to reconnoiter and gather as much intelligence as possible on the disposition and geography of the island. On the 6th of October 1405 A.D three vessels set out towards Gran Canania, but violent Atlantic storms separated the fleet. Adverse winds drove De Béthencourt's ship onto the African coast where it remained for over a week.

The second ship under the command of Jean le Courtois and Hannibal managed to make its way to Gran Canaria. Instead of waiting for De Béthencourt and the third ship, Jean le Courtois,

The Norman church of Notre-Dame de Béthencourt named after Lady Béthencourt (Jean's wife), Betancuria, Fuerteventura

The rugged interior of Gran Canaria

Hannibal and Guillaume d'Auberbose decided to launch a pre-emptive invasion of the island. Guillaume d'Auberbose boasted that;

"With twenty men I could easily cross the entire island and conquer it with ease".

The massacre of Arguineguin

The Normans overconfident in their superior weapons landed at a village called Arguyneguy (Arguineguin). The 45 man strong invasion force succeeded in capturing the village and forced the Canarians to flee into the mountains. After the initial shock, the Canarians regrouped and on seeing that they had the numerical advantage they returned to Arguyneguy in force. As the Normans ransacked the village and gathered up the spoils from the attack they were completely caught off guard. Hundreds upon hundreds of Canarians surrounded and advanced on their position. Within a matter of minutes the Normans were overwhelmed and forced to retreat towards the shore. They were perused by the enraged Canarians who slaughtered the fleeing knights and sailors. On the edge of the beach a final last stand was made by the Normans who were unable to escape the carnage.

The modern day resort of Arguineguin scene of the massacre of 1405 A.D

Guillaume d'Auberose, Jean le Courtois, Guillaume d'Allemagne, Girard de Sombray and Hannibal were hacked to pieces, fighting until the last man. The survivors reached the safety of the ship and watched in horror as their comrades were butchered and torn limb from limb.

When Jean de Béthencourt arrived on the scene he was saddened at the loss of so many men he knew personally. With his fighting force cut by half and the psychological advantage lost to the Canarians, De Béthencourt decided to cut his loses and sail on to La Palma. By chance he found the third vessel which had landed on the island sometime before. De Béthencourt led the Norman invasion force deep into the island's interior. Several skirmishes took place in which the natives took heavy loses (according to the Canarian manuscript over 100 natives were killed to just 5 Normans) After six weeks De Béthencourt returned to his ships and left for El Hierro (ile de fer). De Béthencourt had decided to colonise El Hierro with some of the Norman settlers. He had learnt from Gadifer's previous voyage and exploration that El Hierro was the least populated of the islands and had adequate resources to allow a future colony to prosper and survive. Once on El Hierro the Normans managed to capture 111 Guanches who were later sold into slavery.

← Overleaf: The Norman last stand at the massacre of Arguineguin

1405- 1412 A.D Colonisation

De Béthencourt returned to Fuerteventura to organise the colonisation of the newly conquered Islands of El Hierro and La Palma. In order to keep the natives of Lanzarote and Fuerteventura happy De Béthencourt chose to disperse the new colonists onto El Hierro and La Palma, creating new fledgling colonies. This situation appeased both parties as the newcomers gained land to farm and the Gaunches were not displaced.

The site of Rubicon, Lanzarote (Association Jean de Béthencourt)

Under Norman rule and government the Canaries

Links and trading were once again established between the Islands and mainland Europe. By 1411 Jean left for Spain to pay homage to the new King of Castile (John II). In his absence he left his nephew Maciot de Béthencourt as governor of the Norman controlled Canary Islands.

Jean de Béthencourt's return to Normandy and the English invasion

Jean returned home to Normandy at the very time France was being torn apart by civil war and threat of invasion from the English. From the late 14th century onwards King Charles VI of France suffered a series of metal breakdowns and descended into madness.

On one such occasion he believed that he was made of glass and if anyone touched him he would shatter into pieces. The King's madness led to a power struggle between John the Fearless, the Duke of Burgundy (Charles cousin) and Louis of Orléans (Charles brother) for control of the realm of France. In 1407 A.D Louis was assassinated by the Duke's men in the streets of Paris. Louis' murder caused a civil war and blood feud between the Burgundians and Armagnac's (supporters of the dead Louis and the French Royal family). This split between the French nobility allowed the English to re-ignite the Hundred year's war. In 1399 A.D King Richard II of England (son of famous Black Prince) was forced to abdicate and then murdered by his cousin Henry Bolingbroke. Bolingbroke claimed the throne and proclaimed himself King Henry IV. Throughout Henry's reign, he was plagued by revolt and rebellion from many members of his nobility, who believed that he had usurped the crown.

The Royal arms of England from 1404-1603 A.D, Quartering the arms of "France modern"

These plots carried on after Bolingbroke's death and into the reign of his son Henry V. By re-igniting the Hundred year's war with France, Henry V hoped to unit the English nobility and country behind him, distracting them from thoughts of rebellion.

When negotiations broke down in early 1415 A.D Henry V prepared for the biggest gamble of his Kingship (the invasion of France). On the 11th of August Henry's fleet of 1500 ships left Southampton and set sail for France. Unlike the grand chevauchée's (raids) of Edward III and the Black Prince, Henry had decided on a campaign of outright conquest. His target was the ancestral homeland of the English Kings; Normandy. Henry's invasion force landed on the beaches of Saint Adresse at the mouth of the Seine estuary in Upper Normandy. The English army made its way along the high ground of the Cap de la Héve and headed towards the important port of Harfleur. Harfleur was strategically important for both the English and the French. If Henry could capture the port he would have a secure base to receive supplies from England and more importantly he could control/strangle trading links between Rouen, Paris and the sea.

The siege of Harfleur

The French knight Jean d'Estouteville was entrusted with the defence of Harfleur. When Henry demanded the surrender of the port, D'Estouteville refused and prepared to face the onslaught of the English siege machines and cannons. Over the next five weeks Harfleur was bombarded day and night. Some of the English cannon balls can still be seen today just inside the door of the museum du Prieuré. In the end with no sign of a relief force from the French King the townsfolk could take no more and offered to surrender the town, before the English broke through the defences.

On the 22nd of September Harfleur opened its gates to the English King and Duke of Normandy, Henry V. It is not clear if Jean de Béthencourt was back in Normandy at the time of the English invasion. If he was, the dreadful news from Harfleur would have traveled to Grainville-la-Teinturière with lighting speed. Henry re-fortified Harfleur before heading north on a grand chevauchée towards the English garrison of Calais. The English hugged the Norman coast passing via Fécamp not far from Jean de Béthencourt's fief of Grainville.

On the 25th of October 1415 A.D Henry's depleted army defied the odds and defeated the chivalry of France at the battle of Azincourt. This victory allowed Henry to return in 1417 A.D to commence the conquest of Normandy. Henry landed at Touques in lower Normandy and advanced on Caen. On the 17th of August the English laid siege to Caen. Its 40,000 inhabitants huddled behind the city walls, praying that English would not break through.

The port of Harfleur, Normandy

By the 4th of September, Henry gave the signal for the final assault on the city. Just as before in 1346 A.D Caen succumbed and was overrun by the English. Henry let his troops run riot through the streets and only halted the violence when he saw the body of a decapitated woman with a baby in her arms still sucking at her breast. The Sack of Caen sent shockwaves throughout Normandy. Henry took advantage of the terror and momentum generated by the capture of Caen and secured town after town and village after village. By the winter most of lower Normandy had fallen to the English and only the mighty castle of Falaise refused to surrender. Like Harfleur and Caen, Falaise was invested and subjected to English cannon and trebuchets. After three weeks of intense bombardment the town surrendered to Henry's army. The die-hard garrison of the castle refused to give in and held out for another six weeks. Only when English sappers undermined the walls of the castle did the garrison finally realise that resistance was futile. By the spring of 1418 A.D lower Normandy had being totally subdued, only the island monastery of Le Mont de Saint Michel remained outside English control.

Rouen 1418-1419 A.D

The next stage of the English plan was to conquer upper Normandy. Henry's objective was the capture the second largest city in France and also the capital of the Duchy; Rouen. The garrison and town burgers were determined not to allow the city to fall into English hands.

They decided to burn down the suburbs of the city and lay waste to the countryside; hoping to deny the English any provisions or shelter. The inhabitants were told to provide themselves with one year's worth of provisions or leave. On the 20th of July Pont de l'Arche was captured and the road to the capital lay wide open. When Henry's army arrived outside the city they were met by several thousand refugees that had being thrown out of the city. Rouen was surrounded by nearly 8 Kms of huge walls and towers. Henry decided against a direct assault and settled down for a long drawn out siege. For six months the city bravely held out, but in December with food and supplies running low, the garrison ejected several thousand more of its citizens. These unfortunate people were refused access through the English siege lines and virtually condemned to death. On the 19th of January Rouen agreed to surrender. Henry entered the capital and rode through the streets of Rouen towards the Cathedral, where he paid homage to the tombs of the Dukes of Normandy and to his Crusader ancestor Richard the Lionheart. French rule in Normandy came to an end in 1419A.D and many of its nobility faced a stark choice, submit and pay homage the King Henry of face forfeiture and exile from the Duchy. Jean the Béthencourt was in a precarious position.. As lord of the Canary Islands, he paid homage to the King of Castile, who was at war with England. This meant that he had to choose either forfeiting the Canary Islands or risk losing the family ancestral fief of Graineville-la-Teinturiére in Normandy. Jean decided the best option was to hand over complete jurisdiction of the Canary Islands to his nephew Maciot and remain in Normandy. Sometime in 1419 A.D after the fall of Rouen, Jean made his way to the Ducal Court and begrudgingly acknowledged Henry V as his feudal overlord.

Falaise castle (Lower Normandy), besieged by Henry V in 1417 A.D

The Canary Islands after Jean de Béthencourt

Teguise Church, Teguise was founded by Maciot de Béthencourt

Although Jean was unable to return in person to the Canary Islands he did manage to secure safe conduct from Henry V to sent two ships of provisions and supplies to his nephew Maciot. He also appointed his old Chaplain Jean Le Verrier as Bishop of Rubicon.

In the winter of 1418 A.D Maciot handed over the control of the Islands to Enrique Pérez de Guzman (the Count of Niebla) in the name of his uncle Jean de Béthencourt. Maciot continued to govern Lanzarote and married the daughter of King Guardafia (Princess Teguise). Maciot founded Teguise, naming it after his wife and helped create the layout of the town. The settlement grew in importance and became the capital of Lanzarote until 1852 A.D. When Robert de Braquemont (Admiral of Castile and France) and also De Béthencourt's relative died in 1419 A.D both Maciot and Jean were deprived of a useful ally at the Castilian court in Spain. Although Henry V of England died in 1422 A.D, English rule in Normandy continued for another 30 years. The last of the Norman Conquerors Jean de Béthencourt died at the family seat of Grainville-la-Teinturiére in 1425 A.D.

Maciot's power and influence over the Canary Islands diminished after the death of his uncle Jean de Béthencourt. A series of Castilian and crown officials arrived and attempted to complete the conquest of the unconquered Islands. Maciot led a brutal reprisal campaign on the island of El Hierro against the native Guanches who had revolted against the Norman settlers. By 1445 A.D his relationship and loss of power led him to sell the lordship of Lanzarote to Castile's rival in the region; Portugal. The Portuguese sent soldiers and occupied the island for two years, but a native revolt assisted by Castilian troops brought their rule over the island to an end in 1447 A.D. Maciot also fled with his wife Teguise to Portugal. So ended the direct link of the De Béthencourt family and Norman Conquest of the islands.

The "Conquista Realenga"

In June 1478 A.D a Castilian invasion force led by Juan Rejón and Dean Bermúdez landed on the island of Grand Canaria. Although they destroyed the Guanches in battle near Real, infighting broke out between the Castilian commanders which led to the campaign taking another 5 years to complete. Next to fall was the island of La Palma (1492-1493 A.D). Tenerife was the final island to be conquered. In 1494 Alonso Fernández de Lugo invaded Tenerife with a force of over 2000 men (including 200 armoured knights). Overconfident just as Hannibal de la Salle and the Normans had been in 1405 A.D, the Castilians were annihilated at the Battle of Acentoejo. Alonso Fernández de Lugo managed to escape the carnage and returned again in December 1495 A.D to complete the conquest. He finally secured victory by defeating the Guanches at the battle of Aguere and then the decisive second battle of Acentejo.

Memorial to Jean de Béthencourt, Grainville-la-Teinturiére

Museum of Jean de Béthencourt, Graineville-la-Teinturiére

Chapter 9: Normandy

Richard the Lionheart
"THE LAST WAR"

In order to understand the relationship between the Kings of England and France we must travel back in time to the creation of the Duchy of Normandy. During the 9th and 10th centuries Viking raiders from modern day Scandinavia terrorised most of mainland Europe and the British Isles. The French province of Neustria (North western France) suffered increased invasions when by 911 A.D the King of France, Charles III "the Simple" had no choice but to cede the area of the Seine valley and coastal regions to the Viking Chief Rollo (Hrolfr). The treaty of St Clair sur Epte has been shrouded in mystery ever since. Legend has it that during the conclusion of the treaty Charles demanded Rollo to kiss his foot as an act of fealty and homage. Rollo grabbed the King's foot and hurled him backwards in the air. Clearly vassal or no vassal Rollo was too powerful to be dictated to or punished. The Duchy of Normandy had now been founded in which Rollo was baptised into Christianity, taking the name Robert. He married Poppa de Bayeux and in theory controlled the land as a subject vassal of the French King.

Over the next 150 years the Dukes of Normandy expanded their territory annexing lower Normandy, pushing the western borders with Brittany, to the south Maine and even claiming the disputed Vexin region close to the French capital (Paris). In 1066 A.D Duke William of Normandy invaded England and beat the army of the Anglo-Saxon King Harold at the battle of Hastings. Duke William was crowned at Westminster on Christmas

day in 1066 A.D and became the King of England as well as the Duke of Normandy. After William's death in 1087 A.D the crown and Dukedom passed to each of his sons, William II "Rufus", Robert "Curthose" and finally Henry I "Beauclerc". When Henry Beauclerc's son died in a shipwreck off the Norman coast, Henry forced the nobility to accept his daughter Matilda as heir. Henry's I nephew Stephen of Blois had other ideas and usurped the crown with the help of his brother, Henry of Winchester. For nineteen long years England was ravaged by civil war. Matilda with the help of her second husband Geoffrey Plantagenet (the Count of Anjou) fought on, but it was their son, Henry Plantagenet who forced Stephen accept his succession, finally ending the anarchy in 1154 A.D

The Angevin Empire and the Devil's Brood
1152-1189

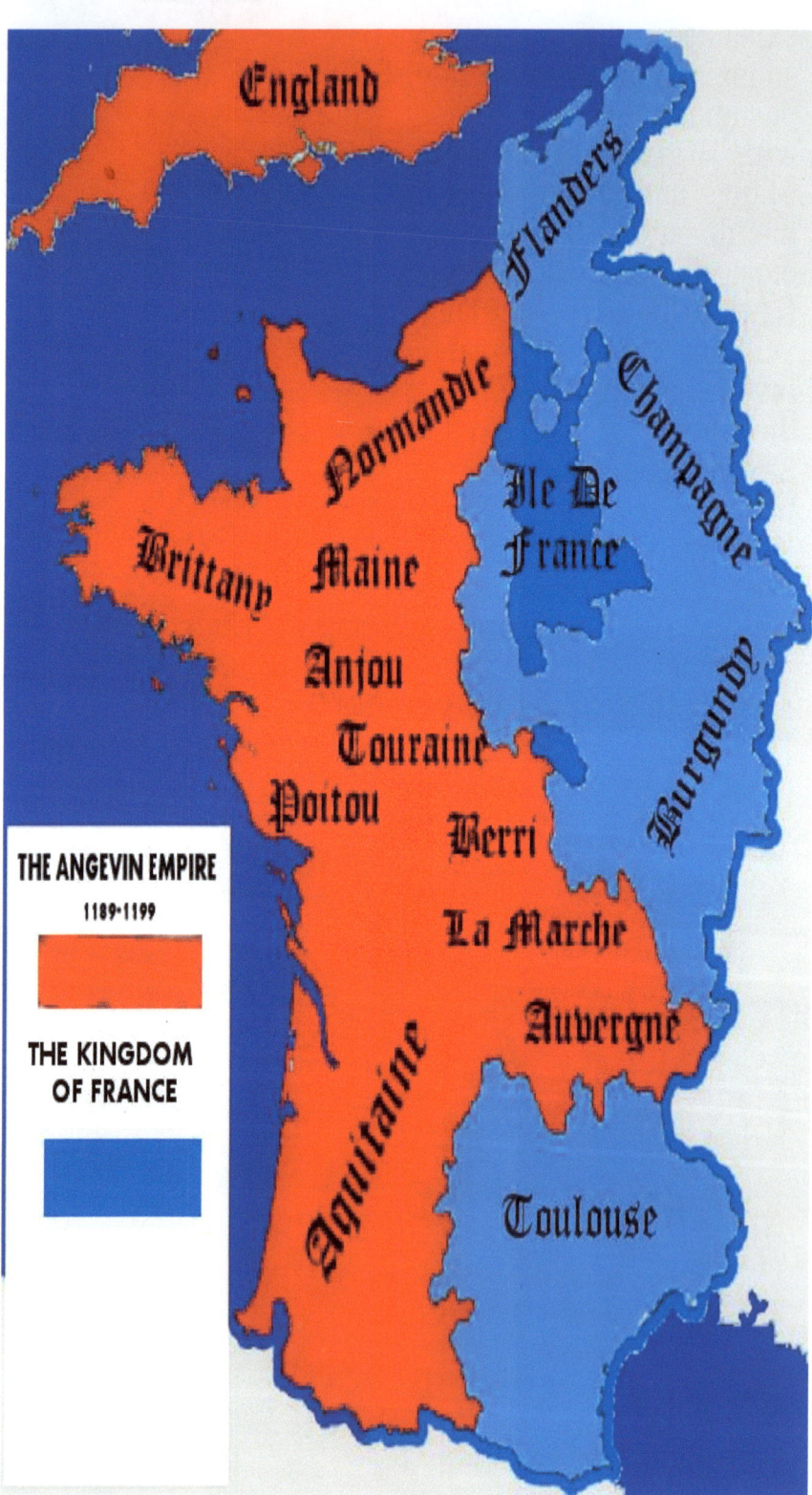

On the 18th of May 1152 A.D Henry Plantagenet married Eleanor the heiress to the Duchy of Aquitaine. On Stephen's death in 1154 A.D Henry became King of England, Duke of Normandy, through his mother, Count of Anjou, Touraine and Maine through his father, Overload of Brittany, Scotland, Wales, Ireland and Duke of Aquitaine though Eleanor his wife.

Although Henry was King of England, in France he was only a Duke / Count and therefore paid homage to the French King for those lands. But now the vassal had become more powerful than his liege lord. The Angevin Empire stretched for the borders of Scotland to the foothills of the Pyrenees and made Henry the most powerful monarch in Europe. The marriage between Henry and Eleanor produced no less than eight children who became known as the devils brood.

There is a legend that of the house of Anjou "the Angevins" were descended from the Devil. An early Count married Melusine the daughter of Satan. This was only discovered when time and time again Melusine refused to attend mass until one day her husband forced her to stay during the service.

Before the service was over, Melusine freed herself from her guards and flew through the window taking her two children with her never to be seen again. From this legend the Angevins were known as the "Devils brood". The curse would iterate that the Plantagenet's would destroy each other; father was to fight son and brother against brother. Richard the Lionheart encouraged the legend be even stating;

"From the Devil we sprang, and to the Devil we shall go".

The curse would indeed come true during the lifetime of Henry Plantagenet. After John was born in 1167 A.D Henry and Eleanor slowly grew apart. Eleanor spent most of her time in Aquitaine while Henry ruled his domains travelling from region to region entertaining his famous mistress Rosemond Clifford (Fair Rosemond). In 1172 A.D Richard was made Duke of Aquitaine in Poitiers. The young King Henry (Henry's eldest son) would inherit England and Normandy, Brittany was to go to Geoffrey and the newly conquered Ireland to John. The only problem with this arrangement was that Henry was still a young man only in his thirties and although he would give all his sons titles, he would not relinquish any of his power.

During the last 20 years of Henry's reign he was plagued by rebellions by his sons, his wife and the French monarchy eager to destroy the Angevin Empire.

But Henry was a remarkable King and each time he crushed the plots and revolts against him. Queen Eleanor was confined in England to deter her from causing any more trouble. In 1183 A.D Henry (the young King) died, three years later Geoffrey was killed in a tournament accident which only left Richard and John. In 1188 A.D Henry was in Normandy fighting against the advances of the French King Philip Augustus. Rumours had been circulating from Paris that Henry intended to disinherit Richard in favour of John, his favourite and youngest son. During the peace negotiations in November the French King proposed that the postponed marriage between his sister Alice (Countess of the Vexin) and Richard should take place immediately, the disputed areas should be given to Richard and that Henry should publicly acknowledge Richard as his successor. Henry confirmed Richard's fears by refusing to acknowledge the conditions. Richard now paid homage to Philip for all his continental possessions. Philip had succeeded in forcing a rift between father and son, and by 1189 A.D they had openly declared war on the old Plantagenet King.

Henry was old and his un-bounding energy was ebbing away, meanwhile Richard had become an experienced military commander during the years of civil strife. The conqueror of the impregnable castle of Taillebourg had now come of age.

Geoffrey Plantagenet (father of Henry II)

In the summer of 1189 A.D Richard and Philip invaded Maine. The local nobility loyal to Henry changed sides believing that the old King would soon be dead. While at Le Mans (Henry's birthplace) the Franco-rebel alliance caught up with the King. Henry rather than face a siege, ill like a wounded lion withdrew and ordered Le Mans to be burned to the ground to slow down his enemies. First heading for the safety of Normandy, but then being forced south into Anjou. Richard chased after his father on route to Chinon, to force him into submission, but the King's entourage was led by Sir William Marshal (the champion of over 500 tournaments and one of the most feared knights in Christendom). William Marshal ambushed the pursuers and unhorsed Richard in the process, only a last minute cry from Richard **"Do not kill me Marshal I am unarmed"** saved his life as the Marshall re-aimed his lace, killing Richard's horse and not the Duke himself. On the 4th of July at Azay le Rideau Henry was forced to accept the humiliating conditions. Henry returned in a litter to Chinon, when reading the list of pardons of those who had conspired against him, he saw John's name. His favourite son had turned traitor against him. Just before he died he turned to Geoffrey his illegitimate son and said **"The others are the real bastards"**. So the life of the grandfather of Europe came to an end.

Richards the Lionheart's confrontation with Sir William Marshal

"By Gods legs Marshal, Do not Kill me! I am unarmed"
I will not kill you, but I hope the Devil may.

Henry's body was taken the short distance from the castle of Chinon to the Abbey of Fontevraud in the heart of Anjou to be buried. Richard followed the procession, entered the Abbey and paid respects to his father. After the funeral Richard rode north to Normandy, in the cathedral of Rouen he was invested with the Ducal sword, and became the Duke of Normandy. While crossing the river Seine Richard nearly drowned. On reaching the safety of the bank, he gave thanks for this good fortune by founding the Abbey of Bonport. The coronation in England followed and by 1190 Richard was again back in France preparing the final details for the Third Crusade to recover the Holy land. Had the events of the battle of Hattin (1187 A.D) and the fall of Jerusalem not happened, it is fairly likely to say that war between Richard and Philip would have started as early as 1190/91. A.D

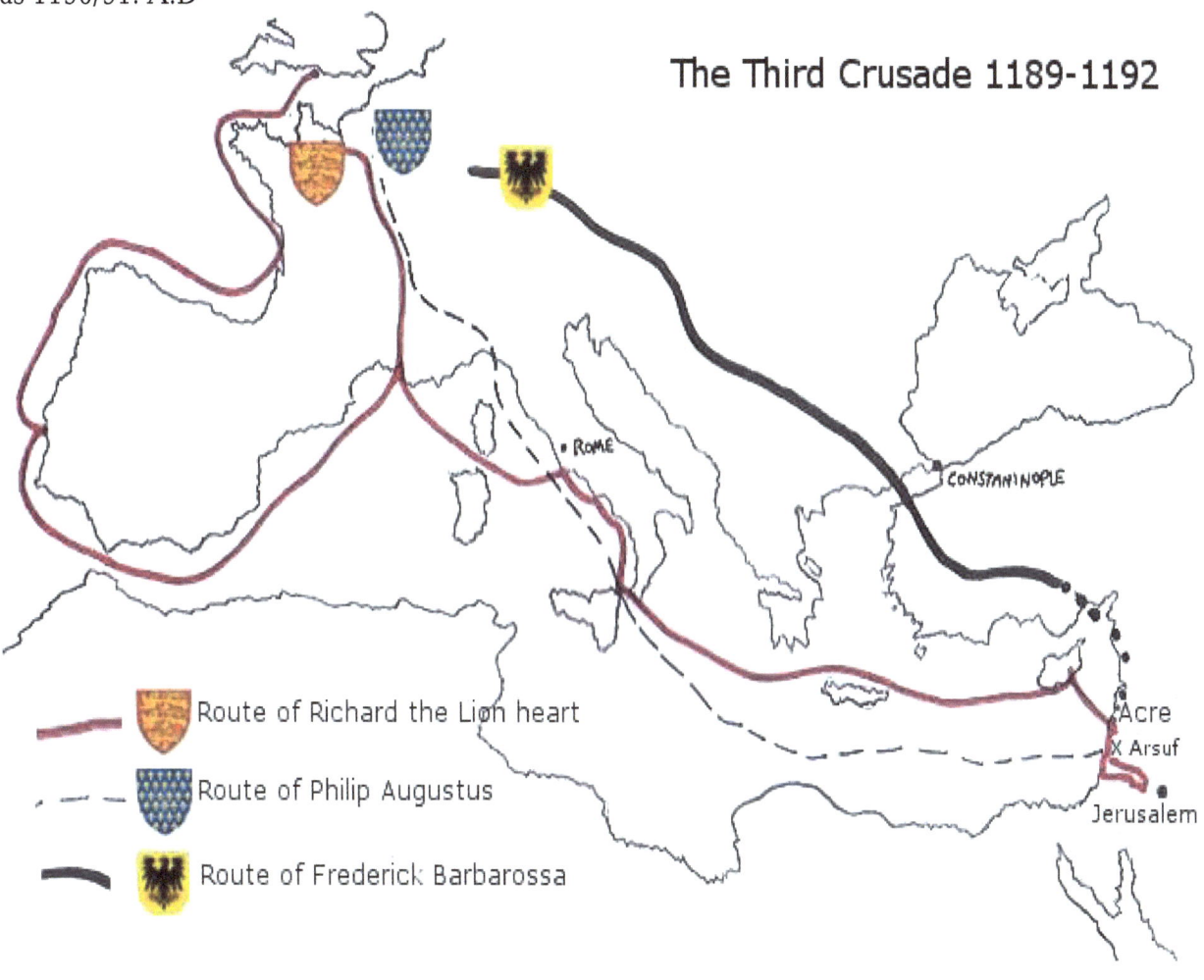

The Third Crusade
1189-1192

The Three most powerful monarchs in Europe embarked on the Third Crusade. Frederick Barbarossa the Holy Roman Emperor chose the land route across the Byzantine Empire, but in a freak accident he drowned while crossing the river Saleph in Turkey.

The remnants of his army reached the Holy land under the banner of his son Henry of Swabia, then Leopold Duke of Austria. Richard and Philip left Vezelay (France) on July 1st 1190 A.D and chose sea routes to the Holy land.

Hauteville Arms, Montreal Sicily

The Angevin and French fleets arrived in Sicily during a crucial time in the island's history. The Normans under the De Hauteville family had conquered most of Southern Italy and Sicily only a century before and Richard's sister Joan had been married to King William II "the good", but after his death the new King, Tancred de Lecce imprisoned Joan and withheld her dowry. After a show of force in which Richard captured and sacked the port of Messina, Tancred gave in.
Philip again raised the question of the marriage between Richard and Alice, but Richard refused on the grounds that Alice had been a mistress of his father Henry and that they had an illegitimate child together. In fact Eleanor of Aquitaine had been secretly negotiating with the King of Navarre to marry his daughter Berengaria to Richard (this marriage would secure the Duchy of Aquitaine from French advances).

Finally in March 1191 A.D the two fleets set sail from Sicily for the Holy land. During a storm Richard's fleet was scattered and after some shipwrecked survivors from the fleet were roughly treated by the rebel Byzantine regime in Cyprus. Richard conquered the strategic island, and married Berengaria in St George's chapel, Limassol. He then sold the island to the Knights Templar for 100,000 dinars. With the arrival of the fresh Crusader armies, the coastal city of Acre which was already under siege surrendered, but Richard's handling of the hauling down of Duke Leopold's banner from the battlements would have repercussions later. Both Richard and Philip contracted dysentery during the siege. In the pact at Vezelay, the two Kings agreed the split the profits of the campaign 50/50, but ill feeling over the spoils of war could not stop them from quarreling. Firstly Philip demanded half of Cyprus, then Richard counter claimed half of Artois in France whose Lord had just died during the siege of Acre. Feeling overshadowed by the Lionheart, Philip tired of the whole campaign and decided to return to France. Before he left, he promised Richard he would not attack any of his lands. Richard took control of the remaining Crusaders and marched on to capture the coastal cities of Caesarea, Jaffa, Ramleh, Ibelin, Darum and Ascalon. He defeated Saladin at the battle of Arsuf, but was unable the take Jerusalem. After many tiresome negotiations a three year truce was agreed, the Crusaders kept the towns they had captured and pilgrims were allowed to visit Jerusalem once again. The third Crusade was now at an end and Richard decided to return home to France. On nearing the port of Marseilles Richard received word that the Count of Toulouse intended to arrest him and hand him over to Philip Augustus for trial over an attack by Richard's seneschal in Gascony on the Counts lands. Headwinds stopped Richard's ships from attempting to circum navigate the Iberian Peninsula, thus the fleet turned about and headed for the Adriatic coast to return home via Germany. Richard traveled through Northern Italy and then Austria making for the lands of Henry the Lion (Duke of Saxony and Bavaria), his brother in law.

The capture of the Lionheart by Duke Leopold's men

Austria was hostile territory and Richard's behavior towards its Duke (Leopold) during the Third Crusade only highlighted the danger. There were several close escapes, once in which a local knight originally from Normandy helped the King escape. Richard's luck finally run out and he was arrested by Duke Leopold's men and handed over to the Henry VI, the Holy Roman Emperor. During this time Philip could no longer resist the temptation of trying to dismantle the Angevin empire and unit France under his rule. Richard's troublesome younger brother, Prince John needed little persuasion into establishing an alliance with Philip, and paid homage to him for all the Angevin lands and even England. In 1193 A.D Philip invaded the Duchy of Normandy. The important castle of Gisors opened its gates to the French King without any resistance. Its Governor Gilbert Vascoeuil's name became a byword for treachery in the Duchy. With the Vexin secured, Philip moved onto the Norman capital Rouen, but the capital was defended by the experienced Crusader Robert Fitz Parnel (the Earl of Leicester) who when showed false documents from Philip instructing him to hand over Rouen promptly replied;

"If you wish to enter, the gates are open"

Philip smelling a trap withdrew back towards the border to consolidate his recent gains. Richard's ransom was set at 100,000 marks, but Philip and John offered 150,000 marks. In the end only Richard's skill as a diplomat in resolving a dispute between the Emperor and rebel Princes from the Lower Rhineland compelled Henry to release the Lionheart on the 14th March 1194 A.D.

Medieval streets of Rouen

On the news of Richard's release, Philip wrote to John; **"Look to yourself, the Devil is loosed"**. Richard returned to England after an absence of over four years and was re-crowned at Winchester in an elaborate ceremony. Almost immediately he set about securing England's northern border by pacifying the King of Scots, then reselling lucrative offices and titles in order to raise the money needed to regain the lost territories in France.

Normandy

Philip's invasion of 1193 A.D had overrun the Vexin and most of eastern Normandy. Richard's agents had secured a rest bite from further French advances at the Treaty of Mantes in July 1193 a.D. The one sided treaty allowed Philip to keep all his recent territorial gains; Richard would also have to pay 20,000 marks and cede the great fortresses of Loches and Chatillon in Tourraine. 1194 A.D, the year of reckoning had come. The last war in Normandy would require all Richard's experience in both warfare and politics to regain the lost lands in an age where the advantage favoured the defenders of strong castles and fortified towns. In spring 1194 A.D Richard left England for the last time and crossed the Channel to Normandy. The King arrived in Barfleur (Contentin, Lower Normandy) to a joyful welcome, old and young came out of their houses to see their rightful Duke. A retainer of Sir William Marshal stated **"God has come again in all his strength"**. The procession continued through the Contentin into Calvados where en route John was reconciled with Richard and begged for his forgiveness. Richard pardoned his brother; **"Do not be afraid John, you are a child and have got into bad company"** Since February Philip had been attacking the remaining Anglo-Norman strongholds on the Duchy's eastern frontier. By May only the border castle of Verneuil sur Avre stood in the way of Philip controlling a line of fortresses following the river Iton within striking distance to attack lower Normandy and the Ducal capital of Rouen.

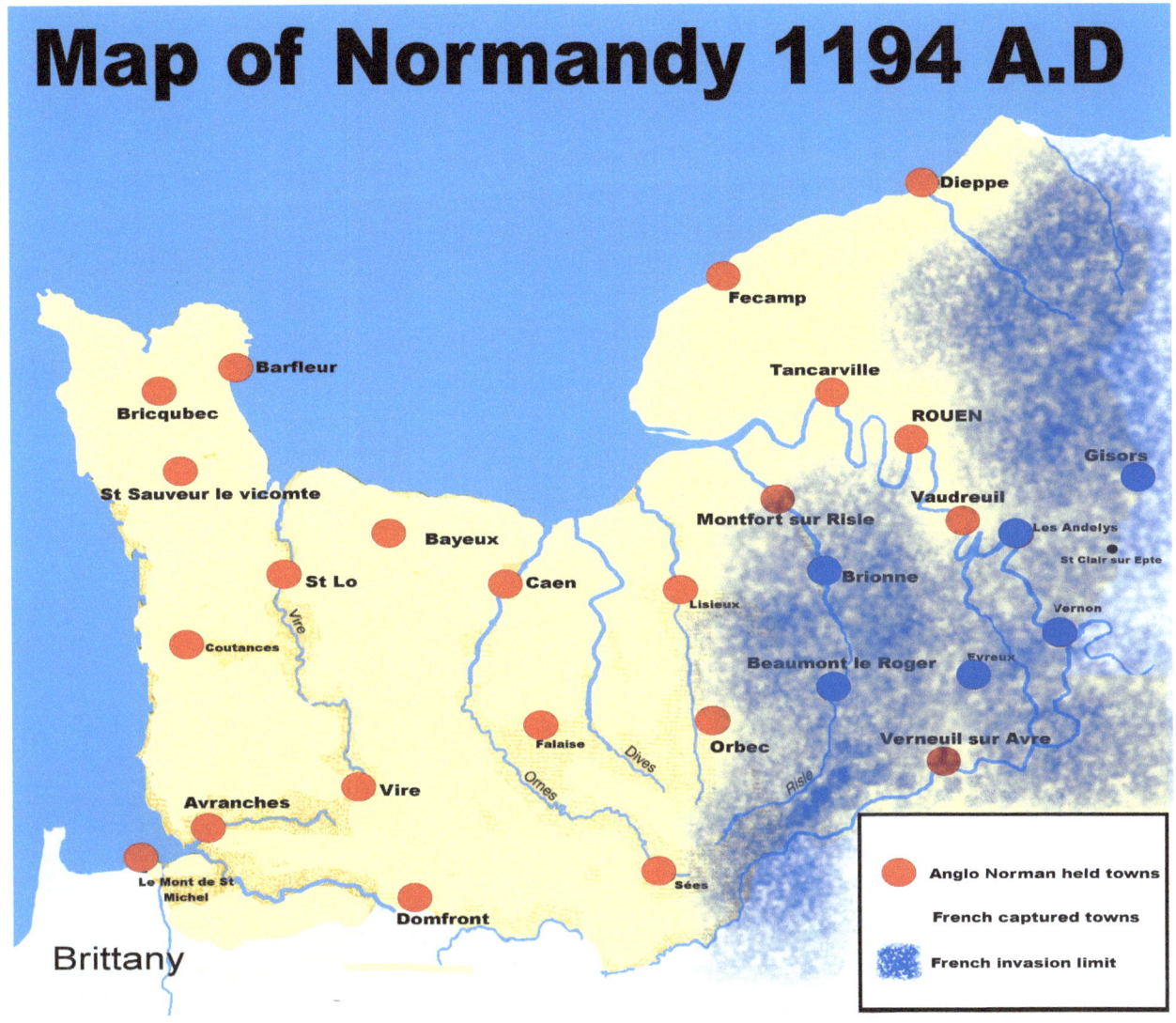

The castle garrison was so confident of withstanding the French assault that they even painted an unflattering image of Philip on their gates in defiance. When Richard heard the news he marched at once to relieve the siege. He sent John to Evreux, where after pretending to be loyal to Philip, John entered the town and had the garrison executed. A gruesome tale circulated that the heads of the French soldiers were hung above the town gates. Philip left Verneuil in order to retake Evreux which he sacked, but the French army at Verneuil now leaderless broke off the siege after news reached them that the Anglo-Norman army was approaching. Richard entered Verneuil at the end of May and personally thanked the castle defenders for their bravery in defending the town. With his supply lines cut Philip retreated back towards Paris. Richard now repaired and reinforced the town and castle walls before turning his attention south. In Tourraine Richard re-took the castles of Loches and Montmirail. Tours opened its gates without any struggle. Richard was intent on bringing order to the southern part of the Angevin Empire and punishing the rebel barons who were in open revolt. Meanwhile Philip instead of attending a peace conference in Pont de l'Arche launched a raid towards Brionne.

In June the French forces managed to capture the Gallant defender of Rouen (Robert Fitz Parnal).

Fretéval, July

The victorious Army headed south again to reduce the last sparks of revolt. By late July the castles of Marcilliac and Tailleborg (the same castle Richard had captured when he was a young man) were reduced. Angouleme was taken in a single evening. The territories of the Count of Angouleme were completely pacified. Richard wrote back to England;

"We have captured all the lands from our enemies and taken 300 knights captive".

Richard returned north to ease the pressure in Normandy and Philip headed south likewise to ease the pressure on the rebel barons. The two armies were now on a direct collision course. Richard encamped at Vendome and Philip only a few kilometers away at Fretéval. Philip sent word that he intended to give battle, but in reality he struck camp, not daring to risk the confrontation and retreated north again. Richard sensed weakness and on the 4th of July caught up with the rearguard of the French army.

Arms of Robert Fitz-Parnell (Beaumont) Earl of Leicester

So intense was his desire to capture or kill Philip that it is said when one horse tired he took another, searching his mortal enemy. Philip only evaded capture by seeking refuge in a church as the battle took place. Although the French King escaped, his baggage train, treasure and royal records did not (of which included lists of those Angevin subjects who had betrayed or intended to join the French). Richard himself during the encounter had also showed his experience as a great general by putting Sir William Marshal in command of the reserve, which hovered the battlefield incase of a French counter attack. Richard acclaimed after the battle;

"The Marshal did better than all of you, if there had been trouble he would have been there, when one has a reserve one does not fear the enemy".

Philip sieving from his defeat at Fretéval, returned to Normandy and had by chance scored his first success against John and the Earl of Arundel; defeating them in a skirmish at Vaudreuil. With the campaigning season coming to an end a

Effigy of Richard at Verneuil sue Avre

truce was agreed at Tillieres in which both sides agreed to keep what they held at the present time.

1195 A.D
Total War

As the year 1195 A.D commenced Richard was in Rouen preparing for the second phase of the war. Rumours were about that the German Emperor Henry IV who had just completed the conquest of Southern Italy and Sicily intended to add the Kingdom of France to his Empire. He indeed sent the Lionheart a golden crown requesting that Richard attack the lands of the French King. Richard sent the bishop of Ely to the German court in order to enquire what Henry was up too. Philip realising the danger of fighting on a double front tried to apprehend the Bishop and declared the current truce null and void. Philip took the offensive and attacked Normandy from his Vexin castles.

Vaudreuil

During the peace talks between the two sovereigns at Vaudreuil the French had continued to undermine the castle walls. An almighty crash was heard as the castles stone defences came crashing down in a cloud of dust. Richard stormed out and swore by God's legs he would have revenge. He immediately gathered his men and charged the French lines, taking the castle and capturing many of Philip's Knights. As Philip retreated, the bridge over the Seine collapsed from under him. Philip not for the last time only just escaped from being drowned.

The campaign of 1195 A.D commenced with French countryside being ravaged, villages were sacked, the crops burned, vines pulled up and all who resisted put to the sword.

The fighting only ended when disturbing news from Spain reached the two Kings. Boyac the Muslim Emir in North Africa had invaded Spain and defeated the King of Castile. The Pope urged both Kings to put aside their differences and help Castile against the Moors in Spain

At Louviers Richard and Philip met to consummate a more long lasting peace. Richard handed back Philip's Sister Alice and a marriage was planned between Richard's niece and Philip's son Louis.

The French raid on Dieppe 1195

The agreement was delayed until the German Emperor ratified the terms, as Richard was still Henry's man because of his oath of fealty when he was a prisoner in Germany. Henry sent back the Bishop of Ely with instructions that there should be no peace between England and France. He also gave Richard 17000 marks to continue the war along with the title "Vicar of Arles".

While Richard was in Chinon, Philip sent assassins (15 in total) to kill him. The plot failed, but the personal enmity between the two Kings was clear. In November Philip attacked the port of Dieppe, the town was burned to the ground and using Greek fire several English Ships were destroyed in the Harbour. Although it was high winter both sides continued to raid and counter raid. Richard's mercenary captain captured the important castle of Issoudun in Berry.

Philip re-captured the town and besieged the castle, but was unable to budge the stubborn Angevin garrison. On hearing the news, Richard marched off from Normandy. Within three days he arrived and broke through the siege lines, relieving the castle. Philip who was afraid of the Lionheart had no choice but to retreat and offer favorable terms towards the Angevins.

My beautiful Daughter

Into the third year of war Richard had regained most of the areas lost to Philip with the exception of the Vexin. The problem remained that Philip was still in control of Gisors and within striking distance of Rouen. Richard's solution to this problem would antagonise the uneasy peace. Philip had demanded the fief of Andely which was under the jurisdiction of the Archbishop of Rouen, who refused to hand it over. Richard sensing the danger if Andely fell into French hands seized the town and commenced the construction of Chateau Gaillard (Le Roche d'Andeli Richard could now turn the tables against Philip with the construction of Chateau Gaillard. The town of Andely is placed where the rivers Gambon and Seine converge in the middle of the Vexin. Richard built his new castle to be able to control river traffic into and out of Normandy and also to be within striking distance to launch attacks against Gisors and the French controlled Vexin. Perched on the cliffs above the town the castle was a masterpiece of military engineering and one of the most modern castles built in the twelfth century.

Château Gaillard, Normandie

All of Richards experience and knowledge of warfare went into the construction. During building a shower of blood from the heavens spattered the walls. Richard ordered the continuation of the work and said **"God himself would not stop the construction of the castle".** In an amazing 13 months the castle and fortified town was complete. Richard remarked; **"How beautiful my one year old daughter has grown".** The castle cost over (£11.000 pounds) an enormous amount of money at the time, dwarfing all the other construction projects in the Angevin Empire. Expensive as it was, it was worth it and would remain Richard's favorite headquarters until his death. Legend has it that Philip came the see the castle and shouted to Richard; **"Even if the walls were made of iron I could take the castle"** Richard replied back; **"Even if the walls were made of butter I could hold it".** Sadly Philip never dared attack the castle while Richard was alive.

Reconstruction of Château Gaillard

The continuation of the conflict in 1196 A.D saw Richard's young nephew Arthur of Brittany being smuggled into Philip's hands. Richard at once invaded Brittany with a large host and forced the Bretons to submit and change sides, forming an alliance against Philip. The Lionheart also destroyed and captured the town of Vierzon (Berry) whose lord had recently appealed to Philip over a dispute. Richard was sending out a message to all the barons that they could not count on being protected by the King of France anymore in grievances against him. Richard named his nephew Otto of Brunswick (who was actually born in Normandy) as Count of Poitou to strengthen family ties. There was also a welcome breakthrough in the south. After much negotiating the marriage between Richard's sister Joan (once of Sicily) and the new Count of Toulouse ended the feud between the Angevins (Dukes of Aquitaine) and the Counts of Toulouse. Philip had lost his only ally against Richard in the south of France. Enraged by the news, he again descended on the Duchy of Normandy, this time from the north attacking the border town of Aumale, and then occupying Nonancourt on the Border. The tit for tat continued to rage back and fourth, John subdued Philip's success by capturing the castle of Gamaches in the Vexin. The Lionheart then attacked and took the important town of Gaillon, just a few kms upstream from chateau Gaillard in which he was wounded by a crossbow bolt to the knee.

The wheel of fortune turns against Philip

1197 A.D was a defining year in the war between Richard and Philip. Since 1194 A.D Richard had slowly been turning the tide against Philip, gaining back the lost ground and forging alliances both internally and externally. The seeds of these alliances came to fruition in late 1196 and 1197 A.D. When Richard was a prisoner in Germany he had forged alliances with the Rhineland Princes, this relationship would in time put pressure on France's northern front, especially the Count of Flanders. By 1197 A.D the economic blockade of Flanders forced Count, Baldwin to ditch his alliance with Philip in order to avoid economic disaster. Richard also gave Baldwin 5,000 marks of silver to pursue the war against his former master Philip. Spring came with the renewal of hostilities. This time Richard took to war to Philip by raiding the town of Saint Valery on France's northern coast. The town was burned and the relics of Saint Valery were taken away to Normandy. During the raid some English ships were found breaking the embargo bringing supplies to Richard's enemies. The English sailors were hung, their cargos seized and distributed amongst Richard's supporters and their ships sunk.

King Richard I of England (14th century manuscript)

Beauvais and Milly

Richard's brother Prince John had been given the task of harrying the lands around Beauvais on Normandy's North Eastern frontier. The warlike Bishop of Beauvais had long been an enemy of Richard and was part of Philip's envoys when the Lionheart was held captive in Germany. Prince John, Mercadier and Sir William Marshal ravaged the countryside, and just outside the gates of Beauvais put flight to the local militia and captured the erstwhile Bishop. They then proceeded to assault the castle of Milly sur Therain, where Sir William Marshal (now over fifty years of age) became the hero of the day once again, saving the life of a Flemish knight. Seeing the brave young Knight in mortal danger, Marshal leapt forward into the fray, he scaled the castle walls and single handedly drove off the knight's attackers, beating the castle's commander to the ground and then sat on him while taking a rest until reinforcements arrived. Marshal's actions helped galvanise the Normans to force open the castle gates and take the fortress by storm. The jubilant Anglo-Norman routiers destroyed the castle, taking their booty and prisoners back to Normandy.

Flanders

Marshal was sent north to seal the ties with Count Baldwin and the other major noble families of Flanders. The Flemish army invaded the county of Artois, took the town of Douai and commenced the siege of the region's capital Arras. Philip now faced with a total collapse of royal authority, gathered his army and marched north to deal with the Flemish. He raised the siege and pursued Count Baldwin back into Flanders.

By Ypres Baldwin set a trap for Philip luring him further into Flanders stretching his supply lines. He gave orders for the bridges in front and behind of Philip's army to be destroyed trapping the French.

Sir William Marshal defending a Flemish Knight on the castle battlements of Milly sur Therain

Philip tried to worm his way out of the situation by acclaiming he had come to make peace with the Count; his pleas fell on dear ears, Baldwin forced him to surrender. He was lucky Richard was campaigning in Auvergne (taking 10 castles off the King of France) or he may well have been taken prisoner and ransommed off to the Lionheart.

In September Count Baldwin and the leading magnates of Flanders came to Chateau Gaillard to consummate their alliance with Richard. Philip who was supposed to attend refused reneging on all the promises he had made with Count Baldwin and returned to Paris.

Also in September Henry VI, the German Emperor died leaving his infant son as heir to the imperial throne. An ensuing power struggle followed between Henry's brother Phillip Duke of Swabia, who received support from the King of France and Otto de Brunswick (Richard's nephew) who received Angevin Support.

The Lion and the Lamb

The election for the new Emperor side tracked events in Normandy at the beginning of 1198 A.D. Also in 1198 A.D Innocent III became the new Pope in Rome. On his agenda was firstly to re-establish the power of the Papacy and secondly to destroy the power of the German Emperor's in Italy and Sicily, who were becoming far the powerful too tolerate anymore. Richard's candidate Otto, offered concessions in order to gain the support of the Holy Father against the Hohenstaufen candidate. The Lionheart also used his influence with his intention of going on Crusade again which deeply pleased the Pope. Innocent had also taken up the cause of Philip's wife Ingeborg of Denmark whom the French King had repudiated since their marriage in 1193 A.D. Philip tried to marry Agnes of Merania a German princess to counter Richard's recent political successes, but to no avail as the Pope declared the marriage illegal as Philip was still married to Ingeborg.

Arms of Otto IV Holy Roman Emperor

By July Otto had been crowned in Cologne by the bishop as the new Holy Roman Emperor and Philip was on the verge of being excommunicated because of the unjust treatment of his wife. With only one cause of action left open to him, Philip embarked the disastrous campaign of 1198 A.D. Count Baldwin had followed up his successes of 1197 A.D by reducing the last remaining royal French strongholds in Flanders. This time there was no relief force to save Arras. The Flemings took the capital of Artois by force along with many other towns including St Omer.

The Battle of Gisors 1198 A.D

In the summer of 1198 A.D Philip suffered another defeat at the hands of the English King. Somewhere in the Seine valley between Jumieges and Vernon a skirmish took place in which Philip lost over sixty knights and forty plus men at arms. The French army including the King were forced to flee, and were chased all the way back to the border fortress of Vernon.

Following up this victory Richard invaded the French Vexin, destroyed the harvest and captured the castle of Corcelles les Gisors. Philip who retired to Mantes had heard a false report that the Castle of Courcelles les Gisors had not been captured and was still holding out. He gathered his knights and the local militia and set out to relieve Courcelles les Gisors. As the French army approached, Richard sent out Mercadier and Hugh de Corni to reconnoiter the position and strength of the enemy. Richard's main army lay in wait at Dangu a few kilometers away. Marcadier and Hugh advised it would be possible to surprise the French. The Lionheart sent them back to Dangu to mobilise the main army, while he and a small contingent of knights went forth to observe Philip's movements. On accessing the situation, and against the advice of some of his men to wait for the reinforcements to arrive, Richard leapt forward on his war horse and charged directly at the French.

"Like a hungry Lion upon its prey"

Like a hungry lion upon its prey Richard charged into the fray cutting through deep into the ranks of the French army. So fierce was the charge that the French soldiers buckled under the pressure and began to panic. Richard and his knights hacked their way towards the Fleur des Lys banner and King Philip himself. Philip fearing for his life panicked and trampled down his own men in order to escape and reach the safety of Gisors. Richard relentlessly pursued him and unhorsed three of his knights (Matthew de Morenci, Fulk de Gilerval and Alan de Rusci) with a single lance. Before the town gates could be opened the bridge on which the French knights were gathering collapsed from under their weight. King Philip fell into the river head first and had to be dragged out to avoid being drowned. The remnants of his army lay shattered; some dead in the rout, some drowned in the river and others were captured. Over thirty knights were captured and may well have been executed by Mercadier who believed no ransom would be fore coming.

It seemed even God had forsaken Philip as Richard said:

"It was not I who had defeated the French, but God as we are fighting a just cause"

. This is where England's national motto stems from **"Dieu et Mon Droit"** (God and my right). Richard no longer considered himself as a vassal to the King of France, but unto God himself. With the lack of siege equipment Richard returned triumphantly back to Chateau Gaillard with the victorious campaign of 1198 A.D at an end.

Peace and the end of the Lionheart

In the winter of 1198 A.D Walter Hubert Archbishop of Canterbury came to Normandy apparently by the request of Philip to arrange peace between the two Kings. In January Richard who was at Domfont on Normandy's southern Frontier marched off to Chateau Gaillard to seal the peace with Philip. The hatred between the two Kings was so strong that the Treaty had to be concluded with Richard coming to the river Seine from Andeli by boat and Philip on horseback on the other side of the river. In the end only a truce for five years could be agreed. The truce was nearly broken when Marcadier and his routiers were attacked while crossing the lands of the King of France; Philip denied all connections concerning this attack.

← Overleaf: The Battle of Gisors 1198 AD

In early spring 1199 A.D Philip started the construction of a new castle by Gaillon, taking wood from the forest which belonged to the Normans. Richard collected his army and forced Philip to dismantle the castle before war was declared. The Lionheart headed south into Anjou, then Poitou while emissaries from England and France tried to hammer out a permanent peace.

The Legend of the lost Gold

Legend has it that a peasant in Limousin found a horde of Roman gold. The treasure found its way into the hands of the local Lord Achard of Chalus a vassal of the Count of Limoges. Some of this treasure should have been handed over to Richard, but Achard refused. Richard laid siege to the castle of Chalus Charbol. The garrison offered to surrender the castle if they were to be allowed to go free. Richard was so angered by their boldness that he swore to take the castle by force and execute the entire garrison. Richard and Marcadier reconnoitered the castle looking for the weakest point, during which a cook /crossbowman took aim and hit the King in his shoulder. Richard who had been careless in not wearing his armor broke the arrow off, taunted the garrison and rode back to camp. The King's doctor (who became known as the butcher) tried to remove the arrow head, but infected the wound in doing so. Gangrene or septicemia set in and the Lionheart was on borrowed time. He sent word for Eleanor his mother to come to him. When the castle fell to Richard's forces he asked for the man who had shot him to be brought forward.

Richard asked: **"What harm have I done to you 'so that you have tried to kill me"** the man replied **"You have killed my father and my brothers and you would have killed me"** magnanimous to the end the Lionheart forgave him and ordered the man to be set free.

On the 6th of April Richard made his last rites to his chaplain Milo. He had not confessed in seven years because he could not let go the hatred he fostered for Philip of France. He asked to be forgiven for the wrongs he had done against his father and died.

The unfortunate crossbowman who had been set free by Richard was arrested by Marcadier and flayed alive. Eleanor mourned her favorite son and acclaimed **"I have lost the staff of my age and the light of my life"** Richard was laid to rest in the abbey of Fontevraud, beside his father. His brain was buried at Charroux Abbey in Poitou, his body lay in rest at Fontevraud abbey in Anjou and the heart of the great warroir was given to the cathedral of Rouen in Normandy, For England there was nothing just the legend.

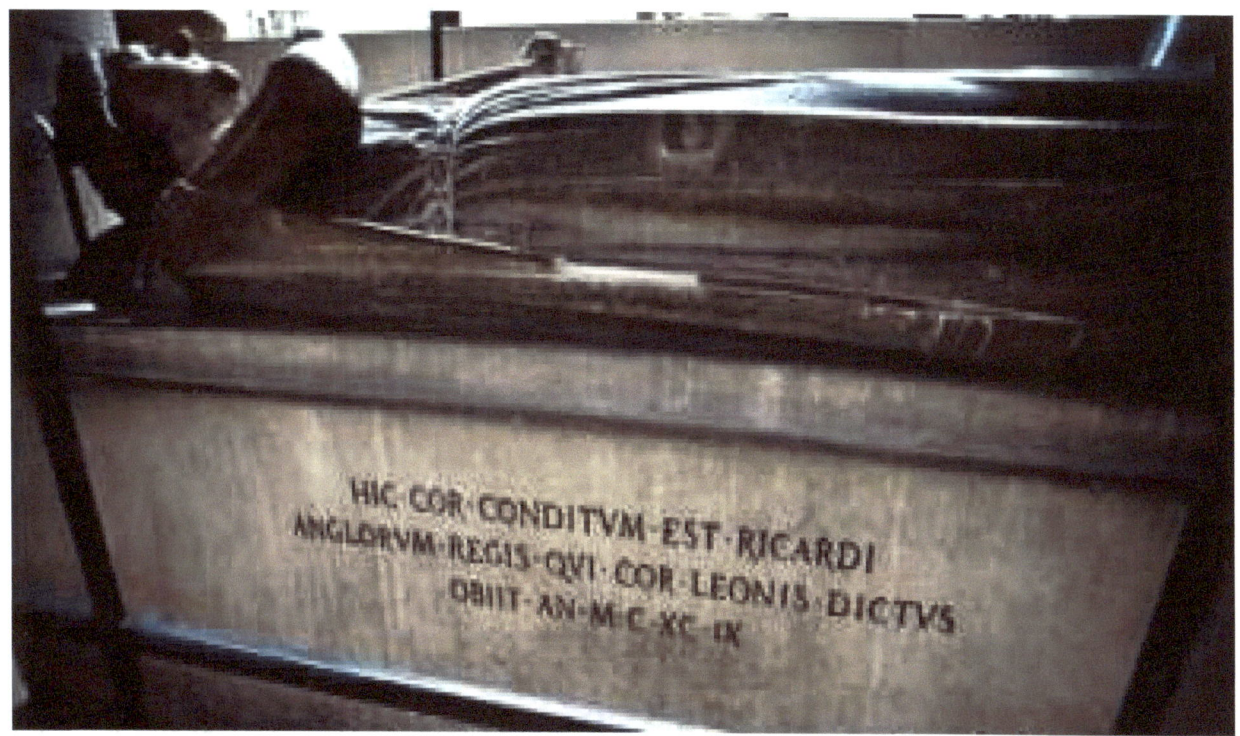

Tomb of Richard the Lionheart (Rouen cathedral)

Aftermath

Had Richard survived, the war would have recommenced at some stage. If the last six years would be anything to go by Richard would probably have extinguished the Kingdom of France, but it will remain one of histories what ifs ? Prince John became King of England, Duke of Aquitaine and Normandy in 1199 A.D but within five years Normandy and all the Angevin lands in France with the exception of Aquitaine were lost to Philip who in time became known as Philip "Augustus" but that is another story in its self.

A comment from the chronicles of William Marshal states:

"The Normans in the days of old were grain, but now they are like chaff since the death of King Richard, they have had no leadership. With the Lionheart gone, the Normans were blown about by a puff of wind from France".

Other Titles from the author:

 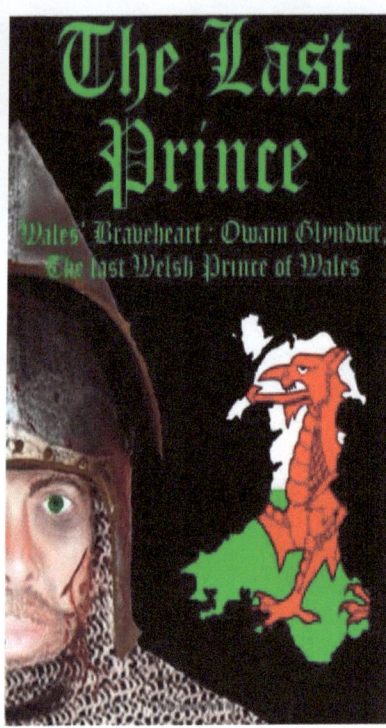 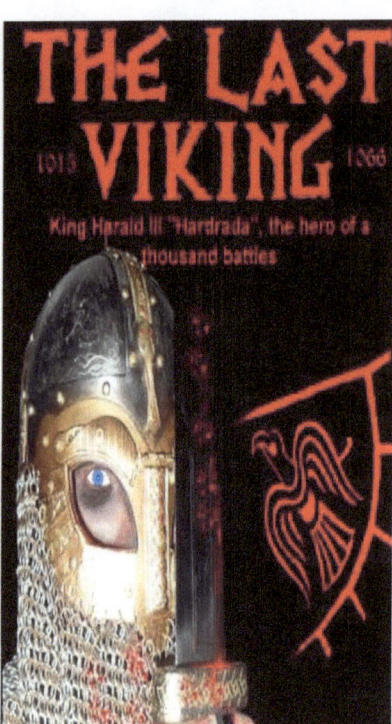

THE GREAT HEATHEN ARMY
Ivar "the Boneless" and the Viking invasion of Britain

THE LAST PRINCE
Wales' Braveheart: Owain Glyndwr, The last Welsh Prince of Wales

THE LAST VIKING
King Harald III Hardrada, the Hero of a Thousand Battles

www.ingramcontent.com/pod-product-compliance
Lightning Source LLC
Chambersburg PA
CBHW041150290426
44108CB00002B/25